Strategic Management for School Development

Published in Association with the British Educational Leadership, Management and Administration Society

This series of books published for BELMAS aims to be directly relevant to the concerns and professional development needs of emergent leaders and experienced leaders in schools. The series editors are Professor Harry Tomlinson, Leeds Metropolitan University and Dr Hugh Busher, School of Education, University of Leicester.

Titles include:

Performance Management in Education: Improving Practice (2002)
Jenny Reeves, Pauline Smith, Harry Tomlinson and Christine Ford

Strategic Management for School Development: Leading your School's Improvement Strategy (2002)
Brian Fidler

Subject Leadership and School Improvement (2000)
Hugh Busher and Alma Harris with Christine Wise

Living Headship: Values and Vision (1999)
Edited by Harry Tomlinson

School Culture (1999)
Edited by Jon Prosser

School Improvement After Inspection?: School and LEA Responses (1998)
Edited by Peter Earley

Policy, Leadership and Professional Knowledge in Education (1998)
Edited by Michael Strain, Bill Dennison, Janet Ouston and Valerie Hall

Managing Continuous Professional Development in Schools (1997)
Edited by Harry Tomlinson

Choices for Self-managing Schools: Autonomy and Accountability (1997)
Edited by Brian Fidler, Sheila Russell and Tim Simkins

Strategic Management for School Development

Leading your School's Improvement Strategy

Brian Fidler

P·C·P

Paul Chapman
Publishing

ISBN 0-7619-6526-2 (hbk)
ISBN 0-7619-6527-0 (pbk)
© BELMAS 2002
First published 2002
Reprinted 2003, 2005

Paul Chapman Publishing Ltd
A SAGE Publications Company
1 Oliver's Yard
55 City Road
London EC1Y 1SP

SAGE Publications Inc
2455 Teller Road
Thousand Oaks
California 91320

SAGE Publications India Pvt. Ltd
B–42 Panchsheel Enclave
PO Box 4109
New Delhi 110 017

British Library Cataloguing in Publication data
A catalogue record for this book is available from the British Library

Library of Congress Control Number: 2002101931

Printed on paper from sustainable sources

Typeset by Dorwyn Ltd., Rowlands Castle, Hampshire
Printed and bound in Great Britain by
Athenæum Press Limited, Gateshead, Tyne & Wear

Contents

About the author

Brian Fidler teaches and researches at the University of Reading. He is professor of education management and course leader for the MSc Managing School Improvement. He has authored or edited 12 books with others on school leadership and management and is editor of *School Leadership and Management*. He is a past treasurer of the British Educational Leadership, Management and Administration Society.

Acknowledgements

The publishers wish to thank the following for permission to use copyright material:

Cambridge University Press for material from B. W. Vaughan (1978), Planning in Education

S. J. Murgatroyd and C. Morgan (1993), Total Quality Management and the School, Open University Press

Every effort has been made to trace the copyright holders but if any have been inadvertently overlooked the publishers will be pleased to make the necessary arrangement at the first opportunity.

Series Editor's Foreword

Brian Fidler has been central to the development of understanding the importance of strategic planning and its links to school development for a number of years. This workbook is based on a thorough understanding of strategic planning in theory and practice and offers clear practical guidance on how to carry through the associated processes. The distinction between the strategic and the long term is clearly presented. The need for schools to determine strategy in the light of a rigorous analysis of the future places ownership firmly within the school community and in particular on its leadership. School development and school improvement planning are aligned through strategy.

The process of strategic analysis, strategic choice and strategic implementation is explored in considerable detail. This requires recognising and using the school's core competences and its capacity to respond imaginatively to its environment. Brian Fidler links, through strategy, the leadership team, an analysis of the school as organisation, its values and a requirement for a rigorous and honest evaluation of performance. This leads on to an examination of team roles and performance, the wider school self-evaluation and reaches out to understanding the school culture, and the school's capacity to develop as a learning organisation. Strategic management determines the unique school vision and develops the school's capacity to make strategic choices.

This practical workbook provides both a thorough understanding of strategic management for school improvement and practical activities to support a school in achieving its improvement strategy. It is a book in the best tradition of the BELMAS series in that it presents new developments, encourages best practice, supports professional development and will lead to school improvement.

Professor Harry Tomlinson, BELMAS *Series Editor*
Leeds Metropolitan University

1   Introduction

Background

In 1991 Geoff Bowles and I with the help of John Hart produced the *Effective Local Management of Schools Workbook: Planning Your School's Strategy* as an aid to schools that wished to engage in longer-term thinking about their future. This was a companion to the book *Effective Local Management of Schools* (Fidler and Bowles, 1989) which contained theoretical ideas and case studies of the constituents of school based management as applied in schools in England and Wales following the 1988 Education Reform Act. The workbook contained our ideas on formulating and implementing strategy in schools and it also contained activities on a variety of school management processes. We intended that either individuals or groups of staff in schools could work on them to apply our general ideas to their particular school and its context. The present book is a development of that workbook. I have continued to work on strategy in schools and develop my ideas about how to incorporate strategic ideas into school planning.

My thinking has been expanded by my increased study of the literature on strategic planning in business organisations and by teaching a course on strategic and school development planning on the part-time MSc Managing School Improvement degree at the University of Reading. Succeeding student groups have helped me better understand the theoretical ideas and they have also worked on activities based on the workbook and have applied the ideas of strategic analysis to their schools. Since they are all senior staff in schools, my ideas have been 'reality tested' by their attempts to work out what strategy would mean and its practicality for their own schools.

The original workbook has gone out of print and there have been substantial changes to the school context in England so that the activities needed updating. This combined with my evolving understanding of the difficulties of formulating and implementing strategy suggest that a new book would be timely. This brings together a comprehensive presentation of the theory and additional and updated activities to help apply strategic thinking to school improvement.

This book is primarily intended for practitioners – those staff in schools with a responsibility for leading and managing their institutions – who need to understand and apply the principles of strategy but are under great time pressure in their work. Thus this book does not make use of extensive references and there are just a few sources that are suggested for additional reading. For those taking advanced courses I hope to produce a more theoretical book which details the researched base for these ideas.

The book is intended for those in schools where there is a context of a high degree of self-management including staffing and finance with some degree of curricular decision-making even if there is a national curriculum. It takes the situation in England as its basis, although where it takes a particular example from England this will be specified. This should help those in other countries to apply the ideas in their context and also, as the situation in England changes in the future, particular considerations which are time-bounded should be easier to recognise and adapt.

Reason for book

❏ The importance of improvement and the need for a long-term approach

In many countries education is a high priority and there is great pressure for the school system to produce better results. The form of the pressure and its emphasis may vary from country to country but there are some common features. There are pressures to improve:

- student results
- participation rates
- inclusion and results for previously disadvantaged groups
- parental satisfaction with schooling
- employer satisfaction with the products of schooling
- cost-effectiveness of schooling.

Whatever the particular pressures nationally and locally, it will be for the staff of any particular school to ascertain the needs of that school and formulate a development plan suited to its needs. It is unlikely that any school would need to tackle all these issues with equal vigour and, even if it did, there would be a need to prioritise which of the issues to tackle first. There are important considerations about what to improve and how.

There are a number of reasons for taking a long-term approach including that:

- major change cannot be accomplished quickly
- some changes need extensive preparation before the time is right
- future needs will be different to current ones.

Although major change cannot be accomplished quickly and may need to be pursued over a number of years, there has to be a start. However, the start also has to be continued. Whilst it is important to get started it is also vital to press on through a sequence of stages which are expected to reach the final destination. Strategy both identifies the final destination and also a route map of how to get there.

> **You can't get there from here.**
> (Wilkins and Patterson 1985)

Some changes are not possible in one step. They may need to be accomplished in stages over a number of years. Some changes may not be possible unless conditions are right. This means that extensive preparations are required. This may also mean waiting until the time is right.

Another reason why improvement needs long-term planning is that the final destination needs to take account of current requirements, and also incorporate the best of current thinking about the future. The education of children who are in school now needs to take account of the world into which they will emerge from schooling some years in the future. Unless some thought is given to prospective requirements it is likely that children will be being prepared for the past rather than the future.

A cautionary tale

Whilst improvement may need long-term planning, decline can also operate over the longer term. Without an understanding of strategy the full significance of each step in a long-term decline may not be appreciated. Strategic thinking deals not only with long-term success but also with the implications of decline if action is not taken.

> **The steady state is very precarious:**
> **organisations are actually either declining or improving.**

This is an example of the decline of a secondary school. A secondary school recruited from a very mixed and large catchment area – semi-rural, suburban and inner urban. Much of the catchment area was some way from the school and there were children who lived nearer but were in the catchment area of a neighbourhood school at the centre of a council estate. The secondary school received more applications than there were places because the school appeared more attractive to a number from the inner urban area than their local school. The school expanded slowly. However, this and a generally complacent

attitude in the school led to continuing poor examination results. There were also some exa
indiscipline and the public image of the school declined.

Some parents from the suburban area of private sector housing began to search for alternative ͙   ͦ.
Other schools began to organise transport to attract children from the suburban area. Lack of public
relations and recruitment efforts in the semi-rural area led to a movement of these children to other
schools. The number of children entering the school was constant but the composition was slowly
changing: fewer well-motivated children from the middle-class semi-rural and suburban areas, and more
children from the council estate with less supportive parents. This had not been noticed as a multifaceted
effect, particularly as numbers had remained constant. Only the lower reading scores of children entering
the school raised the issue.

All the ingredients were now in place for a downward spiral to continue which incorporated several
vicious circles where each action made the situation worse. Some parents, anticipating what might happen
to their children if they attended the catchment area school, avoided the school. These tended to be middle-
class supportive parents. The changing composition of students led to poor results despite efforts to
improve. In fact the school in some senses was improving, it was maintaining results despite a less able
entry which meant that its value added was rising. But the exam result figure appearing in the published
league tables was not improving like those of other schools. This further reinforced a wish to avoid the
school by ambitious parents. Declining numbers of students began to reduce the income of the school, and
economies had to be made. Additional resources were no longer available to tackle the children's lower
reading scores at entry and curricular options had to be narrowed. More and more behavioural problems
worsened the school's image and things got worse because of the flight of the better behaved.

The major point I want to make is that any one of these changes could have been dismissed as
insignificant, but cumulatively they posed a severe if not fatal challenge. Without a sense of strategy the
effect would not have been spotted until it was too late. By the time the numbers had declined, the
composition of the school had already changed, which meant that exam results were unlikely to improve
for the next five years and it would take increasing efforts to stabilise them.

This illustrates the insidious nature of slow but inexorable change. Each year the situation is only a little
worse and so is tolerated because there is no immediate threat. When this has gone on for some time
though, the effect is large and threatening but is much more difficult to tackle. No one should doubt that
this is a very prevalent effect.

The classic illustration of this, and I suspect it is only apocryphal so animal lovers need not worry, which
catches the imagination is the following.

> If you place a live frog in cold water and slowly heat it, you can continue until the water boils and the frog dies.
> However, if you drop a frog into boiling water it jumps out and saves its life.

❑ Schools responsible for their own future and success

In addition to planning what improvement can be made to children's education, there is also an
organisational dimension to improvement strategy. Whatever intentions there are for what a school as an
organisation can achieve, there is also a need to ensure its survival, continuation and success if it is to be
able to carry out its intentions. However laudable the intentions, if a school struggles because it does not
have the appropriate quality of staff or does not engender the confidence of local parents, its intentions
may be unrealisable. A confident, thriving school can achieve what a struggling school cannot, however
good its plans for the education of its students. Thought must be given to the future of the organisation as
an organisation, in addition to the task it performs for its community.

In schools with a high degree of delegated powers there will be the greatest scope for individual decision-
making but there will also be an attendant expectation that the school's future will depend on the actions
of the staff of the school. In this case the need for an understanding of strategy and the ability to put it into
practice is obvious. However, I believe that where schools or other educational institutions have any degree
of influence on their future, they also have a need to understand strategy. Whilst the scope for individual
decision-making may be reduced, there is a heightened need to understand the policy intentions of those
who will impose decision-making from above. Where the scope for school-level decision-making is smaller,
there is a need to be clear about and to exploit what opportunities are offered.

❏ **Need to attract students and public support**

In English schools there is a need to attract students because the funding of a school is directly dependent on the number of children. The imposition of a funding scheme which attaches a sum of money to each child, which is paid to the state school they attend, makes the enrolment of sufficient children an imperative for schools. In other systems the correspondence between funding and the number of children in a school may be more indirect but will still be related. Over and above this financial incentive to attract sufficient students to fill a school there is a need to attract public support. A school which is well thought of in its community will receive a range of benefits which are both tangible and intangible. The community may give direct or indirect financial support and can help a school in a range of ways. Such community support will make it more likely that parents will have confidence in a school and wish to send their children there.

In addition to the viability of a school, if it has a large measure of community support it will be able to achieve more with the resources it has got. Parents and the community are likely to see working in partnership with such a school as a normal expectation. Parents and teachers working together on the education of children are far more likely to be successful than if parents are suspicious of a school's work and constantly challenge its operations. A school which is trusted by parents and the community will find it easier to implement change and to try new initiatives. In its turn this trust imposes on the school greater moral responsibility to ensure that it uses this trust wisely.

❏ **Building on school development and school improvement planning**

In England a process of school development planning was commended to schools as they became self-managing in 1989. The stages in the process have become more sophisticated and schools have acquired a good deal of experience of these processes. However, these have been used by schools as a means of implementing much innovation imposed by government rather than as means of independent planning. Further, these procedures have generally been used to plan changes in teaching and learning for students, and the organisational dimension – the future of the school – has been neglected. Finally, these plans have been relatively short term.

Where an organisational dimension has been included in school improvement initiatives such as Improving the Quality of Education for All, it has only dealt with developing the school's capacity for improvement. Whilst this is important it is not the same as ensuring the school's capacity for survival and success. The future of a school is more fundamental than developing its capacity to improve teaching and learning.

Although there is a superficial similarity between school development planning and strategic planning, there are fundamental differences and, if these are not fully appreciated, what is called strategic planning, and carried on as such, will not yield the long-term success which is its rationale. Thus experience of school development planning can be an advantage but it can also be confusing if the differences are not adequately appreciated.

❏ **Training and expectations of headteachers**

Explicit strategic planning is not the norm in most schools and, so, those who become headteachers are unlikely to have experienced it on their way to becoming headteachers. Thus the principles of strategic planning need to be introduced to prospective headteachers. As I shall show in the next chapter, the concept of strategy is not an easy one to understand and the experience from the business and commercial sector of trying to formulate and implement strategic plans suggests that practice is also not straightforward. I think this shows that it is important to understand the concept fully in order to have a thoughtful approach to practice which will enable a manager to 'see the wood for the trees' and to be able to adapt practices to circumstances. I believe that any attempt to follow a set of instructions slavishly will be unlikely to lead to success. Instead, I favour a good understanding so that a manager can improvise once he or she has acquired an overview of the whole process.

In England the 'strategic direction and development' of a school is one of the key areas of training for headship. I hope that this book will contribute to that training by providing information and by provoking thought and discussion which help exemplify the ideas.

Importance of school improvement

❑ What is school improvement and where does it come from?

In England, school improvement has largely been promulgated by government, and has become synonymous with improving the results of children in examinations and tests. This is a rather narrow definition.

In this book the definition of improvement used by the International School Improvement Project (ISIP) is used. This is very broad and all encompassing.

> A systematic, sustained effort aimed at change in learning conditions and other related internal conditions in one or more schools, with the ultimate aim of accomplishing educational goals more effectively. (Miles and Eckholm, 1985: 48)

The definition assumes that a school has aims which it is trying to fulfil and that school improvement contributes to the achievement of aims. This definition leaves open such questions as the validity of the school's aims, the prioritisation of aims and the origin of school improvement initiatives. I consider that this is a strength since it focuses attention on the need to tackle such questions and the inevitably subjective nature of the responses.

School improvement is not a purely technical matter, it calls for judgement of content and the manner of its introduction.

What is judged an improvement depends upon what a school is trying to achieve, and in whose interests it is being judged. Thus a strategy for school improvement calls for answers to some fundamental questions such as:

- What are we meant to be doing?
- Who are we meant to be serving?
- What are their present and future needs likely to be?
- Are we doing as well as we should?
- What more can we do to supply those needs?
- How can we ensure organisational survival?
- What can we do to increase organisational success?

The answers to these questions will need inevitably to take account of any government or state agendas for the future of schools, but they will also need to take account of wider issues including a more detailed appraisal of local circumstances and the community which the school might serve.

Some authors wish to go beyond the ISIP definition and to require some internal changes to the school's capacity for improvement or add still further requirements. This would make school improvement prescriptive rather than contingent. There are many ways of improving a school's capacity to improve and no certainty how any of these work in the longer term. Here it will be assumed that schools which enter and sustain a regular strategic planning cycle will be well prepared for sustained school improvement.

In terms of doing things better I find the distinction proposed by Argyris and Schon (1974) to be a helpful one. Improvement needs both

---

- **single-loop learning and**
- **double-loop learning.**

They distinguished between trying to improve current processes – which they termed single-loop learning – and trying to rethink operations in a more fundamental way – double-loop learning. A rather small illustration of this is the case of reporting to parents. In schools that produce reports in teachers' own handwriting, a perennial problem is how to ensure that they are produced without spelling mistakes or other errors. Single-loop learning concentrates on improving the current system either by trying to produce reports with fewer errors or by more efficient checking for errors. Double-loop learning asks if there are alternative means of producing reports, which do not require handwritten comments, or even ask whether reports are needed at all.

This distinction provides a way of assessing improvement initiatives when they come along:

- Do they offer a rethink of existing practices?
- Would they work in this school?
- Do they attempt to solve existing problems in this school or problems in other schools?
- Do they attempt to improve current practices?
- What do they add to existing know-how?

It seems to me that there is too great a search for 'silver bullets' or innovations which will revolutionise practice and a somewhat uncritical acceptance of plausible ideas which have little empirical support. Some of these will be valuable but many more will prove to be illusory.

The strategic planning model of processes and stages

The use of the word planning in the title – strategic planning – can be very misleading if, by that, the usual form of operational and action plans are brought to mind. Strategic planning is not like that. It is concerned with identifying a future state and trying to plan a route map to get there. This route map has only very general directions rather than detailed instructions about what to do at each road junction. A strategic plan has broad courses of action to follow. These need detailed action plans for a succession of relatively short-term steps. Each action plan might only cover the following year before the next set of detailed plans are required to continue progress.

The concept of strategy can be likened to a guiding star. A detailed course can be plotted to take account of current conditions for the next stage of the journey but the longer-term aim is fixed. All analogies have their limitations and this one is capable of misleading in terms of thinking that the guiding star is fixed forever rather than being the guiding star only for the foreseeable future. As time passes another star might be the one by which the organisation is steered.

Based upon previous work by Geoff Bowles and I, a model of strategic planning suitable for use in a school or other educational institution has been formulated. This is a heuristic device to help conceptualise the process to aid understanding. The model has a number of sequential stages. Whilst this staged model provides conceptual clarity it should not be assumed that in practice strategic planning is a linear process by which one stage is completed before the next is started. The real world is rather more messy. However, being able to analyse what is going on in practice and relate it to the model will help keep the process on track and ensure that essential stages are not missed out.

Although I shall return to this later in Chapter 3, I want to draw attention here to the importance of this form of mental processing. It requires an ability to:

- conceptualise practice
- relate the concepts to a mental model
- change scale of the mental model so as to be able to move between the 'big picture' and particular details.

I believe that these abilities are vitally important in leading strategy.

The strategic model (Chapters 2 and 6) combines decisions about how to carry out the stages of strategic management and decisions on the strategic processes themselves. These are called process or operational decisions (about how to carry out strategic planning) and conceptual stages (concerned with assembling the information on which to make strategic decisions and implement them). The operational decisions are designated 'O' and the conceptual stages are designated 'C':

- Getting started – decide how to organise (O).
- Strategic analysis (C).
- Choosing – decide how to choose (O).
- Strategic choice (C).
- Plan – decide on plan format and how to implement (O).
- Strategic implementation and change (C).

I believe that it is vitally important to try to understand the strategic planning process before embarking upon it. The importance of understanding the nature of the change before trying to implement is has been rather neglected recently. In England schools have recently spent much energy responding to a spate of central government initiatives The task of schools has been seen as implementing centrally determined improvement policies. However, this strategy does not appear to have recognised the vital process of understanding and interpretation within the process of implementation. Any change needs to be interpreted, as decisions will be required in order to implement it. The practices which are finally implemented depend on this initial interpretation. Even when there are attempts to be faithful to the original intentions, misunderstanding will mean that the new working practices are not as policy makers expected. Thus understanding of intentions is vital

Illustrations of this abound. Evaluations of many new working practices shows that they are not being carried out in accordance with the basic theoretical principles which underlie them and, so, it is not surprising that they do not lead to the claimed advantages. A typical example was an account of total quality management (TQM) which demonstrated that the philosophic underpinnings of the approach were absent. Hence the claims that TQM did not work should more properly have been presented as TQM had never been tried.

Strategic planning is a particularly complex operation and theoretical understanding has its limitations. It is only by embarking and learning from experience that deep understanding can be gained. The probability of learning from experience is much enhanced if this is anticipated rather than expecting that trying something new will be unproblematic. So it is important to combine theoretical understanding with learning from experience. This leads to a general finding which I shall refer to many times:

> **EITHER-OR thinking should be replaced by AND-ALSO thinking.**

It is not that theoretical understanding and learning from experience are alternatives, they are both necessary and complementary. The purpose of this book is to provide a way of achieving theoretical understanding and also to provide activities and techniques which can be used in practice.

In addition to formal strategic processes, this book is also intended to draw readers' attention to the importance of strategic thinking – the capacity to think ahead in a strategic way. This is not just long term thinking but takes account of a changing environment, changing organisational and individual competence and changing priorities. It searches out opportunities and recognises threats. It helps integrate streams of small decisions into the furtherance of longer term aims. This is a skill which understanding and experience can develop.

Plan of book

This book aims to bring together material to allow a school to plan how to tackle strategy and go ahead and produce its strategic plan for school improvement. It interprets school improvement more widely than solely being concerned with directly improving the experiences of students; it also includes an organisational dimension – survival and success of a school as well as its students. The activities which are associated with stages of the process should stimulate thinking, discussion and decision-making.

The book begins with a discussion of the concept of strategy and the conceptual stages of developing strategy – analysis, choice and implementation. There is a consideration of the well-known difficulties of developing and progressing organisational strategy. This is mainly based on the literature from commercial organisations but a section examines ways in which schools are different and the strategic process in schools will need to be different. As school survival in England depends on attracting sufficient students, a section examines what is known about parental and student choice of schools.

A chapter examines the relationship between leadership and strategy. It is pointed out that successful strategy involves leadership, management and administration but the proactive and symbolic elements are associated with leadership. A contingent style of leadership is proposed which takes account of its effect on followers. The difficulties of evaluating effective leadership are discussed, particularly the strategic component. The effects of mental frameworks on the thinking of leaders and their effects on strategy are identified. Finally, the value of theoretical frameworks for analysing organisational practice are discussed.

There is a major consideration of the ways school staff can work together and the differences between consultation and participation. The advantages and disadvantages of different ways of working together are analysed. This is the chapter in which the use of the activities for planning school strategy are examined. A range of ideas for generating ideas and communicating and recording them are suggested. A further range of techniques deals with problem-solving and managing change.

The following chapter examines school improvement and the issues of how to determine what to improve and how to go about improvement. A brief section examines knowledge gained from research on school effectiveness and school improvement. There follows a systematic analysis of types of improvement approach and their strengths and weaknesses. Three major contributions to organisational strategies for long-term improvement are identified – organisational learning, core competences and benchmarking.

The next chapter brings together the three conceptual stages of strategic management and the three operational stages in a strategic planning model for schools. The relationship of this approach to current school development planning practices is examined. The operational stages are discussed in detail since these provide the practical steps to formulate and implement strategy. There is a brief discussion of strategic cultural change and the value of process consultancy.

The final three chapters consider in turn the processes of strategic analysis, strategic vision and choice, and strategic implementation and monitoring. These discuss in detail each step of the strategic model for schools. Most of the activities are associated with these three chapters and provide the vehicles for staff discussion to aid the process of systematic strategy formulation and the planning of implementation.

A brief concluding chapter invites schools to begin to plan more strategically. It suggests realistic expectations of the outcome from a first strategic plan. In addition to the value of the plan itself, a first experience of trying to plan in this way provides a learning opportunity to improve practice for the next plan. With an understanding of the potential of the process it should be possible to refine strategic skills particularly those of strategic thinking. The value of a strategic approach is twofold: it should ensure the survival and success of the school as an organisation but it should also enable it to give a better education to children and young people over the longer term.

Much of the book reifies the school – it treats the school as if it were a person. Partly this is for economy of writing but also because it does not presuppose how decisions are made in a school. When 'the school decides' this may mean that it is the school leader or headteacher who decides. On the other hand it may mean that the governing body of the school decides, or it may mean that staff participating together make the decision or it may mean that a complex process of micropolitics takes place involving all these groups and others. This means that schools which are run in very different ways can read this book, each envisaging a particular form of decision-making which is customary in that school. There is a section of this book which specifically examines decision-making and so that section should provide an opportunity to consider afresh how decisions are made rather than only customary ways being continued.

A further convention which should be noted is to use the term management as a general term to include leadership, management and administration. In Section 3.2 these terms are distinguished but where all three are involved management will be the term used unless it is important to distinguish between the three.

2   Strategy

Introduction

This section gives a general overview of strategic concepts. Much of this comes from the business world although there has been increasing work on strategy in the not-for-profit sector. The concept of strategy and related ideas are abstract and need definitions and examples to try to clarify them.

A major contribution is an explanation of a conceptual model of strategy. This introduces the concepts of strategic analysis, strategic choice and strategic implementation and change. Some of the acknowledged problems in dealing with strategy are discussed and positive suggestions made about ways of tackling them.

Some of the issues involved in translating strategic ideas to schools are discussed. A strategic management model for schools is introduced which combines operational stages with the conceptual stages identified above. This model is further developed in Chapter 6.

Finally, the effects of a competitive market in school places is discussed. This presents the findings from research on parental choice of schools and school responses.

What is strategy?

❑ Concept and definitions

Strategy is a rather elusive concept. It originates from usage in military situations where it serves to distinguish an overall plan of action from the tactics which are its constituent parts. It is the broad overall direction that an organisation wishes to move in.

Thus there are a number of key features which identify a change as strategic. Strategic change involves the whole organisation in a holistic way and it is concerned with the longer term (five years or more). It takes account of pressures and influences from outside the school and takes steps to ensure than the planned activity will be sustainable over the medium term. A checklist which helps to decide on whether a change should be regarded as strategic is if it is concerned with:

- the whole scope of a school's activities
- the school's long-term direction
- matching its direction to environmental pressures
- devising activities which are sustainable given the school's level of resources.

A comprehensive definition has been developed by Johnson and Scholes (1999: 10)

> Strategy is the *direction* and *scope* of an organisation over the *long term* which achieves *advantage* for the organisation through its configuration of *resources* within a changing *environment*, to meet the needs of *markets* and to fulfil *stakeholder* expectations. (Original emphases)

This sentence contains all the key words which help identify features of strategy.

Other succinct statements which help clarify its meaning are

> A strategy is the *pattern* or *plan* that *integrates* an organization's *major* goals, policies, and action sequences into a *cohesive* whole. (Quinn, 1980: 7) (Original emphases)

This incorporates two views of strategy: (a) as a pattern of actions seen in retrospect, and (b) as a plan to guide future actions. It has been pointed out that the word strategy has a variety of meanings and, although they tend to be used interchangeably, in fact they imply a very different understanding and view of the concept.

Bryson (1988: 5) identifies the essence of strategic planning for the non-profit sector as

> a disciplined effort to produce fundamental decisions and actions that shape and guide what an organization . . . is, what it does, and why it does it.

Strategy takes account of

- long-term intentions and aspirations
- the external environment (both now and future predictions)
- the internal strengths of an organisation
- the prevailing organisational culture
- expectations of stakeholders
- likely future resources.

Finally, this is the place to explain the interrelationship of terms which will be used throughout the remainder of the book.

The term strategy incorporates both a strategic aim and the means of achieving that aim. It is the destination and the route map to get there.

Strategic planning refers to processes involved in formulating a strategic plan. This is a plan to operationalise strategy or put strategy into practice. It is the planning component of strategic management.

Strategic management is the process of planning and implementing strategy. It involves strategic analysis, strategic choice and strategic implementation.

Timescale

Whilst strategy is concerned with the long term this is somewhat vague and needs some discussion. How long is 'long term'? Whilst there can be no precise answer to such a question, it is possible to narrow down the range of possible answers by consideration of the hierarchy of timescales shown in Figure 2.1.

In this hierarchy I think that strategy extends to around what I have called 'middle term'. Whilst I first wrote about strategy in 1989 I suggested five years, which at the time was regarded as unrealistically long, I now think that was too short. I think that strategy should be devised for between five and ten years. It should cover feasible developments but also verge on the more aspirational 'desirable developments' of what I have called 'long term'.

Although the actual timescale may be between five and ten years, this needs to be set in an even longer-term perspective of the future of schooling. Some decisions which are made now may have long-lasting implications – strategic decisions – for example, decisions about capital investment in new buildings. Unless these are taken with some consideration of the use of the buildings in the longer term, they may be unsuitable for future needs before their expected lifespan is completed. This suggests that some consideration should be given to the future of schooling. What will schools be like in the future? Although this soon develops into futurology with all its attendant uncertainties, some writers have suggested global trends which may operate in the longer term. In such future thinking they identify global trends and possible implications for schools. They also offer some suggestions for re-engineering or rethinking how schools should operate. Whilst such considerations are a small part of devising strategy they do need to be incorporated into strategic thinking (Chapter 2). Keeping track of such trends in thinking, whilst inevitably speculative, may help generate insights into longer-term trends. This is important because current decisions and future plans need to be set in an even longer-term perspective

Plans and their timescale

The nature of plans has to be appropriate to the timescale. Plans for the longer term inevitably lack detail but have to be sufficiently clear to indicate a direction that can shape other decisions. The route needs to be indicated rather than the precise road. Plans for the shorter term have to be more precise and for the very short term have to indicate what should be done, by whom, by when, to what standard, and with what resources. One set of plans should lead into the other (Figure 2.2).

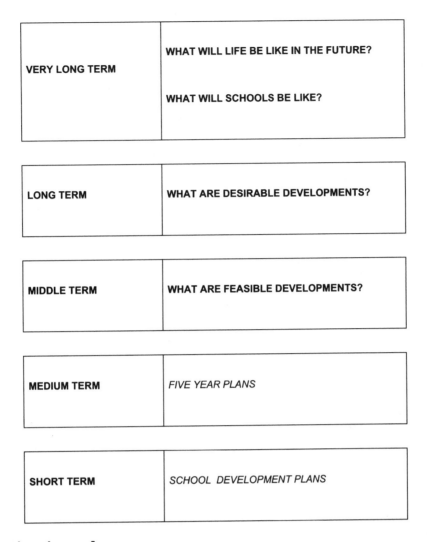

Figure 2.1 *Planning timescales*

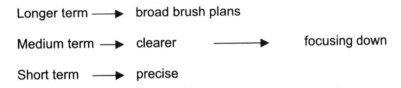

Figure 2.2 *The interrelationship between long-term and short-term plans*

These can be envisaged as on a conveyor belt with short-term plans being completed and dropping off the end to be followed by the next short-term plan. In its turn this has appeared from the focusing down of medium-term plans etc.

An analogy which may be helpful to explain the connection between the plans required for the implementation of strategy is the concept of 'design and build' in engineering. Let us take the example of design and build of a tramway. The start and end points of the tramway need to be determined. Between these two points an approximate route is planned. Then, rather than wait for all the route to be designed in detail before beginning to build, the two go on together. The first stage of design is completed for the first stage of the track before building work begins on this first stage. Whilst this building work is going on, the design work for the next stage is being completed. The design of the second stage can be finalised when it is clear where the first stage of building will terminate. The simultaneous building of one section whilst designing the next, continues until the project is completed. Although this system of engineering saves time, it is its other strength which I think is particularly helpful in understanding strategic implementation. The other advantage of design and build is that it is flexible enough to take into account any detours or adaptations which have to be made during the project whilst still keeping the end point in view.

There are parallels with strategic implementation. Once a strategic aim has been decided, a strategic route map can be sketched to get from the present to the strategic aim (Figure 2.3). Detailed planning work for the first year of the journey can then begin. As this plan is put into operation, the next stage of the journey can be planned. This cannot be finalised until the point likely to be reached by the first stage becomes clear. This process can be repeated until the strategic aim is realised.

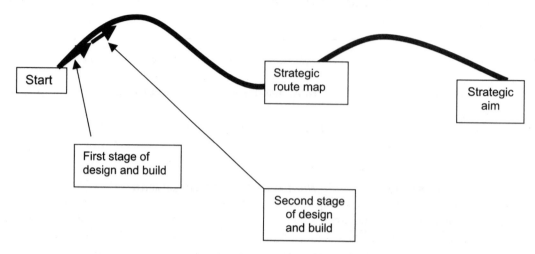

Figure 2.3   *The strategic route map and stages of design and build*

❑ Need for a strategy

Although there are many difficulties in trying to carry out strategic planning, a consideration of the alternatives usually convinces people that it is worth developing the skills for strategic planning.

For small organisations 'creative muddling' has been suggested as an alternative to a formal strategic planning process. This is the situation where there is a gifted intuitive leader who knows the strengths and weaknesses of the organisation and can see immediately what will be opportunities and threats. Such a person can operate without a formal process because it all goes on in his or her head. A person who is good at this can jump in and take advantage of opportunities, but if the person is less talented it can finish off an organisation. In any case the situation is very vulnerable to anything happening to the leader.

As Kast and Rosenzweig (1985) so aptly put it, the extreme choices are 'extinction by intuition' when there is no formal planning and 'paralysis by analysis' when planning is taken too far. It is getting the balance right that is difficult.

> **If you don't know where you are going you will end up somewhere else.**
> **(Anon)**

A fundamental feature of strategy is that of trying to map out and follow a course of action which meets current demands on a school and also takes account of the future. This involves trying to foresee, anticipate and influence future demands such that they can be incorporated into the school's plans. The alternative is to wait until the demands are acute and then react in a piecemeal way.

The value of a strategic plan is that:

- unexpected opportunities and threats can be dealt with in the context of a plan rather than in an ad hoc way
- assumptions on which it is based are identified and hence can be monitored for any changes
- priorities can be recognised and chosen rather than discovered by default
- efforts can be synchronised and co-ordinated to produce a greater effect
- a sense of purpose can be engendered for all staff
- students and staff are able to make more informed choices about whether they wish to join a particular school.

❏ Strategic thinking and strategic decisions

Strategic thinking is a mental attitude which tries to keep long-term objectives constantly in mind and considers all short-term decisions in this long-term perspective. Good school leaders have probably implicitly always worked in this way. When all decisions are consistent with long-term aims and tactics are part of a greater strategy, this is strategic thinking. Strategic thinking and strategic management are complementary. Both are needed. To go through formal strategic management procedures periodically and to ignore such considerations in between would be partial and wasteful. Equally, to have strategic thinking going on only in the head of one person is wasteful and involves only 'muddling through'. Such thinking has not been tested against a formal process and is not easy to communicate to others without a more formal process to relate to. Thus successful strategy requires both a formal process of strategic management and also strategic thinking in the minds of senior managers.

Any selected strategy needs continuously to be borne in mind because decisions have to be made, often very quickly, on a whole range of issues. These need a guiding steer so that they are consistent and not contradictory. Some of these decisions may have strategic implications and these may not be obvious at first sight. Progress on implementing any strategy will not be straightforward or continuous. There may be reversals, detours and adaptations, and there may be marking time, but these need to be set in the context of making progress on a strategy in the longer term.

In any managerial situation decisions are constantly required on a whole range of issues. These will vary in their importance and their urgency. Strategic decisions can either come along in a non-urgent way, be carefully considered and then made, or they can be part of a stream of urgent decisions which have to be made very quickly. It is those decisions which have important long-term consequences which are strategic. Clearly it is vital to recognise a strategic decision which comes along as part of a string of other operational decisions which need to be taken urgently. If time has been spent devising a strategic plan it should be easier to recognise a strategic decision – how does this decision fit into the plan?

> **Fortune favours a prepared mind.**
> (Louis Pasteur)

Strategic decisions are those which, once made, have long-term consequences. They may restrict other possibilities or they may open up options in the future. The first requirement is to recognise a strategic decision and to examine its possible implications. The second, and no less difficult, requirement is to assess these implications and prioritise them against others.

Strategic decisions may involve:

- buildings
- staff
- alliances and competition with other organisations
- curriculum.

Any decision concerned with new buildings is likely to be strategic, for once built they are expected to last for many years. Thus they may set the context for future decades. Another area of likely strategic decisions is in the appointment of staff. Again these are likely to be with the school for some time and will either advance the strategy or represent an opportunity forgone. Other areas of potential strategic decisions are less easy to identify in general terms. Actions which involve alliances with other organisations or engender competition are likely to be strategic as they may start a chain of events with long-term consequences.

Decisions which involve creating a relationship with one or more other organisations are likely to have long-lasting effects. Such relationships, whether alliances or competition, cannot be ended and returned to their pre-existing state on demand. Alliances will require actions for joint benefit. Competition once begun is likely to develop in a way which none of the parties individually can control. This means that the long-term consequences of a relationship with one or more other organisations are likely to be strategic.

Whilst it might be expected that most curricular decisions will be strategic, the extent of the implications might not have been fully appreciated. The curriculum offered may have an effect on the perceived attractiveness of a school and hence affect parental choice of school. The curriculum requires staffing expertise which affects the development of existing staff and the selection of future staff. Resources in the form of specialist accommodation or equipment may be needed and, finally, there will be timetabling implications. In secondary schools a timetable is a great stabilising force. Curricular provision needs to be planned and co-ordinated throughout the school. There needs to be continuity for children as they progress through the school. This restricts the kind of changes which can be made and the speed of changes.

❑ A conceptual model of strategic management
This formulation is based on the model devised by Johnson and Scholes. The three conceptual stages of strategic management are

- strategic analysis
- strategic choice
- strategic implementation and change.

Each of these stages is divided into three parts.

Strategic analysis or taking stock
This is the stage for taking stock of the present situation and trying to foresee future external influences on the organisation. It is more conveniently divided into three components:

- internal resource audit
- environmental scanning
- analysing culture and values.

Internal resource audit
Internal resources are those features of an organisation which can be used to achieve a strategy. These include not only tangible features such as buildings, staff and finance but also such intangibles as reputation. The analysis should cover not only the presence of such resources but also how they are being used or exploited. Thus a school might have untapped potential in, for example, its buildings or staff. It might have further potential in its relationships with local industry or potential funders.

A realistic assessment of possibilities needs to be made as this will form part of any evaluation of possible future strategies. It is essential not only that all possibilities are assessed but also that over-optimistic assumptions are not made since this would place the viability of any strategy in jeopardy. Strengths and weaknesses of the school's current operations should emerge from the resource audit.

Organisational performance will need to be assessed. Such an assessment needs to use comparative data. How well is the organisation performing compared with like institutions and particularly any local competitor institutions? For schools this means an analysis of test and examination results and other outcomes of schooling.

Surveys of the opinions of staff, parents and students will provide data on strengths and weaknesses as perceived by these groups. Such information is essential to the formation of strategy. These opinions will be based upon perceptions of strengths and weaknesses but a more objective analysis may refute the factual basis of such judgements. Cases of this kind throw up issues for the way in which the school promotes itself either to reverse misapprehensions or to highlight unrecognised strengths.

Environmental scanning
Strategy places great emphasis on an organisation keeping in step with its environment. The intention is that there should not only be a fit at the present time but that as far as possible the two should remain in step.

The concept of the environment may need a little elaboration. This arises from the systems theory of organisation by which an organisation is surrounded by a boundary and everything outside the boundary is termed the environment. Of particular interest are factors which could influence an organisation and its future. These will include general socio-technical trends which influence the whole of society and more specific influences on a school including those of other organisations. A very general list of socio-technical influences is PESTE.

- Political
- Economic
- Social
- Technological
- Educational.

The political will include both trends in national politics and local politics. Political trends will be most influential in future planning as elections approach. It will be as an election is approached that political trends, particularly where there may be a change of the party in power, might harbinger radical changes. Opposition spokespersons and documentation may give clues about what might emerge as policies. Strategic plans which are being formulated in the run-up to a general election where there may be substantial changes may need to have two scenarios, depending on which party is elected. Political policies may offer opportunities if they are spotted at the right time. Grant maintained (GM) school status in England in the late 1980s offered an escape for schools which were under threat. This was especially true in the early stages when the government was keen to swell the numbers of GM schools. Specialist school status may offer opportunities for a curricular specialism and extra funding, particularly for schools in deprived areas at the present time in England.

The significance of economic, social and educational trends should be clear, although deciding which are the ones affecting particular institutions and predicting their future influence will be more challenging. Technological trends are somewhat more complex as they may influence teaching methods and school management, and also the content of the curriculum itself.

An analysis of environmental influences should not only examine the current local and national influences on an organisation but should also try to anticipate future influences. For example, these might involve fewer children in the traditional catchment area and greater emphasis on test results in basic subjects.

Although the main emphasis is on spotting environmental trends, where the opportunity arises a school should be proactive and seek to influence its environment. Influencing local political discussion and media stories may offer possibilities. For example, how a school is currently viewed by its community, can be influenced by promotional activities by a school. However, in the main, the scope for changing the environment may not be great and so the major activity should be recognising current, and anticipating likely growing, influences on the school. These can be classified as opportunities and threats for any future strategy, depending on whether they are positive or negative.

For a school one of the most fundamental items of intelligence is future pupil numbers. This involves discovering the number of children in the school's area and assessing future trends. This will also involve acquiring intelligence on the activities of neighbouring schools and the preferences of potential parents.

Trying to anticipate future influences should reduce the possibility that any strategy is abandoned half completed because some external imperative has intervened. The scanning of the current environment will be partly based on hard (often numerical) data and partly on a product of 'soft' qualitative data. In strategic decisions soft data is likely to be particularly valuable. For example, inferences about what other schools are likely to do in the future may be based on a combination of hearsay, chance conversations and knowledge of the people involved. Such soft information will be particularly partial and judgemental. Although more difficult to interpret than more factual material, it is likely to prove more valuable, particularly for making informed guesses about the future. Such intelligence gathering, whilst it should never be expected to be wholly an accurate prediction of the future, should improve with experience.

The results of the analysis of environmental factors and internal resources can be embodied in a SWOT (strengths, weaknesses, opportunities, threats) analysis. Figure 2.4 gives a summary of actions indicated by the findings.

This SWOT analysis recognises that a combination of an external opportunity and an internal strength represents a growth point, whilst an external threat and an internal weakness needs to be reduced. The possibilities offered by the other two positions are less clear. Where opportunities coincide with internal weaknesses, it may be worthwhile to seek to deal with the weaknesses or ignore the opportunity. Where

	Internal resources	
	Strengths	**Weaknesses**
Environment — **Opportunities**	maximise	remediate/ignore
Environment — **Threats**	deflect/reduce	minimise

Figure 2.4   Actions indicated by a SWOT analysis

there are external threats to internal strengths it may be worthwhile to seek to deflect the threats or allow the internal strengths to decline.

Organisational culture

The dimension which is missing from a conventional SWOT analysis, and which immeasurably reduces its value, is an assessment of the prevailing culture in an organisation. Organisational culture is a powerful influence on the thinking of school staff and, more importantly, it is largely an unrecognised one. It has a powerful conditioning effect. Unless cultural influences are made explicit, they may lead to strategic possibilities being prejudged with the rejection of those that are not consistent with the prevailing culture. This will be particularly disastrous in a failing or near failing school. A failure to question current cultural assumptions condemns the school to more of the same. For some schools, external help may be needed to assist staff to examine a very dominant culture.

The effect of the prevailing culture will be self-reinforcing unless attempts are made to stand back and recognise the implicit values and assumptions which are operating. The observations of new members of staff and outsiders are particularly valuable in pointing out actions, habits and ways of seeing the world which are specific to that school. Trying to recognise how the school would appear to a new member of staff or a new pupil helps to bring to the surface those cultural assumptions.

Recent work has drawn attention to the nested nature of cultural influences. National culture influences the local culture, and both influence the culture of the organisation. Figure 2.5 helps draw attention to cases where the organisational culture of a school may not be consonant with the culture of the local community.

A vital element in assessing the viability of any new strategy will be to compare the values implicit in it with the prevailing values in the school. This will indicate the difficulty of getting the strategy accepted and also the difficulty of implementing it. This represents a key choice: should an attempt be made to change the culture of a school and who should decide this?

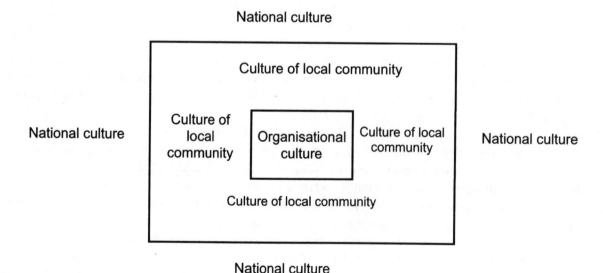

Figure 2.5   The nested nature of cultural influences

The three aspects of strategic analysis are summarised in Figure 2.6.

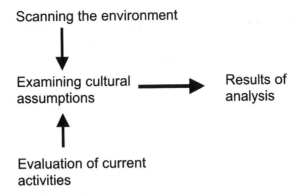

Figure 2.6   *Summary model of strategic analysis*

Strategic choice

Strategic choice has three components:

- generating options
- evaluating the options
- making the choice.

Generating options

Having carried out an analysis indicating a school's current strategic position, the next stage is to formulate possible strategies for the next five years or so. These could be based only on remediating those aspects of current performance which are not reaching acceptable standards, but to do this would be to miss an opportunity to inject a creative, proactive element into the process. As Figure 2.7 indicates, strategy should be formed by a combination of analysis, which is essentially backward-looking, and vision, which is essentially forward-looking.

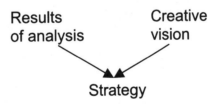

Figure 2.7   *Strategy resulting from analysis and vision*

A strategy has to deal with issues revealed by the SWOT analysis. These may be pressing, in which case most other options will be precluded. Where pupil numbers are falling, then such considerations have to take precedence because of their strategic importance. There are fewer options in a school which is perceived as poor by potential parents. A likely order of precedence in terms of pressing problems is likely to be:

- pupil numbers
- pupil behaviour
- academic achievement of students.

When these primary issues have been satisfactorily resolved there are likely to be many more possibilities for future strategies. This means that the choice stage will take longer, both because there is less urgency and because there are more options to consider. There will always be a wish to further improve students' performance but if the gains from this are likely to be small because students are working near their assessed potential there may be other possibilities in terms of giving a broad and balanced educational experience which may offer a much greater impact, for example through challenging outdoor group activities.

Some possibilities for secondary emphases when the primary issues have been dealt with are

- academic curricular emphases, e.g. technology, languages, sport, creative arts
- community involvement
- creative use of information and communications technology (ICT)
- music performances
- art exhibitions
- drama performances
- sport performances
- charitable work
- varied work experience
- preparation for adult life.

Although the primary and secondary issues are presented as independent ideas, in practice they may be interrelated. Enrolment below expectations may be due to poor behaviour and poor results. Poor behaviour may be partially due to an unstimulating curriculum and poor teaching. Thus they are presented individually and in an order of precedence for heuristic reasons rather than suggesting that they should, or could, be tackled independently.

Forming a strategy is an opportunity to make a move forward towards a vision of an improved future. It should attempt to be aspirational. Substantial steps towards this vision should be possible – it should not be some idealised picture that is unachievable. For example, a vision could be of a much greater degree of self-selected learning by students in the future, whilst its embodiment in a strategy could involve a multimedia centre bringing together library and computing resources leading to a greater degree of directed self-study by older students. The possibilities are endless and will need to suit each school and its situation in its current state of development. It represents an opportunity to skip steps in incremental development and make a bold and imaginative leap forward.

Some generic strategies are

- diversify – teach additional age groups or subjects
- federate – join with schools of a similar kind
- integrate (vertically) – join with schools with complementary age groups
- liquidate – close the school.

Other means of formulating strategies are by considering strategic issues These are crucial questions which, when answered, help define strategy. The questions need identifying and then placing into some kind of logical order such that, having resolved one question, this leads on to the next, and so on. Some scholars of strategy in not-for-profit organisations consider that the identification of strategic issues is a vital step between strategic analysis and the development of strategy in not-for-profit organisations. Strategic issues are the fundamental policy questions affecting the organisation's mission and values. These by definition involve differences of opinion and interpretation. They may involve ends (what) and means (how). Each issue should be framed as a question. These should be prioritised according to the consequences of failing to address the issue. This is a way of focusing attention on really important issues such that some resolution is effected even if this is only for a period of time. An example from Bryson (1988: 151) is 'How do we ensure an adequate funding base to fulfil our mission?'. The 'why-why' diagram, on p. 65 may be helpful in identifying why the issue is important and why it is difficult to resolve.

Evaluating choices

To make a valid choice a number of possible strategic options should be formulated. These could be radically different or they could be alternative emphases on a common theme. There are four tests which should be used to choose between options and to apply particularly stringently to the preferred option. These are

- consistency
- suitability
- feasibility
- acceptability.

Consistency requires that the actions that are required to implement the strategy are consis\ that the parts fit together and harmonise rather than appear as discrete and disconnected strar.

Suitability means that there is a strategic fit between an organisation and its environment, sp\ the opportunities and threats from the environment and the strengths and weaknesses of \ _ul organisational resources.

Feasibility is a measure of whether the strategy appears to be achievable. This requires that the match between what the strategy requires and likely resources is a good one.

Finally, acceptability means that key stakeholders – those who make the decision and those who are most affected by it – will be willing to accept the strategy.

Strategic implementation

Strategic implementation has three elements:

- organisational structure and systems
- staff and change
- resources.

Having chosen a strategy, the final step is to implement it. Implementation should not be considered for the first time after a strategy has been chosen but should have been considered in detail at the formulation stage and checked at the evaluation stage for its viability. Thus problems involved in implementation – for example resources, co-operation of others, staff preparation – should have been largely foreseen.

Implementation involves managing a change over many years. A major consideration is the organisational structure of positions and responsibilities which will be required for the future. This may involve change over a number of years as vacancies arise if the full changes cannot be implemented immediately. A major decision concerns the way in which staff are to work together and how decisions are to be made in future. This concerns involvement. In addition to the structure, systems have to be set up to speed progress in the new direction. Staffing needs for the new strategy should have been foreseen. This involves both development of existing staff and any need for staff with new skills. These will depend upon the magnitude of the change which is being planned. Managing strategic change is considered in Chapter 6.

The sources of resources and their deployment over a number of years will need to be considered. These will need contingency plans in view of the yearly funding which schools receive.

❑ Issues in strategic management

Whilst all major organisations are committed to strategic planning, there is a great deal of experience which demonstrates the challenging nature of the activity. Some of these difficulties are related to conceptual difficulties, such as trying to foresee the future, and some are more practical difficulties, for example, finding the time. This section will review such difficulties and put forward such advice and positive suggestions that have emerged from the experience of devising strategy in other organisations.

I think that it is true to say that the conceptual difficulties increase as more ambitious attempts are made to formulate strategy. Practical difficulties apply to any attempt at strategic planning. Thus it is probably wise to work from where the school is now and its state of experience of strategy. If the school is starting from a low base of experience, it will be a challenge to set up a realistic strategy for five years. With this aim it will be mainly practical difficulties which need to be solved. These involve mainly managerial activities where there is a good deal of wisdom about how to proceed. For organisations which have worked on these problems and have realistic five-year plans, the greater challenge is to engage in more futuristic thinking and to devise even longer-term and more ambitious plans.

Uncertainties of the future

A cardinal feature of devising strategy is that a view has to be taken about what is likely to happen in the future both outside and inside a particular organisation. This is made more difficult by the fact that this becomes increasingly error prone the further into the future the predictions go. For the purposes of strategy this deals increasingly with a period more than five years into the future.

Once the realisation is made that no one has the perfect answer to the problem of foreseeing the future, it becomes a little more manageable. A realistic intention is to try to identify broad-brush trends. There is likely to be a fair amount of agreement on these – it is only as their timescale is made more specific and their likely consequences anticipated that greater difficulties begin.

One obvious measure to improve long-term prediction is to regularly update the prediction by taking account of what has happened, what new evidence has come to light and by taking account of informed thinking. This is the process of monitoring. Whilst this should be going on continuously in an informal way, there should be formal assessments periodically so that too long does not elapse before any action is taken as a result of the monitoring process. On the other hand, plans cannot be revised too often or they lose their value as a secure basis for planning.

Flexible planning is an oxymoron and only suitable as a crisis reaction.

Monitoring needs to take a number of forms. First, there is monitoring of progress on implementing the existing strategy. This involves both short-term plans which have a timescale associated with them and also their implications for the next stages. Actions will be needed if, as is almost inevitably likely to be the case, implementation is not going exactly to plan. Secondly, there is monitoring of the external environment. This involves the assumptions which were made about external trends and external reactions on which the strategy was based. If any of these change there may be implications for part of the strategy or, in extreme cases, it may be that as a result of legislative changes some parts of the strategy are now ruled out.

Inevitably as new opportunities emerge some organisations take them up more quickly than others. Partly this may be as a result of the situation being more fruitful, but often it reflects a predilection of the school and particularly its leadership. Such organisations which are first into every new development are called 'prospector' organisations. Their experience can be very helpful to other organisations who may follow a similar course in the future. However, in the early stages the difficulty is to recognise and differentiate the genuine experiences from the hype and the 'Hawthorne effect'. The Hawthorne effect is the colloquial name given to the experiences at the Hawthorne plant of General Electric in the USA in the 1930s when Elton Mayo's experiments on increasing productivity all succeeded. This was attributed to the reaction of workers to the concentration of attention on them and not any one of the particular measures which was expected to have an effect on productivity. New initiatives may appear to succeed initially due to this effect, but it is transitory. As attention is directed elsewhere the Hawthorne effect is also transferred elsewhere and previous innovations fail to live up to their early promise.

A suggestion from Hamel and Prahalad (1994) with respect to strategy has been the identification of the concept of 'core competences'. These are not individual competences but organisational competences. Hamel and Prahalad proposed three tests. I have interpreted these for schools. Core competences represent organisational strengths which matter to clients and which are capable of development. It is easier to identify such organisational attributes which will be increasingly important in the future than to foresee the future itself. Implicitly, some idea of the future is necessary in order to identify these core competences but these can be identified as a result of broader trends. If the core competences have been developed, then any particular developments which will be required in the future can be refined from these more general competences. An example cited for commercial organisations is the low number of defects per vehicle achieved by Japanese manufacturers in the 1970s. For schools such competences might be social learning, using ICT, monitoring and assessment, or working with external organisations. The argument is that it is easier to identify these capabilities as likely to be important in some form in the future rather than to try to foresee the precise details of how they might be used.

This involves the idea of successive approximation or increasing clarity of vision. The future is always easier to foresee if predictions are short term rather than long term. However, a series of short-term plans do not necessarily add up to what would have been a good long-term plan. The concept of core competences tries to offer staging posts in long-term planning. Thus, to take the example of ICT, although it may be difficult to predict the way in which ICT in schools will develop, it is rather less speculative to suggest that a capability to adapt to and develop the use of ICT will be important in the future of schools. This is more about staff and organisational capabilities than about particular hardware and software. An

ICT capability provides the best jumping-off point to assess hardware and software needs at appropriate times, and to see how these can fit into teaching patterns.

Core competences should be acquired by groups of staff and not a single individual. If the competence is held by one person this is a situation which is very vulnerable if the person leaves. Such a person is highly likely to leave if a valuable competence has been spotted, since other schools who have failed to develop such a competence may wish to poach and 'buy-in' expertise. A further advantage of a more widely shared competence is that a group is likely to be far more productive in generating ideas than a single individual.

Conventional strategy or not?

The difficulties of predicting the future are at their greatest when the environment is turbulent. Turbulence is not usually defined and appears to be used as a reason for not trying to develop environmental scanning skills. I think that there are skills to 'reading the environment' which improve with reflection and experience. I contend that this reduces apparent turbulence to more acceptable proportions. With these skills many more occurrences in the environment will be anticipated and fewer will be complete surprises. When major features in the environment can be recognised and their influence assessed I think that conventional strategy as covered in this book is appropriate and worthwhile. However, I accept that there are a few environmental contexts which are not susceptible to worthwhile prediction and this precludes planning of the kind suggested here.

One situation which I can recognise would not be amenable to conventional planning is one where political reorganisation of the structure of schooling was known to be likely to take place but its timing and nature were not known. Where such decisions depend on political support which itself may be unpredictable, I can see that an individual school cannot make worthwhile long-term plans until the position becomes clearer. However, I believe that circumstances like this are relatively uncommon.

Stability versus development

All organisations have to prioritise the respective demands of stability and development. The balance is different in different types of organisation and different within organisations of the same type. As a type, schools are high on stability. So many processes are ongoing and interlocking. The curriculum is planned to be coherent for students across a year and from year to year. In England options chosen as subject choices in year 10 lead into GCSE examinations in year 11. Pre-university study requires a two-year course. Indeed, parents expect schools to be stable places and for many children at particular times schools may provide one of the few points of stability in their lives. So stability is important to schools. Teaching which goes on from year to year needs to be of enduring high quality. Since there is so little slack in the system, few teachers have the time to sit and ponder the future. How is this to be combined with new priorities and new developments?

Organisations deal with this issue in different ways. Large organisations have a planning department and may well have strategic planners. It is their job to dwell on these issues uninterrupted by ongoing operational issues. This is not an ideal solution since such planners do not have the front-line experience and operational intelligence to fit into their plans and may well encounter difficulties when presenting their plans to more hard-pressed colleagues dealing with more routine operations. Such options are not open to schools. Few, if any, professional staff are not engaged in teaching. Thus whilst 'not invented here' is much less likely to be a problem, having the time and organisation to be able to deal with and progress long-term issues is the corresponding difficulty.

Information demands

For strategy to be well informed a great deal of intelligence must be amassed, communicated and assimilated. Such intelligence is both of the 'hard' and public kind and also the 'soft' and informal kind. Worthwhile intelligence may be possessed by anyone in the organisation – a classroom assistant may be a local councillor, a teacher may be a chief external examiner or a teacher's partner may have commercial contacts. In view of the lack of time for management in general, and intelligence assessment in particular, schools find these issues are formidable problems.

Problems in this area are not restricted to small public-sector organisations. Large commercial companies have been accused of being so preoccupied with what other competing firms are doing that they lose sight of, and put far too little resource into, primary intelligence gathering from clients and consumers. This is a danger which also could overtake schools in highly competitive environments.

One suggestion which has been made especially in the context of not-for-profit organisations is to concentrate on gathering intelligence which informs decisions on 'strategic issues', as discussed previously. These are the large issues or dilemmas which are particularly important for a particular organisation. In the case of schools such issues might be how to improve results in a primary school, whether parents are sufficiently involved in the work of a school, or whether a small sixth form is viable. These provide a focus for data gathering and assessment but should not be interpreted too narrowly nor chosen too parochially or they may defeat the object of intelligence gathering for strategic planning. This is to have a good appreciation of prevailing external forces and not to be taken by surprise by external initiatives.

Making time

As I have already alluded, the problem of finding time is particularly acute in schools. The more corporate the activities the greater the time demands. I regard this as sufficiently important that I have devoted a section of the leadership discussion to time management. This seems to me both a personal and an institutional issue. Individuals have different priorities on their time but some time management issues can only be alleviated by institutional decisions. Some issues such as strategy should be institutional priorities which require everyone's time in some measure. One has to have faith in the old adage that planning saves time. The big difficulty is finding time in the first place to be the launch pad for future time saving.

Questioning spirit

Finally, and not least, is the requirement to combine optimism and vision in devising strategy with a questioning, sceptical spirit. One of the greatest enemies of devising effective strategy is complacency. It is all too easy to accept that the status quo is good enough and that greater efforts at planning are not sufficiently likely to pay dividends. With such attitudes it is all too likely that this becomes self-fulfilling. Strategy needs to be pursued with a restless questioning spirit which is not ground down by the relentless flow of essential but time-consuming and stressful work. Devising strategy needs to incorporate the prospect of improvement, an aspiration that the future will be better and all the effort worthwhile. This involves a tension between a critical appraisal of ideas whilst working harmoniously and optimistically together.

This is an enormous challenge since there is all too much evidence that firms in the commercial sector seem too easily to slip into complacency. This is despite the rhetoric which identifies them as intensely competitive. They appear to continue in ways that were formerly successful long after that has ceased to be a wise course to follow. Processes become institutionalised and cease to be subject to scrutiny. To prevent this happening is a challenge for all organisations.

Strategy and schools

❏ To what extent are schools different?

For those who are accustomed to strategic planning in commercial organisations there are differences in applying these practices to schools. It has been observed that much that is called strategic planning in commercial organisations is in reality little more than long-range financial planning. This suggests two differences for strategic planning in schools.

First, financial planning plays an important but smaller part in school planning. This is because schools have less control of their income and their output is not measured in financial terms. Whilst income depends on the number of students, which schools can influence, the quantum of resource which accompanies each child is not within the control of a state school and depends on a yearly lo authority (LEA) decision which is dependent on public finances.

Secondly, schools are much more regulated than most commercial organisations and sub political influence and decision-making. Thus there is a greater need for strategic rather than Ɡ Ɡrange planning which only extrapolates current plans into the future in an unchanging environment. Following the failure of long-range planning in commercial organisations I agree with Mintzberg that there should by as much emphasis on the strategic as on the planning in strategic planning.

Some reasons that I have previously suggested as differences which school need to take account of are

- *Value laden* – unlike most services offered, there are large differences of opinion about the purposes of schools which depend on value positions.
- *Majority of professional workers* – the majority of full-time members of staff are highly educated and share professional assumptions.
- *Combination of professional and managerial work by most workers* – most organisations have a group who manage and a larger group who provide the service.
- *Dual client* – parents and children are the primary clients, in addition to others whom the school serves.
- *Restricted client choice* – in rural areas and areas with over-subscribed schools there may be little choice of school for clients.
- *Clients do not directly pay for the service* – state education is largely funded from general taxation and those who directly benefit do not pay. This removes a basic accountability mechanism which operates in the commercial sector by which satisfaction with the service is judged against its cost.
- *Funding is not directly related to need* – the income of a school is related to the number of children educated but the quantum for each child depends on the state of national finances and not on a costing of needs.
- *Professional standards set by national inspection* – there are standards which will be inspected, and results published, by other professionals who are neither funders nor clients.
- *Legal requirements to follow a curriculum* – a substantial part of a school's curriculum is determined by regulation and so a school has limited freedom to offer its own curriculum. This reduces the extent to which a school can make itself distinctive.
- *Difficulty in measuring outcomes* – there are difficulties in assessing professional outcomes and these may, or may not be, the basis on which clients make their choice of school and express their satisfaction.
- *Ambiguous employer for LEA schools* – personnel responsibilities are shared between the LEA and the school.

Whilst there may be differences which need to be taken account of, I believe there is much that schools can learn from the experience of other organisations which have extensive experience of planning strategy. To paraphrase a pithy saying:

> **Those who do not learn from experience are condemned to repeat it.**

❏ Advantages which schools have for planning

Schools have many advantages as regards strategy and strategic management:

- purpose
- size
- professional workforce
- behavioural skills
- decision makers.

Purpose

Schools have as their prime purpose the education of children and young people. They do not have the difficult task of deciding which business to be in. They are in the education business, although they may be able to offer a curricular specialism and in other ways make themselves distinctive.

However, within an educational remit the precise purposes of schools and stakeholders are very diffuse and difficult to prioritise.

Size

All the staff of a school can be collected together in one hall and can participate in strategy formation; compare this with a multinational company where all the workforce are not even on the same continent. This is not to say that all staff should be involved in all stages, but that communication and involvement are smaller problems in smaller organisations.

Largely professional workforce

Teachers and most people connected with schools have many shared assumptions about how schools should operate. Teachers through their professional training have acquired experience and been inducted into the values of educators. By their education they have acquired the powers of critical, open-minded and constructive thought. On the other hand, this shared culture can be an impediment to radical thinking.

Behavioural skills

Teachers by the nature of their work are good at acquiring and explaining ideas to others. They are used to discussing, synthesising ideas and working together. Whilst teachers have these natural advantages compared with many organisations, there is still a need to consider and develop these behavioural skills and to manage the processes of consultation and participation.

Decision makers

For most schools the decision-making body for strategy will be the governing body. This has the advantage of having members from a number of constituencies including a majority from outside the school, for example the parents of children in the school. However, since the governing body are part time and unpaid, most of the work involved in devising strategy will be the responsibility of those inside a school. Involving some governors in this process has the advantage of retaining an outside perspective and of ensuring a nucleus of support on the governing body able to explain and defend the proposals.

The decision makers are local rather than remote. The governing body represent the community and clients. They are close to a school and should be aware of local pressures and a school's particular circumstances.

❑ Advantages of a formal process

I think the advantages of a formal planning process are that

- important factors are less likely to be neglected
- information and reactions can come from a wider group
- others in the organisation develop a whole-organisation view
- the opportunities and constraints are known to everyone and others can propose developments which take advantage of opportunities
- other decisions can be made in the knowledge of the strategy
- implicit strategy can be tested and improved by the constructive criticism of others
- strategic decisions can be more easily recognised.

❑ Strategy connects with other management functions

A strategy does not encompass all the activities of a school. It does, however, potentially involve them all. Much of the work of a school is ongoing or maintenance. It involves sustaining current efforts. A strategy is concerned with new emphases. This may involve some new activities but almost certainly will involve changes to some existing activities to co-ordinate them and harness them for the new strategy, as indicated in Figure 2.8. The strategic plan gives a unity to development efforts. Uncoordinated efforts will achieve less because some actions undermine the effects of others.

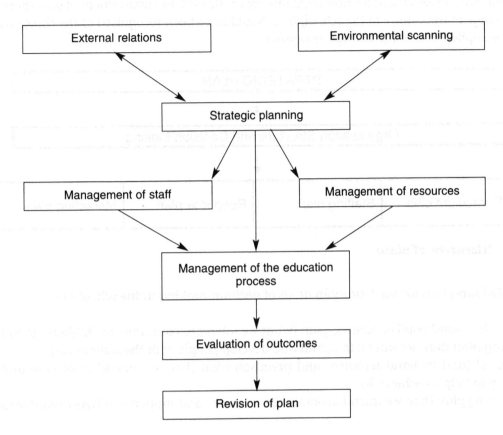

Figure 2.8   A summary showing the relationship between strategy and other management functions

The strategic plan contains a *focus statement* which is a succinct statement of the current strategy. It is a statement of the hoped-for progress over the next few years which the strategic route map signposts.

The school will have a *mission* statement which gives its long-term purpose and the groups which it intends to serve. This should have been questioned as part of the strategic analysis. In addition, the strategic plan will involve the creation of a short, compact, memorable, meaningful *focus statement* outlining the specific development of the school in this strategic plan. The wording of this statement should have been refined to be as concise as possible whilst retaining as many of the nuances which are the keys to the direction of many other aspects of the school's work. It should be capable of being 'unpacked' to yield the core values of the school and its vision of the future. The most basic feature of the statement is that it should be *a guide to action*.

This is the situation which Harvey-Jones describes at ICI when major change was contemplated:

> We need at the end to have simplified to a stage where one sentence, almost a slogan, will describe what we believe, and what we can accept and work to. This process of simplifying down involves attacking the 'weasel words'. We aim to make the simplifying process one of distillation and concentration, rather than trying to make 'umbrella' statements which are unobjectionable. We haggle and argue over single words. But we know when we have 'got it', and when we have 'got it' we believe it and can work to it. (Harvey-Jones, 1988: 55)

The strategic plan should have implications for each of a series of more detailed sub-plans. It should include implications for both what to do and also what not to do. In short, it should indicate (implicit) priorities.

The focus statement may be amplified by lists of long-term objectives which indicate intended progress on a range of fronts. These should be consistent with each other and, where there are potential internal inconsistencies, the means by which these are to be resolved should be indicated.

The first level of detail of the strategic plan (see Figure 2.9) is the plan of the organisational structure and decision-making machinery of the school, including the involvement of governors. The strategic plan will have implications for the structure of responsibilities in the school and that combined with the culture of the school will have implications for how decisions are made and the involvement of governors. Where this implies a change in the culture of the school, this should have been recognised at the choice stage and the extent of the implications of the change recognised.

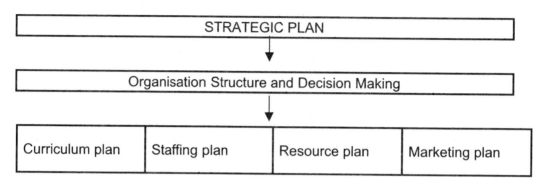

Figure 2.9   Hierarchy of plans

The detailed sub-plans for the four main areas of decision-making in the school are

- curriculum (and pupil outcomes) plan (what we intend to contribute to children's learning)
- staffing plan (how we intend to recruit and develop people with the skills to do it)
- financial (and material resources and premises) plan (how we intend to acquire and spend the money to help us achieve it)
- marketing plan (how we intend to obtain the resources and support of others to enable us to achieve it).

Each of these plans will be interrelated and consistent with the overall strategic plan.

In each of these plans there will be long-term and short-term objectives. For example, in the staffing plan there might be a long-term aim to move to a more balanced age-profile of staff, to take on more specialist classroom assistants and to take on more part-time teaching staff as a way of giving enhanced flexibility in the future. Another part of a longer-term plan might be to make full-time core teachers into curriculum managers, and change their role to planners and managers of learning.

Limited progress on some long-term aspects of the plans may be possible but, until some full-time teachers leave by promotion, retirements or other reason, major progress may not be possible if finance is tight. However, the purpose of this aspect of the plan is to keep these issues in mind for the occasion when a full-time teacher leaves.

❑ Some examples of school strategies

Some further examples of strategies in addition to the more obvious structural ones given above may be helpful to illustrate the variety of possibilities.

Earlier the generic strategies of differentiation and niche differentiation were mentioned. In a school context differentiation would most obviously apply to the curriculum. Thus whilst offering the National Curriculum a school could plan to achieve a higher reputation for innovation or high standards in a particular subject or range of subjects, for example music, technology or sport. A niche strategy would involve offering this curriculum only to selected children either by having a generally selective entry or selection on the basis of a special aptitude and interest in the school specialism.

If a comprehensive school with a balanced curriculum considers becoming a technology school, or other specialist school, it needs to foresee the associated decisions which will be required to make a success of such a change. These will need to be weighed for their possibility and desirability before making the larger decision and committing itself to this course of action.

Where a school has a falling roll, a strategy will be needed to address the situation. This may range from reversing the fall in numbers to identifying and facilitating a merger with another school if it is not possible for demographic reasons to prevent the fall in numbers in that school. Where the fall in pupil numbers can be reversed, then that is the strategy and it will take concerted action from a number of people on a number of fronts to achieve this. It is the choice and co-ordination of efforts of numbers of people which is at the heart of strategy. It should be noted that falling rolls has often been a factor in a decision to engage in strategic planning.

Denominational schools, particularly Catholic schools, often have an admissions policy which requires children to be baptised and may have further requirements such as regular church attendance. In an area with a falling birth rate such a school has a strategic problem. If there are no further Catholic children who can be admitted there are only two choices. The school can reduce in size with the fall in numbers or the school can consider admitting non-Catholics. This is a major decision. How far and by what means can the school retain its distinctive ethos if it widens its admissions policy? What is the limit to such a policy once started? These are strategic issues.

To take a more proactive example: a multiracial school contemplates its future and considers the possibilities of seeking to achieve a more balanced intake of students from different ethnic groups, on the one hand, or considers seeking to be an excellent school of its type, on the other. This is a strategic decision. What follows will depend on which of these two choices is made. Once the major decision is made other smaller decisions are contingent on, and need to be consistent with, this larger decision.

Raising student achievement is a strategy in that it requires many consistent actions for it to be achieved. There are many different possible choices that could be made but the guiding principle is that they should be consistent, mutually reinforcing and all play a part in facilitating the total enterprise of raising pupil achievement.

In cases where student achievement is already high, there are many more possibilities to consider for a strategy for the future. One might be to develop children as more independent learners. This may be desirable for their longer-term future as it will develop desirable skills and encourage a more independent attitude of mind.

The competitive market

In England and Wales the degree of choice of schools which parents have has been progressively increased over the last 20 years. This involves an expression of a preference for a particular state school. If the school has spare places the child has to be accepted, whereas if the school is over-subscribed there should be a formal set of criteria by which children are admitted. Whilst this has reduced a source of parental dissatisfaction compared with when they were allocated a school place based mainly on a designated catchment area for each school, it has raised expectations among parents about their degree of choice which cannot always be satisfied This degree of parental choice was intended to introduce a market in school places which would create competition between schools and allow more desirable schools to prosper and unpopular schools to decline. The system was 'given teeth' by directly allocating finance to schools on the basis of enrolled student numbers.

To facilitate a rational choice of school by parents more information has been made available about each school. Each school has to produce a brochure stating its aims and giving factual information about a prescribed range of school activities. In addition, the results of external key stage tests at ages 7, 11, 14 and external examinations at 16 are published. The form in which individual school information is produced for potential parents and any additional material which is produced is a school-level decision. The principal documentary forms of information which parents have available are

- school brochure
- test and examination results
- school inspection reports.

In addition to the information made available to potential parents, more information about children's progress and an annual report by governors to parents have been instituted. Parents may try to move their child to another school if they are not satisfied with their current school. These moves have intensified efforts by schools to attract children and to satisfy parents.

All schools are not affected by competition to the same degree. Primary schools and secondary schools are affected differently, and rural schools are affected much less than urban schools. This means that knowledge of the local market in school places is vital. Parental choice of school and parental satisfaction are strategic considerations. These will be included in the data which is gathered for strategic analysis in Chapter 7, p. 97. Here general findings on parental choice and associated conceptualisations will be covered to help interpret and to set in context data for an individual school.

❑ Parental choice of school

In England and Wales there has been research on the bases of parental choice and some of these findings and conceptualisations may be helpful in interpreting school data. As has been pointed out by commentators, the research findings on parental choice are varied and often appear contradictory. This may be explained by differences in the methodology by which the research was conducted – specifically, how data was obtained, the timing and who provided information. Most investigations have been of transfer from primary to secondary schools.

Much of the research assumes that parental choice of school is made when a form is filled in at the time of transfer. Whilst this may finalise the choice, undoubtedly for most parents this started many years before. For some the choice of primary school was already influenced by the desired secondary school. In areas of high competition for students promotional activities by secondary schools start when children are age 9.

A three-stage model has been put forward to help analyse parental decision-making:

- Step 1 – parents decide on type of school eg independent. This is often many years before transfer to secondary school.
- Step 2 – parents decide on a range of possible schools of this chosen type.
- Step 3 – parents and child decide on a school from this range.

Not all families will go through all stages and this is an idealisation, but it does help explain why there are contradictory research findings on the part which children play in the process. In addition to bias from the choice of respondent (parent or child), they may simply be describing different aspects of the whole process.

Although most choice is analysed in terms of the pull of the chosen school, there is also evidence in some cases of a push from an undesirable school when it is the catchment area school. There are straightforward reasons for rejecting schools when a very large number of potential schools are being reduced to a smaller number, for example, such as distance from home. However, it is cases where nearer schools are being rejected which signals the kind of rejection which indicates an unpopular school.

Although there are research findings on the reasons which parents give for choosing particular schools, there are some doubts about how seriously these should be taken. The way in which the choice process is modelled may distort the results (weighing up a series of factors at one point in time), the timing of the research and choice of respondent may influence recollections and lead to post-hoc rationalisation, and there are doubts about the honesty with which parents are willing to declare their reasons where these are not socially acceptable. They may give proxy reasons which are more acceptable but will mislead if taken at face value. Finally, there must be doubts about how far parents are aware of their own thought processes when making a complex decision over a substantial period of time. We know professionals have difficulty in explaining their thought processes in similar circumstances (Chapter 3, p. 34) and so it is to be expected that others will have similar difficulties.

This may seem overly negative about the results of research on school choice but it is intended to give warning that the results may need interpretation and, in any case, may not match parental actions at a particular school. The range of findings for particular groups of parents may be helpful in alerting a school to the range of factors which may be affecting parental choice so that a more informed and detailed study can be made in each case.

A typology of choosers has been put forward which indicates the degree to which a range of schools has been considered and whether this is associated with either independent or state schools:

- Fatalist – this group make either a single positive choice or a negative one – either it chooses a particular school (independent) or it accepts that which is offered by the local authority (state).
- Child centred – as the final time for choice arrives the decision is left to the child (state).
- Parent centred – the parents decide alone (independent).
- Eclectic – a full consideration of all types of school is given and the child is included.
- Consumerist – an early decision is made about which type of school with the choice of a particular school following later.

Factors influencing choice

Rather than just list the range of factors which have been found to be involved in parental choice I want to comment on some key ones and their implications. Undoubtedly a school's reputation is the central basis for choice. This does not help very much since it raises questions about just how schools acquire and change their reputation. Clearly there is factual information available, but only some parents will consult this first hand and many more will rely on others to evaluate this. This 'grapevine' effect is likely to be influenced by opinion formers in the local community. These may have first-hand experience of dealing with the school or may interpret and pass on the experiences of others. In most communities the 'grapevine' is likely to be a very powerful effect and needs investigation. Whilst many schools invest effort in gaining good media coverage particularly in local newspapers, there is little evidence about how this contributes to the image of a school. However, rapport with local media may help in the case of a bad news story when it comes after a series of positive stories reporting school events and successes. But local reporters change frequently and so a constant rapport needs to be kept up.

The research on school choice identifies the importance of objective indicators like examination results but gives few clues about how these are assessed and how much schools can do to massage the acceptance of the results in a positive way. Examination results appear to provide a threshold – schools above some level are considered and other factors then come into play. The importance of academic standards may vary by social class, acquiring most importance for aspiring middle-class parents. For these and other parents, perceptions of discipline and the behaviour and appearance of students can be particularly influential factors and changes in school uniform can have a major effect.

In addition to the outcomes of schooling there are two process effects which have a bearing. The first concerns the process of schooling and the second concerns the process of choice. Parents generally want their children to be happy at school although some may discount temporary unhappiness following a change of school on the basis that the child will be happier when settled. They take into account the personality of their child and how it will fit into a particular school. This appears to be particularly important in the choice of primary school together with distance from home.

The process of choice effect incorporates such factors as the education of siblings, relatives and school friends. Parents with several children may not make individual decisions about their schooling but may have made decisions which involve them all. They may be basing the choices on the present education of the others or their own past experiences of education. The effects on some children of the choice of secondary school of their friends should not be underestimated. Identifying opinion-formers – children or their parents — who may be influential to others, and their reasons, may be disproportionately important.

School responses

It is fairly obvious that there are limitations on what a school can do in response to findings on school choice particularly where it has a poor reputation which is due to the nature of its surrounding catchment area. Whilst undoubtedly there are barriers to any response to parental choice, one that should be singled out for particular attention is the perception of senior staff that nothing can be done and the situation is inevitable. There are a range of responses. Some involve a rational consideration of the evidence against a checklist of possible areas to work on, but others require more lateral thinking and a one-off response for a specific school situation.

A framework which has been offered from research suggests the following when a school is under pressure from lack of students:

- Competitive response – a substantive attempt to change school performance and image.
- Raising income – raising additional income to support the school's activities when the formula budget is inadequate.
- Efficiency savings – trying to carry out activities more efficiently and cutting some activities which are not core.
- Political responses – trying to exert influence to obtain more favourable treatment for the school.
- Collaborative responses – either using combinations of the above or trying to work with other schools to reduce the effects of competition.

Two final thoughts that may have resonance for some schools. First, there are indications that some parents plan their child's route through the school system rather than make a separate choice at each stage. This involves identifying a linkage of one or more primary schools and the associated secondary school. Schools caught in such a pattern where there is some degree of rejection of another school in the group may have limitations on what actions they can take to become more popular without involving other schools in the grouping. A recognition of this effect can save effort on promotion and redirect it to trying to enlist the co-operation of the other schools. Secondly, whilst distance from home is one criteria for choice of school, travel patterns and access can also be factors. Examining commuting and transport patterns may offer fruitful ways of seeking to increase the number of students. This may require the provision of supervision and meals where children will be dropped off and picked up well outside school hours.

3   Leadership and Strategy

Introduction

This chapter examines the role of leadership in generating strategy. It distinguishes leadership, management and administration. It suggests that particular leadership styles will produce particular responses from followers. The role of values in leadership and the assessment of leadership effectiveness are discussed.

The final section of the chapter examines the mental processes of leaders and role of personal theories and mental constructs. It commends the analytical value of the four organisational perspectives – structural, human relations, political and cultural.

Leadership, management and administration

Much current educational writing in England has emphasised leadership as the activity for headteachers. It is not clear whether this is a change of emphasis in the activity or merely a change of name. Since, as I shall argue, leadership represents an entrepreneurial and proactive end of a continuum, it is particularly ironic that such a change should happen at the present time. Commentators have noted the greater degree of central prescription which is increasingly imposed on headteachers and that their function is becoming that of administrators – quite the opposite end of the continuum.

The changing name of the UK association for the study of this area illustrates changing usage:

- British Educational Administration Society (BEAS) 1972–79
- British Educational Management and Administration Society (BEMAS) 1979–2001
- British Educational Leadership, Management and Administration Society (BELMAS) 2001–.

Any reading of the literature on management quickly reveals that there are cycles in the popularity of the terms leadership and management. As interest in one wanes or disillusionment sets in the other is brought forward as the solution to the problem. But any keen eyed observer would note the similarity of the ideas and concepts which are put forward under the two terms. For example, the leadership grid at one point in time may be found as the management grid at another (see Figure 3.2). These are both demonstrations of the two dimensions of leadership/management – a concern for people as individuals and a concern for getting the job done.

Such changes of fashion rather than substance do not help to make progress in trying to understand the complex and contradictory area. To try to make progress I have suggested that rather than have swings of fashion, the two terms should be used for complementary aspects of the direction/motivation/organising continuum. For what is quite evident is that successful organisations require both leadership and management, but not necessarily combined in one person and certainly not at all times. Both leadership and management can be dispersed within an organisation.

My formulation which is widely shared is the following:

Leadership ⟷ **Management** ⟷ **Administration**

Person centred-------------system centred

Proactive--------------------steady-state/reactive

I make the distinction that:

Managers are appointed but leaders emerge.

This formulation puts management at the centre of operations and I think this is right. It is the responsibility of managers to ensure that the other functions are in place. It is the job of a manager to ensure that for any operation there is leadership, whether provided by the manager him or herself or whether it is delegated to others. As I shall argue later, leadership can be in many forms and if it is to be flexible, responsive and comprehensive it needs to be provided in more than one form. It follows from this that unless the manager is unusually talented and multiskilled, a range of individuals will be needed to supply different facets of leadership at different times.

❑ Leadership
Leadership involves such roles as

- entrepreneur: identifying new opportunities
- motivator: inspiring and motivating others to commit
- figurehead: representing the organisation
- spokesperson: articulating meaning or what the organisation stands for.

Leadership is recognised by the presence of followership. If people are not willingly and confidently following then there is no leadership. Leadership provides meaning for those within an institution by defining and espousing the values of the organisation.

This identification of leadership with action means that leaders cannot be appointed. Individuals may be appointed to leadership positions but whether they show leadership is an empirical question. Of course, those who are appointed to heads of institutions have a number of sources of power which help to establish and sustain leadership credentials.

Leadership is a complex area with many apparently contradictory requirements. Suggestions that particular approaches to leadership should be universal, for example transformational leadership, should be resisted. Any particular formulation of leadership highlights some actions and ignores others. Any such simple formulation should be taken as one aspect of leadership rather than a comprehensive articulation of leadership. Leadership will need to exhibit many actions in different styles on different occasions.

It is clear that strategy requires leadership as we have identified it above. Strategy identifies new opportunities and is central to an organisation's goals. It has to be in line with the values that the organisation stands for and staff and others need to have confidence in the new organisational direction and enthusiastically play their part in making it succeed. There are two separate aspects to this. The first involves the strategy formulation process and the second is the strategy implementation process. Both of these processes need to be led.

❑ Management
Management involves such functions as

- planning
- organising
- staffing
- resourcing
- monitoring and controlling
- liaising and negotiating
- communicating.

These functions are essential if any project is going to be successfully completed. They combine work on systems and influence on people. The nuts and bolts of ensuring that the right people are at the right place at the right time with the right resources and know what to do constitute the essence of management. It is clear that if strategic resolutions are to be put into practice then management is essential. Much management practice has been broken down into well-developed skill areas.

❑ Administration

Administration is concerned with

- establishing routines
- ensuring the smooth running of systems
- collecting, storing and analysing data.

In the steady state administration should work efficiently and effectively to ensure that routine operations run smoothly. This provides a stable base for change. Good records provide a source of information which can be invaluable in making informed decisions. Any new strategy is likely to require changes to routines and systems in order to accomplish change and to institutionalise the new procedures.

Thus it is clear that as strategy moves from formulation through implementation to institutionalisation all three aspects will need to play their part. How this is done and who is involved may depend on circumstances. In primary schools the headteacher will almost certainly be involved in all three aspects although others will play appropriate parts whilst in secondary schools the greater number of staff in senior positions and the availability of support staff will mean that different people may be the mainstays of different aspects of the process.

Approaches to leadership

One of my worries about the use of the term leadership is that is tends to be associated with a heroic vision of leadership – the Arnold of Rugby, great headmaster, syndrome – and this is most unhelpful. For that reason I have separated what leaders need to do from how they go about doing it. I have given above a sketch of what good leadership involves and here I want to offer some thoughts about how leadership might operate. A great deal of attention has been paid to leadership in the management literature and, whilst progress has proved to be elusive, some worthwhile ideas have emerged:

- contingent style
- personal preferences
- leaders emerge
- organisational model.

First, there is general agreement that leadership should be contingent, that is, it should depend on circumstances. A number of scholars have developed ideas on 'situational leadership'. These have focused on the internal situation within an organisation Based on the strategic model I have suggested that actions should depend on two organisational factors:

- the external context in which the organisation finds itself
- the internal situation or conditions within the organisation.

I shall use the term contingent leadership to distinguish it from the more restricted situational kind which only considers internal factors. I think that the standard presentation underemphasises the importance of the external context and the requirements which this imposes on leadership and management. For a school, for example, there are great differences between the leadership required in an environment where there is great demand for high-quality education compared with one where the community is uninterested.

At first sight it is reassuring that different approaches can be successful. On the other hand, it throws up the problems of how to diagnose the context and situation in order to match an approach to the circumstances.

Secondly, there is an intensely personal dimension to leadership. The personal characteristics of the individual leader have to be accommodated in any approach to leadership. If a leader is not to be an actor, he or she must have authenticity and this must come from their inner character.

Thirdly, leadership does not only come from those in 'leadership positions' and may not come from those in management positions who are expected to lead.

Fourthly, as there are different ways of conceptualising organisations so there are different ways of looking at leadership – structural, human relations, political and cultural. Whilst these could be viewed as alternatives they are probably best viewed as different dimensions of leadership and that more than one may be required to be effective.

These points could apply to the leadership of any organisation but there are two further points which are particularly poignant for schools:

- professional staff
- moral function.

First, schools are one of a small group of organisations which have a staff who are professionally qualified. Thus, in addition to generic aspects of leadership, leadership in schools is expected to show professional leadership in education and teaching. These two are not the same. Whilst headteachers may be able to gain some credibility from their colleagues by demonstrating their practical teaching ability, as heads of schools they also need to be able to show their credentials as educators. This involves an overview of the curricular needs of children, their learning propensities and appropriate educational approaches.

Secondly, it has been pointed out that leadership of schools may need to be different to the leadership of commercial organisations because education is a moral activity. Education does not only involve the learning of facts but also how to behave. Whilst that has implications for the activity which is being led, it may also have implications for the way in which it should be led. It is the age-old means–ends dilemma but with the added complication that the ends themselves have a moral aspect (this is discussed further on p. 36).

I want to discuss briefly the first four points. This is intended to raise issues which individual leaders might use to examine their own practice and to think about extensions to their leadership approach or alternatives if their approach does not appear to be working.

The Johari window (Figure 3.1) is a device for explaining the relationship between personal understanding and competence and suggests ways of developing competence.

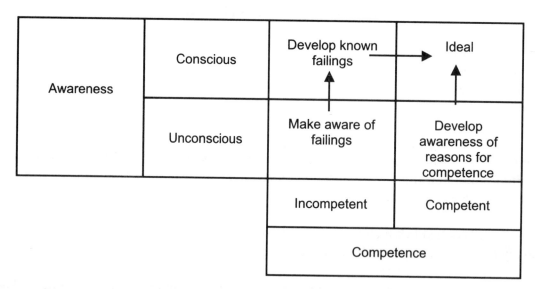

Figure 3.1 *Johari window of awareness and competence*

Situational leadership assumes that an approach to leadership in a particular context should be tailored to the circumstances. This may require a different approach to the leadership of groups from that dealing with individuals. And each individual may need treating differently and these differences may change over time. Most sensitive leaders are likely to find themselves operating with individual members of staff in this way without even being aware of it. They will be aware of the expectations of others and integrate these with their own personal preferences to formulate an approach that they are comfortable with. Two characteristics delineating different approaches to leadership and management are concerns for people and results (see Figure 3.2). These are treated as independent characteristics rather than alternatives.

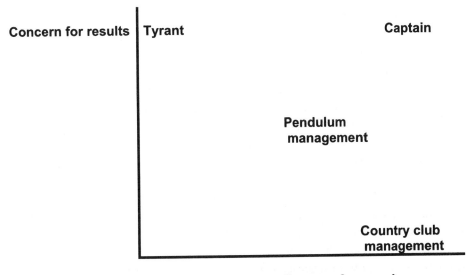

Figure 3.2   *Different management styles showing different degrees of concern for results and concern for people*

Whilst these positions are mainly self-explanatory, pendulum management may need a little explanation. This is a situation where there is no consistent concern for either results or people. This style sometimes displays one and sometimes the other.

Those who have studied situational leadership suggest an appropriate balance between these two concerns depends upon the state of the organisation and the maturity of the staff. For example, where a school is failing a more directive style of leadership may be needed to obtain results quickly to reassure parents and others that an improvement is taking place. If confidence is not restored swiftly, the more substantive task of improvement may be made even harder because parents have begun to take their children elsewhere. Also, where a staff is particularly inexperienced it is suggested that a more directive style of leadership may be required. Of course, it is a truism that an organisation's most important resource is its staff and so any short-term expedients in terms of particular styles of leadership should be balanced against the long-term needs for enthusiastic and innovative staff.

Leaders need to discover a style of leadership which is comfortable for them. Each will have strengths and weaknesses from the organisation's perspective and individuals need to understand themselves and seek to minimise their weaknesses. This can often be done by using other strengths within the management group of a school. Instead of expecting one person to possess all the desirable skills and qualities, a much more feasible alternative is to identify one's personal attributes and also the strengths and weaknesses of others who could also play leadership roles. There are three aspects to this.

- complementary styles
- dispersed
- developer of others.

The first point is concerned with the complementary perspectives from which an organisation can be analysed and the corresponding type of leadership which is required. A valuable heuristic formulation is to view leadership from the four organisational perspectives (see Chapter 3, p. 47) – structural, human relations, political and cultural. Each of these requires a different form of leadership to be successful. The structural view requires a leader who can plan and organise the structural elements to ensure appropriate staff and resources operating through efficient systems. The human relations perspective requires a leader who can communicate and empathise with individual members of staff so as to motivate and develop them to achieve the organisation's objectives. The political view requires someone who knows how to use power and is adept at negotiation and bargaining, and knows when and how to form alliances and coalitions with others. Finally, the cultural view recognises the importance of symbolism and rituals to convey meaning to organisation members so that they 'understand' what is required of them and feel that what they are doing is important and valued.

The second point identifies a different need. Whilst the need above is for complementary skills, there is also a need to ensure that leadership is organisationally dispersed. If the organisation is divided into departments or sections with different functions, each of these will need leadership of its area of operations if it is to do more than follow orders from the centre. For all except the smallest organisation, some delegation of responsibilities is necessary if leadership is not to be remote, lacking in situational knowledge and decision-making log-jammed by the sheer volume of decisions required.

The third point is concerned with developing future leaders. In addition to compensating for the deficits which any particular leader might have, there is also an issue about how future leaders are developed. It is difficult to see how future leaders can emerge if they have never been given an opportunity. Thus for developmental purposes other members of the organisation need to be given opportunities so they can gain experience and show their abilities. At times this may mean that although there are more senior staff who might be expected to lead a particular activity and are well able to do so, more junior staff are given the opportunity in order to facilitate their development. This should be part of a staff development policy which involves preparation and coaching for such activities.

A conundrum for leaders is how to balance their personal ideas and the suggestions of others. Leaders who are infinitely malleable and willing to take on any ideas from others do not inspire confidence, whilst those who have their own fixed ideas are unlikely to receive enthusiastic support and positive suggestions for improvement from others. The leader's stance on this dilemma needs authentic feedback from the perspective of followers if the leader is to have confidence that they have got the balance right. Without this leaders may be unaware of misgivings of their followers.

❑ The leadership style will condition the behaviour of followers

The style of leadership also conditions what is expected of followers and may also limit what is possible for followers in the future. Whilst initially this may not be serious, in the longer term this reduces the options open to the organisation. Where an autocratic head has reduced the need for, and may even have suppressed, the initiative of other members of the senior management team (SMT) this may have repercussions for the next head. Although he or she may wish for a more participative and shared style of leadership, this may be very difficult where the SMT have been selected for, and have become habituated into, a different way of working which has expected much less of them. It may even mean that there is a lack of other leadership talent in the school to take up positions as they become vacant.

Figure 3.3 shows four leadership positions depending on whether the leader is proactive or reactive and whether he or she is autocratic or democratic in terms of participation of others. Here strong leadership combines emphasis on active leadership in an autocratic style. When, however, an autocratic style is combined with a reactive stance then the leader will be viewed as someone who needs to be pleased. The leader will hear only good news in addition to being presented with decisions only he or she can make. The corresponding positions when the basic style is democratic are the captain for an active stance and a co-ordinator where the stance is reactive.

Figure 3.4 gives the followership style which can be expected to correspond with particular leadership positions.

The role of values

There has recently been more articulation of the importance of personal values for leaders and institutional values. Partly this interest has been spurred by the study of organisational culture and the values which are embedded within the taken for granted actions of organisation members. Partly this has been engendered by the more explicit recognition of the role of schools in developing the morals of children during their education. Finally, there has been a longstanding tradition in England of associating headmasters and headmistresses with a strong moral stance.

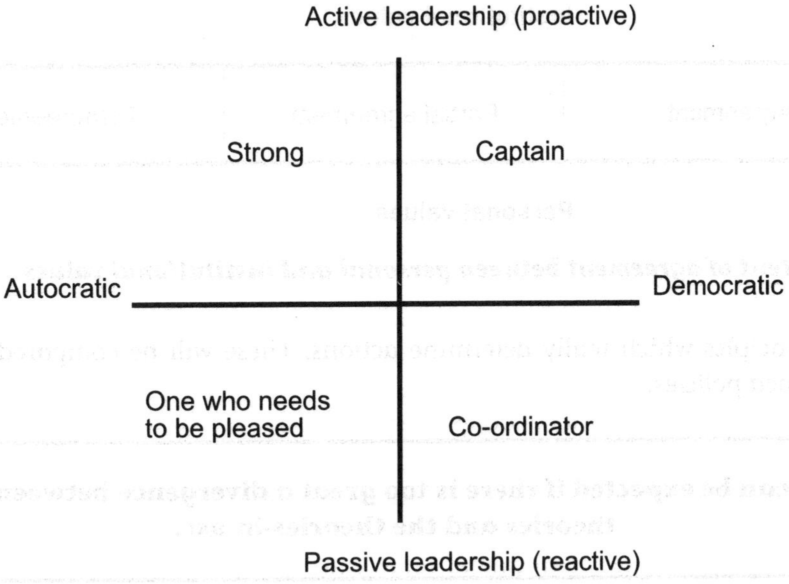

Figure 3.3 Leadership descriptions of four forms which differ in terms of personal involvement and the involvement of others

Leadership style	**Followership style**
Strong	Dependent
One who needs to be pleased	Courtier
Captain	Team member
Co-ordinator	Independent operator

Figure 3.4 Corresponding leadership and followership styles

This is not the place for a long discussion of this subject but I want to raise a number of complexities which do not appear to have been recognised by those who sloganise on this issue. Values appear to be treated as straightforward and unchanging. Some issues which need consideration are

- the relationship between personal and institutional values
- the consistency between the values implicit in institutional processes and proclaimed personal and organisational values
- the complexities which arise when values conflict.

How far does the leader have to subscribe to and exemplify the values proclaimed by the institution? There are three possible cases (see Figure 3.5).

At one extreme it is difficult to imagine a mismatch between the two being tenable without there being great cynicism at the hypocrisy involved, but there may be a middle ground of partial agreement which is quite tenable. This provides some flexibility for future change.

At the behavioural level people will compare the actions of a leader with what is the publicly proclaimed moral stance of the organisation. From an analysis of actions they will infer what are the 'theories-in-use'

Institutional values

Agreement	Partial agreement	Disagreement

Personal values

Figure 3.5   The extent of agreement between personal and institutional values

or what are the principles which really determine actions. These will be compared with the 'espoused theories' or proclaimed policies.

> **Cynicism can be expected if there is too great a divergence between espoused theories and the theories-in-use.**

Whilst there may be arguments about whether management in business organisations is a moral activity, there can be little doubt that leading an educational organisation is. There are two clear reasons why this should be so. There is still a presumption of *in loco parentis* for schools in England. The school takes the place of parents for the young and immature whilst they are in attendance. Secondly, schools play a part in the moral development of children both within the formal curriculum and implicitly in the hidden curriculum. Whilst an academic approach within the curriculum may not be problematic, actions of staff and the headteacher which will be observed as part of the hidden curriculum certainly are. This reduces to the age-old ends and means debate. Whilst there may be clear and consistent moral answers provided by philosophers, many pragmatists will see a need for judgement which takes account of such factors as

- the desirability of the ends
- the possible mismatch between the means and proclaimed institutional values and the example this may set.

A final area which illustrates the difficulty of any high-profile value stance concerns the frequent conflicts between espoused values. Those who do not see a difficulty should beware of engendering a great deal of cynicism when practice does not match proclaimed values. An acid test of the degree to which values are espoused is not what is proclaimed but what happens when two espoused values are in conflict. Inferences will be drawn about which are the truly held values by studying which prevail when they are in conflict. Where judgement is being exercised in deciding an order of precedence for the conflicting values, any particular example may give a misleading picture of which are most deeply held. Any realistic discussion of values has to recognise that few are absolute and that judgement will be needed in particular cases. This makes the whole area much more complicated than the simple prescriptions allow.

Leadership effectiveness

There are two criteria for judging the performance of a leader:

- outcomes
- process.

The first way of judging the head of an organisation's performance is by what he or she achieves in terms of organisational outcomes. This should be reflected in the performance of the organisation. In its turn this raises two further questions. First, to what extent should the head be held accountable for performance and, secondly, how should performance be judged? The next section (p. 39) will deal with these issues.

The second way of judging a head's performance is by evaluating the processes by which the out his or her work. First, this requires some framework to analyse the work of the headt secondly, it requires an assessment of how well the headteacher performs on each aspect of the The section on page 40 will pursue these issues.

❑ School performance

First, I shall discuss the difficulties of assessing the performance of a school before returning to the issues as to how far a school leader should be responsible for school performance.

There are a number of criteria which could be used to assess the performance of a school:

1. Output performance measures, e.g. examination results, attendance and other published indicators.
2. Progress or value added measures of children's progress.
3. Office for Standards in Education (OFSTED) school inspection findings.
4. Systematic satisfaction ratings from parents and students.
5. Popularity of the schools in terms of parental choice and reputation.
6. Achievement of aims.

Each of these criteria has some difficulties. In the case of (1) there would need to be appropriate comparators so that the school's value on any indicator could be judged to be adequate or not. Deciding what are similar schools in order to perform a valid comparison is not easy. Having found valid comparisons it is likely that the school will be adequate on some indicators and not on others. However, it is not only the level of the indicator as compared with similar schools which is important. A further factor to be considered is how these indicators are changing year by year. A school improving from a low base would probably be judged differently from a school declining from a high base.

Criterion (2) requires data on input scores of children when they enter the school and when they leave. If these are available then it is possible to calculate whether the school is helping children make as much progress as other schools. Again, in addition to relative progress, there should also be a consideration as to whether progress is rising year by year or declining.

Office for Standards in Education school inspections judge a school on a wide range of performance measures but these are only carried out every six years for a typical school, although schools with weaknesses may be inspected more regularly. In addition to poor performance of the school, the inspection report is also likely to express a judgement on the leadership and management of the school.

Schools which have begun to collect systematic satisfaction ratings from parents and students have a further source of information with which to judge the performance of a school. A particular difficulty with this source of information is that there are no systematic comparative results from other schools although there are some schemes operated by LEAs or universities which can give some comparative results using a specific instrument. In general, such measures of satisfaction could only be used as a means of indicating rising or declining trends over time as yearly statistics are built up by an individual school.

Satisfaction ratings from staff are another possibility. Although not strictly an output measure, such ratings would be an indicator of staff morale and could be assumed to demonstrate the extent to which they are actively pursuing school aims. Other things being equal, high staff morale would be highly desirable and low morale would indicate some problems with leadership. Any ratings would need to be viewed in context and in their historical trend. There may be good reason why morale is not high at a particular period but continuing low morale would need investigation.

The popularity of a school can act as a crude barometer of parental approval although any trends would need to take account of demographic data. Numbers on roll varying in proportion to the number of children of the appropriate age would indicate a neutral trend. Clearly this indicator is very crude and may reflect all kinds of irrational decisions by parents. However, it is an indicator of which a headteacher should be aware and be taking appropriate action.

The achievement of aims is placed last not because it is least important but because it is so difficult to assess unless a particular school has formulated its aims in a precise way. This would also need indicators which had been set up to monitor the achievement of aims. Where a school believes that participation in after-school clubs, or sporting activities, or musical tuition or other activity is important and has set up a valid means of assessing success at such activities, these would provide important data for assessing a school's success. The lack of comparative data from other schools would still restrict any judgements to relative trends over time.

In the case of strategic aims, judgement will be particularly difficult because of their long-term nature. Progress will be dependent on circumstances and much planning work may not show concrete results for some time. Process indicators of strategic activity would be a better guide that actions were being taken, although these would not necessarily lead to successful outcomes.

It should be clear that no one of these indicators alone should be taken as the measure of school performance, however, some combination of them could assess success across a wide range of activities. The precise weighting of such indicators for a particular school would need a good deal of discussion and should have been agreed well before the headteacher's contribution to the achievement of these objectives comes under scrutiny. As governing bodies begin to agree performance targets with their headteachers these need to include both remedial targets for correcting any current aspects of poor performance and the more demanding developmental targets which may be connected with pay.

Having identified ways in which the performance of a school could be assessed we move on to examine the contribution of the headteacher to the performance of the school. Although it is generally accepted that the headteacher makes a great deal of difference to the performance of a school, the situation is rather more complicated than the performance of the school being a direct reflection of the performance of the headteacher. A crucial element of the process is to identify a fit between the skills and attributes of the person and the needs of the post at a particular point in time in this individual school. A candidate may be a capable candidate in a generic sense but not for a particular job and its requirements. This is especially true of headship. A headteacher may have the qualities to lead another school in different circumstances but not to lead this school at this time. This situation, however, is rare and cases which are so bad as to be prominent are likely to involve fairly substantial omissions in terms of competences.

A lack of fit and capability is likely to show up more quickly in challenging circumstances. Schools in favourable circumstances and with capable staff are likely to provide a satisfactory performance under indifferent leadership. Over time, however, poor leadership will show up. On the other hand, a school with serious weaknesses will fail to respond successfully to anything but very good leadership and leadership which is appropriate to those circumstances.

❑ Leadership and management processes

There is a case for assessing leadership effectiveness by examining the performance of leadership and management tasks irrespective of their effects on organisational performance. First, there may be external influences on organisational performance about which leadership and management can do little. Secondly, however satisfactory organisational performance may be there is the possibility that it might be still better with improved leadership. Finally, examining the performance of leadership processes may be necessary to discover why organisational performance is not more satisfactory.

Decisions will be needed on what should be assessed and how it should be assessed. There are three possible areas of assessment:

- leadership processes
- outcomes of leadership processes
- impact of these outcomes on organisational performance.

These might be expected to be connected as shown in Figure 3.6.

Leadership processes ➡ Outcomes ➡ Impact on organisational performance

Figure 3.6 Connection betwen leadership processes and organisational performance

First the leadership processes might be assessed. This would require criteria or some model of the process against which actual performance could be compared. One such leadership process could be formulating a strategic plan. Secondly, the outcomes of the process could be assessed. In this case that would be the plan itself. The strategic model of Chapter 6 provides criteria against which to assess a strategic plan. Finally, the impact of the strategic plan on organisational performance could be assessed. This would be quite difficult in view of the long-term nature of strategic planning.

A comprehensive assessment would require a specification of the job of a school leader. I have formulated such a specification when considering how to advise governing bodies about how they might recognise poor performance by a headteacher.

❏ The job of the headteacher

The job of the headteacher can be divided into:

- reactive maintenance aspects
- proactive developmental aspects.

The first aspects are the ones most likely to be covered by a job description and the ones which are most likely to be noticed if they are not done or not done well. However, it is likely to be the more proactive elements which, if they are missing, will, in the longer term, be recognised as having handicapped the school in more subtle and more important ways. Strategy is in this second group.

The proactive elements of a job include those tasks which a good headteacher does which help to ensure the future success of the school – enhancing the reputation of the school, obtaining financial and other support, dealing with problems at a formative stage rather than when they have escalated into a crisis, etc.

The model of headship proposed here is based on two aspects of headship identified by researchers some time ago. It has two principal dimensions, each of which have a number of components and these are presented in increasing order of proactivity. The two dimensions are 'leading professional' and 'chief executive'. The leading professional dimension covers those aspects of headship which explicitly require a professional educational background, whilst the chief executive dimension covers more generic leadership and management skills:

- Leading professional
  - teaching
  - educational vision
- Chief executive
  - management
  - relationships
  - leadership.

In each dimension this ordering probably represents the order of difficulty in diagnosing and improving performance. This is not to suggest that it is easy to deal with poor teaching but, rather, to suggest that it is more difficult to deal with the others since they also involve an effect on other adults.

Teaching

The procedures here are likely to be similar to poor performance by other teachers with the exception that all judgements about poor performance will need to be made by outside professionals. Any starting point for judging performance should not be that the headteacher should be better than other teachers in the school. Headteachers should be chosen for their ability to lead and manage a school. They should be professionally competent as teachers but it is primarily as educators that they will lead and manage the education of children in school. They should not, however, be poor teachers. This becomes an absolute for a teaching head. In a small school where the headteacher is required to take a permanent teaching load it might be thought that their performance standards should be similar to that for other teachers. However, there is an added complication. In addition to their teaching they are also required to carry out functions similar to those of headteachers of larger schools but, since they spend time teaching, they have less time in which to carry out similar management and leadership responsibilities. Research on teaching heads in small schools shows that the only way in which they can fit in all their work is by spending less time than they would like on some aspects of the job – often this is preparation and marking. They are generally still able to teach at least satisfactorily because they are experienced and good practitioners.

Educator

Heads of larger schools are likely to be able to choose the extent and nature of their teaching and thus it is more likely to be their skills as educators which are more critical than their ability as teachers. Heads are required to have a base of knowledge and expertise about how children should be educated. This is not the same as their being able to teach. As heads they are required to take an overview of all that goes on in a school. They need to be able to diagnose what is needed and ensure that they and their teachers deliver it. They need to keep abreast of educational developments and have ideas about worthwhile innovations and improvements which could be introduced at an appropriate stage. Although others in schools can contribute to these, and may be a source of ideas, the head is expected to be the leading professional adviser to the governing body and be capable of offering advice both about external requirements which the school is expected to meet and about the priority which should be given to internally generated improvements.

Management

The foregoing provides the professional base on which a head manages a school. The headteacher needs to ensure that there are systems in place for:

- curriculum development and monitoring
- staff management
- financial management
- external relations.

It is probably in the area of financial management and particularly the more routine aspects of budgetary information and control where governors are likely to be aware of any shortcomings. Whilst the other areas are likely to require professional judgement, governors should be able to judge the extent to which planning is based on information, the implementation of plans is monitored and activities are systematically monitored and evaluated. Warning signs are likely to be a lack of administrative systems, frequent crises, paucity of factual information, and frequent unplanned reactions to events.

The headteacher needs to be capable of taking an overview of all the operations in a school and appreciating the interrelationships between the different aspects. This, and an appreciation of longer-term progress, is at the heart of strategy. There should be processes in operation which demonstrate that any strategy is soundly based.

Relationships

Management and leadership rely upon a relationship with children, parents, staff and governors. There are also relationships with the community, the LEA, etc. At the heart of many relationship problems is communication, either currently or in the past. The need to explain and provide information is fundamental to good management. Where there is poor communication people are left to make their own surmises about what is happening and why. This may lead to mistrust and provide a fertile breeding ground for those with imagination.

From time to time there will be genuine differences of opinion which spring from deep-seated differences of values between individuals. Often the differences between such values are implicit rather than being made explicit. The apparent differences are about opinions and priorities, and there seems to be no respect for the other person's point of view. Relationships are unlikely to be repaired if respect, honesty and shared confidence are lacking. These are difficult issues because there are at least two parties involved and both need to co-operate for good working relationships.

Leadership

Finally, there is that indefinable quality of leadership. Leadership is only demonstrated by followership, therefore, if the headteacher has little impact on staff and students, there can be no leadership. There are many forms of leadership rather than the heroic 'Arnold of Rugby' model but all need to have the effect of causing others to move forward and have confidence that the school is in good hands. Where there are administrative systems in place which work and the routine aspects of management appear to be taking place, any failure to bring about improvement in a school must involve some failure of leadership. This may be a failure to diagnose a need for movement or an inability to lead the improvement. The leader needs to convince others of the importance of the school's work and help them recognise a value and meaning in their activities. He or she needs to recognise and share a need for change and improvement, and to convince others that he or she has a strategy for the future of the school. Good leaders delegate but the leadership of the whole school cannot be delegated: this is the task of the headteacher.

Leadership is where the generic aspects of leadership and the professional skills of the leading professional come together. Formulating an educational vision and implementing it will be key requirements. This is the essence of instructional or curriculum leadership. It will require the harnessing of organisational and educational knowledge to appreciate how structural, human relations, political and cultural components can be applied to improve the teaching and learning of children.

How does the leader figure it all out? The role of personal theories and mental constructs

There is a great temptation to assume that people who use words understand the meaning of the words that they use. A few moments' reflection and experience of similar processes in children will soon bring to mind rather a lot of contrary examples. The use of terminology may only indicate the most superficial acquaintance with the ideas and in some cases may indicate a misunderstanding. And as all examiners know it is very difficult to probe deep understanding.

> **ASSUME makes an ASS out of U and ME.**

Part of this difficulty is that understanding is a very individual process. My understanding is not the same as your understanding of the same concepts. They should have much in common and amount to the same thing but my mental model and the way that I think and express the ideas will be different from yours. This raises very profound and complex issues about how we can discuss with others complex ideas which we have difficulty putting into words. Such tacit knowledge is very difficult to investigate and yet it is at the heart of much of the expertise of professionals. Through their training and experience they have absorbed much knowledge, but in uncodified ways.

❏ Heuristics and mental schemas

Individuals have personal mental models which they use to assimilate and store new knowledge. This is the means by which they make sense of the world. By analysing their past experience they have acquired a personal understanding of why things happen as they do. One example of differences in the way which individuals do this is the extent to which they attribute results to personal agency or themselves and how far they see external forces including luck as the main reason that things happen as they do. This is the theory of attribution – some individuals tend to attribute success and failure to factors internal to themselves, whilst others tend to attribute similar successes and failures to chance or external factors seeing themselves as powerless. On the basis of similar experiences individuals build up their own personal theories of why things happen. They use this personal understanding to make predictions of what will happen in the future if particular actions are taken.

The description 'personal theories' may imply a greater awareness of the bases of the assumptions involved than is the case. Individuals are usually not aware of these personal assumptions. The unconscious use of these personal theories carries with it the great danger that such assumptions through long use will be assumed to be fixed and reflect reality rather than only being a personal interpretation of reality. Long use of personal models in this implicit way may mean that the 'model becomes the world'. When external events change the nature of past certainties such fixed mental models need to be questioned so that some assumptions which worked well in previous circumstances can now be revised. Such revisionism is particularly called for when external circumstances are changing and a new culture is required within an organisation. As is indicated in Chapter 6, p. 92, if the organisational culture changes this may be a very fruitful and productive time, but only if previously fixed assumptions are questioned and some are changed. This is an important mental process and probably needs to be done both privately and also in combination with others. Discussion with others can both help identify personal assumptions and suggest new possibilities. Where individual understanding is difficult, discussion with others may play a part in the clarification process.

One of the aims of many of the activities in this book is to raise points for discussion that might never be raised in the ordinary processes of running a school. Many of them would be implicit and taken for granted, and never consciously acknowledged. Differences of understanding or differences of opinion would never come to light in the ordinary course of events. This is undesirable because discussion of differences of understanding can help to improve and clarify the understanding of all. Differences of opinion may indicate differences of underlying value. It is important to separate differences arising in these two ways, although of course the two causes may be linked. There is a hope of moving to a common understanding but differences of value and priority may always remain.

Some techniques have been used to gain insights into personal models in use for managers engaged in strategy in commercial organisations. There appears to be a role for concept maps, causal maps and repertory grids (see Figure 3.7) as ways of making these internal mental processes more accessible both to individuals and also to facilitate group discussion. Concept maps help identify which concepts individuals use in particular situations and how the concepts are related. Causal maps identify how individuals assume that actions are caused. Such maps deal with which effects produce which results though which mechanisms. Whilst there are indications that this may be a very fruitful field, trials are needed of the different ways of eliciting such maps since results differ according to the way in which thinking is probed. Repertory grids have been used for some time within education to identify ways in which individuals compare and discriminate in their thinking.

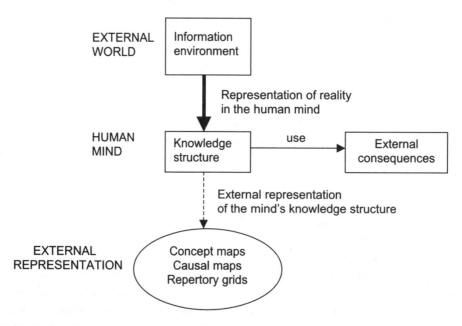

Figure 3.7 The distinction between the external world and internal representations of it and external representations of internal knowledge structures

A study of this body of literature indicates that decision-making is both more complicated and simpler than prescriptions to engage in rational decision-making assume. As Sir Herbert Simon demonstrated in the 1950s, the assumptions of optimal decision-making are hopelessly unrealistic. Whilst his suggestions of satisficing may be nearer a description of what happens, the actual processes of individual decision-making are only weakly understood. When individuals are asked to explain how they reached a decision they appear to defend a decision they have intuitively reached rather than describe how they reached the decision. Whilst it is possible to assume that a range of relevant factors were weighed in the balance as the decision was made, there are known limitations of the human memory.

> **The best is the enemy of the good.**
>
> (Voltaire)

The two effects that I wish to raise concern the extent of short-term memory and its selective nature. Psychological experiments since the 1950s have shown that typically individuals can recall about seven unrelated pieces of information. The normal range being five to nine. This finding presents problems for those who suggest that obtaining large amounts of background information improves the quality of decisions. A question arises: how is this information to be used in view of these memory limitations? A second set of issues concerns the accuracy of facts recalled from longer-term memory. There are a range of potential psychological biases which have been identified and their dangers considered in management training courses. These have not generally been brought to the attention of education managers. The ones I particularly want to dwell on here are ones caused by memory being selective:

- High-profile events acquire disproportionate significance – the unquestioned anecdote becomes the generality.
- Recent and vivid events are more easily recalled.
- The way that issues are posed and the starting estimates heavily influence the subsequent discussion in ways that are entirely arbitrary.
- The difficulties of changing from the status quo are frequently exaggerated.

These effects have implications for strategic decision-making. First, there is a need to ensure that any data, whether quantitative or qualitative, has its representativeness assessed. Is this effect typical? Secondly, there is a need to consider a large number of potential effects but these must be prioritised and, if possible, conceptualised as a smaller number of multifaceted effects. Thirdly, there is a need to be aware of and attempt to reduce the potential of the range of biases to influence the result. Fourthly, there is a need to reflect on and learn from past decisions. Finally, to develop good judgement which takes account of the relative probability of different outcomes rather than being dominated by the favourableness of the outcome.

❏ Figuring it out: the role of organisational analysis

One of the findings resulting from studying successful chief executives of commercial companies is that they appear to have developed a 'helicopter view'. This is the ability to move between an overview of a situation and its detail. This has been likened to changing the scale of a map or changing the magnification of a lens. Not only is it important to be able to change scale between the 'big picture' and the detail, but also to comprehend how the two relate to each other.

Following from the previous section the question arises – what are the features on the map and do they change as the map changes scale? These are empirical questions for which more work on conceptual mapping might begin to provide answers, but what I want to raise in this section is the value of organisational analysis for deciding what should be the features on the map in each case.

If one takes the view, as I do, that management and leadership involve choosing appropriate actions in particular situations, then this raises issues about how such choices should be made. One school of thought is prepared to assume that such decisions are made intuitively as a result of much experience and reflection. There appears to me to be a number of problems with such a formulation. First, it suggests little certainty about the quality of the next decision which is made, even if it follows a successful track record. Secondly, it offers little help in developing the skills to carry out such a task and, thirdly, it provides little help in checking the basis for the decision either before or after the event. So I propose an alternative mechanism which meets these objections.

My proposition is that although rational analysis has its limitations as the previous section has alluded, it can assist other more complex and intuitive processes. I make no assumption about the nature of the intuitive processes and their rationality, only that the processes are subconscious, complex and do not meet the formal tests of rationality. There may be a rational basis but there are great difficulties in trying to investigate such thinking. Thus I only assume that some formal models can assist in the diagnosis and formulation of actions. In addition to the value of such analysis on particular occasions, there is some evidence that exposure to such formal education at formative stages in the work of professionals does influence the way in which they set up their internal mental structures. It also may help identify similar situations in the past to compare and learn from previous outcomes.

My statement of what management and leadership does presupposes that different situations require different actions. This is a particular example of contingency theory. This assumes that actions should be contingent on circumstances. A few moments' reflection on the alternative – that there are universal actions applicable in all circumstances – will suggest that this principle has at least face validity. I have suggested that contingent leadership will involve taking account of the internal situation within the organisation and the external context in which it finds itself. This is consistent with the strategic model which will be introduced in Chapter 6.

If contingent actions are required, how are they to be chosen? I suggest that this requires:

- a method for analysing the situation and context
- diagnosing needs for action
- choosing from a range of possible actions.

All these processes require knowledge, interpretation, application and judgement. Here I want to deal with knowledge to analyse situations and knowledge to diagnose the possible results of actions. This is where organisational theories and management theories come in. Whilst management theories are generally prescriptive – they indicate what should happen in particular circumstances – organisation theories are descriptive – they model what is happening. Since there is more than one of each kind, the first decision is to choose the most promising.

There have been a number of attempts to categorise organisation theories but the one which I consider combines parsimony with sufficient accuracy is that formulated by Bolman and Deal (1997). There are four main types of theory. Each emphasises certain factors and ignores others:

- structural
- human relations
- political and
- cultural.

The structural view of organisations emphasises structures, systems, policies, job descriptions, etc. It includes such models as bureaucracy. It assumes an ordered internal situation in which people act in accordance with policies and work towards agreed organisational goals.

In contrast the human relations approach emphasises the people in the organisation. Their motivation, development and achievements are main foci. People are treated as individuals and the difference which individuals make to a task is recognised. The fit between the needs of the individual and the needs of the organisation is a major preoccupation.

The political view recognises the importance of power in organisations – both formal and informal. It examines the distribution of power and the various forms of exchange which are available for negotiation and bargaining. At an institutional level this is called micro-politics. Coalitions and alliances are expected. Although rarely categorised in this way, the collegial model of decision-making has the hallmarks of micro-politics.

The cultural approach emphasises the power of habit. This assumes that underlying organisational values influence what goes on in organisations at an unconscious level, that is, individuals have become so accustomed as to how to behave in a particular organisation they are not directly aware of why they operate as they do.

Organisational analysis consists of trying to use each of these 'lenses' to examine a particular organisational event to see what each contributes to understanding and choosing the best for the particular purpose. Within each approach there are implications for which management ideas would be applicable in the circumstances. Having chosen a particular management theory, this will make predictions about how to act and the likely consequences. As described here this may appear very mechanistic, for what is missing in this brief account is the degree of interpretation, understanding, judgement and individuality which a manager uses to make the choices and which are reflected in the outcomes.

Time for leadership and management

One of the observations of Charles Handy (1984), the management guru, when he made a short study of schools in the early 1980s was that management was not accorded sufficient time. More recent studies of headship and particularly the stress experienced by heads as they implemented local management of schools (LMS) in the early 1990s indicated that the greatest single source of pressure was insufficient time to meet their objectives. Studies of those in middle management positions in secondary schools have also found that they felt they were not accorded sufficient time to carry out their management function. Thus it seems at all levels there is felt to be insufficient time for leadership and management.

One question which should be asked is 'is this just a perception or is there substance to the feeling?' On the one hand, any analysis of the tasks to be carried out by managers indicates that these are substantial and need time. On the other hand, managers in other organisations also find they are short of time. Schools are unusual in that those who manage also teach. In other organisations the task of management is separated from that of performing the main tasks of the organisation. Thus schools involve staff in much role switching, for example, as they move from teacher in charge of a class to head of department working with other staff. Such role switching is generally found to be a further cause of stress. Thus on balance I would conclude that insufficient time is accorded to leadership and management activities.

However, as sceptics will point out, in addition to the amount of time it is also a question of how the time is used which can make a substantial difference. As C. Northcote Parkinson wryly observed 'work expands to fill the time available'. However, for some jobs in school the time allocation is so little that with the best will in the world it is difficult to see how the jobs could be done satisfactorily no matter how efficiently time was used. Thus the factors to be considered are

- the amount of time to achieve tasks
- how the tasks are carried out.

My experience of working with school managers on time management is that although there is much that can be done by individuals to improve their personal time management, there is a very large organisational dimension to the usage of time. It follows that only when time management is taken as an issue for the whole school can there be much progress on identifying redundant activities, activities which could be done more efficiently and obstacles to improving time management. This needs to be a whole staff activity to identify the need for deadlines, the existence of artificial deadlines and the problems caused for some staff by the inefficient time management of others. Greater understanding of the effects on others and demonstration of the need for the tasks can go a long way to improving co-operation.

Time management surveys of both staff and students can give a better factual basis to any consideration of time management. This means getting them to fill in diaries for brief periods so that each individual activity is noted. Such an activity is itself time-consuming and one of the practical findings from those who have carried out such activities is that the aims need to be clear. Diaries record a lot of data but the form in which it is recorded greatly affects the ease with which it can be interpreted. A pilot exercise which trials both the collection and analysis of the data will ensure a worthwhile result from a diary exercise.

A further design consideration for a diary exercise is how time is to be sampled? Who will keep diaries and over what period are important questions to ensure that the data is representative if decisions are to be based on the results. Events in a week have a pattern and so do weeks in a year. Thus any survey of staff activities needs to cover each day of the week, and weeks within a year need to be sampled so that Christmas or examination or test activities do not distort the findings.

Some indication of where the time goes – such as time spent on marking – can soon expose differences between members of staff and also unrealistic school policies which, if pursed by the conscientious will prove exhausting. And often any rational assessment of the effectiveness of time spent in this way would indicate it to have been ill-used compared with alternative ways of spending the same time. Thus factual information on how time is spent can lead to a more informed discussion of priorities and alternative ways of achieving similar objectives which take less time.

In a secondary school a survey of parents on homework suggested that for some students the amount of time spent on homework was beginning to squeeze out their ability to take part in social and cultural activities outside school. A diary exercise for a range of students would reveal the actual amount of time spent on homework and the other activities which students also spend time on. This would provide additional data to use to make policy decisions on homework to supplement general impressions of student and parental comment.

The four lines of attack for working on time management are the following:

- Prioritise.
- Increase personal efficiency.
- Co-operate to save time.
- Delegate activities to support staff.

❏ Prioritise

The standard advice on time management courses is to concentrate on the important and not only on the urgent. Whilst this is good advice, it is often less than helpful. Rarely are there examples of urgent but unimportant activities. However, asking the question – 'if I didn't do this activity what would happen?' – can often reveal that someone else would deal with it or that no great consequence would follow if no one dealt with it and that it is a habitual but irrelevant activity or it is only double checking on other information. It is vitally important when changing habitual practice to ask questions and explain why procedures have changed rather than just changing. To others this can appear to be failing to co-operate and is likely to cause resentment.

❏ Increase personal efficiency

If individuals have not recently considered how they might increase their personal efficiency, that is, completing tasks quicker, then there may be considerable scope for this. It is worth those who have previously worked on this taking stock to see if either they have fallen back into bad habits or whether new ways have emerged by which time might be saved. Potentially the greater use of personal computers and placing information on web sites could yield huge time savings. In most cases of large steps forward, an investment of time is needed in the short run in order to save time in the long run. Analysis activities may be possible when data is stored on computer which were not possible manually, and this potentially increases efficiency. However, the temptation has to be resisted to do things just because they are possible. Time-saving measures may turn out to be time-wasting measures if time is taken up with sophisticated but unnecessary activities carried out 'just in case'.

In order to increase personal efficiency the first stage is to make time to take stock and perhaps keep a personal time diary for a little while. This can reveal where time goes – those activities that consume much time, those activities whose purpose can be questioned and those activities where there might be quicker and better ways of doing them.

❏ Co-operate to save time

This has many forms. The organisational dimension has been mentioned and is certainly the most important aspect. Can corporate efficiencies be made? If there is time-consuming double checking of data, are there alternative ways of obtaining the definitive information? Is the data so important that it needs to have such a high accuracy? Accurate information comes at a cost. What takes time to collect, costs. This may be a direct financial cost or more likely it may be an opportunity cost. Other valuable activities are being squeezed out because time is being spent collecting, checking and double checking data. The cost of collecting more data rises disproportionately the more data has been collected. This effect needs to be spotted in time or large amounts of time can be spent increasing the value of data by very little. Approximate data may be good enough – providing that the accuracy of the data is borne in mind. It may be a big mistake to base strategic decisions on approximate data if it is assumed to be accurate data.

The more familiar aspect of co-operating within a school is to prevent situations where one person's time management headache is caused by another member of staff – particularly where discussion of the issue might increase co-operation. Timetabling and examination entries in secondary schools depend on a good deal of information. Unless everyone co-operates in assembling the full information, each part which has been collected is reduced in value. Such issues need to be explained and discussed rather than it being assumed that everyone understands this as a matter of course. Some will not see the vital importance of their small bit of information. The other aspect of such discussion is to see if corporately there may be more efficient ways of collecting, storing and checking information.

Although computers are already used in school administration and management, there is a great deal of potential for their further use. Computers have become faster, more user-friendly and have larger capacity than was dreamt of only a few years ago. The rapid increase in the use of computers has not always assisted their efficient use and there is a need from time to time to take stock. As has been remarked, a core competence for the strategy of any school will be an ability to use ICT. The strategic aspect of this is to have experts in the school who are good at spotting generic trends and who can differentiate passing fads from trends which catch on. Whilst technical excellence is one factor, the power of mass usage is another. Some of us learned painfully that Betamax video recorders were a passing fad because VHS, although technically inferior at the time, had achieved critical mass which meant that the VHS format would survive. In computing, those who backed the IBM compatible personal computer and software from Microsoft (irrespective of their personal preferences) were the strategic thinkers.

Whilst these are trends which are now clear with the advantage of hindsight, there will be further trends to be spotted in the future. Although this is part of the process of environmental scanning, which will be discussed in more detail later, this is an interesting special case. In a technical and specialised field there is a need to take the advice of experts, but experts tend to be more interested in the technical detail and complexity than the general potential for use by non-specialists. It is the age-old problem of 'wood and trees'. Experts who are able to consider developments from the point of view of the general user are invaluable. The advice and technical expertise of boffins without this capacity will have to be complemented by senior staff who need to develop a generic understanding of the major issues and debates. Benchmarking with schools which are recognised to be advanced in their use of ICT will help gain insights into future developments.

There are some general principles which are clear from a systems analysis of the computerised storage and retrieval of data:

- single data entry
- unified database
- multi-access
- provide value to data providers
- obtain feedback from users to improve data accuracy.

❏ Delegate activities to support staff

Although a great deal more use of support staff has followed the delegation of finances to school level, some schools have made much more use of support staff than others. This suggests that there is greater potential in most schools. The particular facet of the use of support staff which is relevant to time management is their use to take away from teachers tasks that do not require a trained teacher. Tasks that are important do not have to be done by teaching staff, they can be done by appropriately skilled and responsible administrative staff.

The general principles of delegation need to be followed:

- Delegate whole tasks.
- Prepare.
- Choose a suitable delegatee.
- Monitor.
- Evaluate.

Although 'letting go', which is at the heart of delegation, is never easy, most objections to delegation can usually be overcome if these are all followed.

Support staff, if they are trained and suitably briefed, will meet expectations. The briefing will need to explain the purpose of their job and how it fits into the school organisation. In this way sensitive support staff will be able to see their job as supporting the smooth running of the school and not as an end in itself.

It should be stressed that time management is not only for teachers. Support staff will soon have time management problems too unless care is exercised in the delegation of activities. Even if the tasks given to support staff were carefully analysed in the past, many more tasks will have been delegated to them and periodically their workload will need to be reviewed and the time management priorities applied.

The strategic dimension to time management is that most changes cannot be made very quickly. There needs to be usual processes of analysis and planning before action. In some cases there has to be a period of preparation to change expectations before the change is made if it is not to produce an adverse reaction. If there is to be a change in policies involving marking students' work, for example, then this has to be prepared for. Explanations need to be given about the reasons for any change in policy, the consequences of changes and the new expectations of what all staff will be delivering.

Where there is to be a reallocation of time which involves the timetable, then considerable lead time will be required. In secondary schools the contact ratio or proportion of available teaching time (c) which is programmed by the timetable has tended to rise. This is accounted for by the smaller size of teaching groups (g). There is a direct trade-off between the amount of non-contact time and the average teaching group size.

$$R = cg$$

(where R is the pupil teacher ratio)

Thus it is small teaching groups which are the cause of high contact ratios and a lack of non-teaching time which could be spent on leadership and management activities. In secondary schools, in the longer term, there is some flexibility. As surveys have shown, any decision about the extent of the contact ratio should take account of the out-turn contact ratio which includes the extra amount of time which teachers spend covering for absent colleagues.

In primary schools there is much less room for manoeuvre. However, in larger primary schools there will be some possibilities and, as extra resources are made available to primary schools, there will be some choices to be made. Clearly any time spent on leadership and management activities needs to have a clear pay-off and add value to the school's activities and performance rather than being taken up in 'busy' work.

For more senior colleagues, in addition to facilitating the improvement of time management in the whole school, their own personal time management needs to be increasingly good. Thought also needs to be given to the consequences of adopting a particular style of management. If there is a wish to be consultative and participative, then unless other accommodations are made this will take up a good deal of staff time. In the past, surveys have been carried out among schools staff as to the extent to which they feel that they have been adequately involved in decision-making in schools. However, such surveys which have tended to identify teachers as feeling deprived have failed to cost out the time which would be required to increase the extent of involvement in decision-making. One possibility is to survey staff asking about the areas in which they would like to be involved, to offer different ways of being involved and to ask them how much time they would be willing to spend on becoming more involved. Where such surveys have been carried out differences emerge between staff. Not surprisingly those new to teaching feel they have other calls on their time. This kind of information makes it possible to tailor involvement (see Chapter 4, p. 51).

It may also be possible to foresee how ICT may be able to open up new, more efficient practices and also provide additional ways of involving people. E-mail is particularly well suited to passing information to many staff but, as some of us have discovered, there is a very fine line between feeling underinformed and feeling overwhelmed with information of rather doubtful value.

We are entering an era of information overload and the challenge is how to discover information when it is needed rather than when it is produced. This requires knowledge of what is available and how to access it. Information management will be a core competence.

4 Working Together and Involvement

Introduction

This chapter examines ways in which staff can work together and be involved in decision-making. Consultation and participation are distinguished and a typology of involvement in decision-making is formulated. Ways of deciding who should be involved in decision-making are examined. Groups and teams are distinguished and some of the potential disadvantages of working in groups are discussed.

The second section of the chapter discusses ways in which the activities may be used to help generate strategy. Various forums for generating ideas and predicting the future are suggested and for recording the results. Finally, various techniques for problem-solving and planning change are presented.

Involving staff

The following discussion attempts to provide knowledge and understanding of staff involvement, however, the choices that a school makes must be consistent with its overall management style and must be made clear to all staff so that unrealistic expectations are not built up.

There are varying forms of involvement with an increasing degree of participation. From this point participation will be used only for the more specialised usage indicated in the following list and *involvement will be used as the more general term covering consultation and participation*. It is important to differentiate consultation from more active forms of involvement. Consultation means listening to new facts and the views of those affected by the decision but not necessarily giving these high priority in the decision-making which will be done by others. Any more active form of involvement means that these facts and views will play some part and that these groups will be involved in the decision-making in some way. If consultation is being offered then this should be made clear since, if more active involvement is envisaged, then disillusionment and cynicism is likely to result when the group find that their views have influenced the decision only marginally.

Involvement in decision-making has two major benefits:

- an improvement in the quality of the decisions
- improved motivation and commitment of those involved.

Involvement is not without its drawbacks. These include:

- It is slower than autocracy.
- It consumes a great deal of staff time.
- The pattern of decision-making is less predictable.
- The pattern of decision-making is less consistent.
- The location of accountability may be less clear.
- Some decisions are expected to be taken by senior managers and participation may be seen as abdication.

The range of styles of decision-making from the least to the most participative is the following:

1. Autocracy
   (a) autocratic – tells
   (b) autocratic – sells
   (c) modification under adverse reaction
2. Consultation
   (a) consultation on tentative decision
      (i) individual
      (ii) group
   (b) consultation on problem
      (i) individual
      (ii) group
3. Participation
   (a) participation
      (i) majority rule
      (ii) consensus
      (iii) unanimity.

The participative decision-making processes are (Murnighan, 1982):

- majority rule – a variety of techniques can be used to indicate preferences but the most popular according to the particular preference arrangement is the chosen one
- consensus – although all members must assent this can be for a compromise which satisfies everyone
- unanimity – this means that all must agree; a single no vote can veto the proposal.

The type of decision-making which involves other people least is autocracy whereby some key decision-maker unilaterally decides. Such a decision may be announced, it may be advocated and its advantages propounded, and it may even be changed in the face of substantial opposition. Consultation with others may take place after a tentative decision has been formulated and may be held either with individuals on a one-to-one basis or a group may be consulted together. Alternatively, consultation may take place after a problem has been identified but before even a tentative decision has been formulated and, again, such consultation may be with individuals or with a group. Finally, in true participation all share in the decision and methods must be identified to take into account differing preferences.

One of the most important decisions that a group makes is to decide how it will make decisions. Unless this is made explicit it is commonly found that people are not aware how decisions are made. Without some formal decision-making machinery people may not always be aware that a decision has been made even when, ostensibly, they were involved. If decisions are made following a chance discussion in an informal setting (a chat in the corridor), it is not surprising that individuals may be unaware of their part in decision-making unless it is made quite explicit that a decision will be made following such a conversation.

Consulting staff about involvement

Before any decision is taken to change the involvement of staff in decision-making it might be wise to formulate a questionnaire which investigates staff's views. This does not preclude change but makes opinion about the present situation clearer.

❏ Investigating the extent to which staff feel that they are appropriately involved

A study in a secondary school showed that teachers in the early years of their career were preoccupied with teaching and wanted little whole-school involvement. It was some staff in mid-career who were most keen for further involvement. Their wish to be involved was greatest in those decisions which affected them and they felt they had something to contribute. Most staff were willing to spend between one and three hours per week on such activities.

The means of involvement which were explored were

- questionnaire
- ballot
- one-to-one interview
- voluntary working party
- meetings – departmental
    – whole-school groupings
        ○ full staff
        ○ heads of department
        ○ pastoral
        ○ standing committees, e.g. curriculum.

The changes resulting from such an exercise are illustrated by Figure 4.1.

Satisfaction with degree of present involvement	Yes	Decrease	No change
	No	No change	Increase
		No	Yes
		Wish for future involvement	

Figure 4.1   *Comparison of present involvement and future involvement*

Factors which could be taken into account in deciding an appropriate form of decision-making concern the degree to which:

- speed is essential either because there is an impending deadline or the situation is unstable
- quality of decision is important
- expertise is available to contribute
- a likely solution is unknown and the situation without precedent
- acceptance is important
- understanding of the situation and the decision is important.

Some problems are best solved by an individual with high expertise and good judgement, and others are best solved by pooling expertise in a group and using group decision-making.

Models of decision-making

Models of decision-making fall into two broad groupings. There are those which assume that decisions are made on political grounds according to power and self-interest and which involve bargaining and negotiation. The alternative approach is to assume that a super-ordinate with power is able to make decisions using rational means (which may mean a participative approach if that appears the best rational solution).

Theories of rational decision-making contribute two broad approaches to the issue of involvement. However, it should be said that these models oversimplify the complexity of the real world and the observed thinking processes of school managers. Whilst that may be true, it would be a mistake to see the models as of little value. Clearly they may be inappropriate for much of the day-to-day decision-making which goes on in schools but are worth considering for the larger issues which occur much less frequently and as a structured way of considering the issue of involvement.

Whilst there is much agreement that participation in decision-making has some advantages, as has been pointed out above, there are also disadvantages. A number of writers make a distinction between programmed and non-programmed decisions, that is, between routine decisions and those where there are no general policy guidelines to follow. It is in this second category that participative decision-making has real value. Thus the crucial question is 'under what circumstances is participation particularly desirable?' There are some for whom this question is already answered by their value position – participation is always desirable – unrelated to the consequences of such an approach. However, for those of a more pragmatic disposition, help in formulating answers to the question would be very valuable.

The approach here uses the concept of a 'zone of acceptance' originally formulated by H.A. Simon (1957). This refers to the realm of decisions which are accepted with little or no questioning when they are handed down from above. Bridges (1967) suggested that participation in decisions outside the zone of acceptance would be worthwhile and puts forward two tests to determine such decisions:

- the test of relevance
- the test of expertise.

The test of relevance asks whether the participating individuals would have a high personal stake in the decision. The test of expertise asks whether they have expertise and knowledge to make a valid contribution. An affirmative to both of the two tests makes a strong case for involvement. However, there is evidence that within their zone of acceptance individuals may show indifference or alienation if asked to participate when they do not consider this necessary.

Figure 4.2 summarises the discussion of Hoy and Miskel (1991).

		Test of relevance	
		Yes	No
Test of expertise	No	Occasional consultation for communication purposes	No participation
	Yes	Participate	Only occasional consultation for quality decisions

Figure 4.2   *Tests of expertise and relevance to determine participation*

Whichever decision-making process is used it is essential that all parties acknowledge their part in the process. Everard and Morris (1996) expand on the relative contributions required of managers and managed under consultative decision-making. They describe this as the 'management contract' (Figure 4.3).

❏ Formation of involved groups

If groups are to be formed in order to be involved in decision-making then the bases can be:

1. representatives of interest groups
2. volunteers from those expressing interest in taking part
3. those having particular expertise for the problem
4. according to status in the school
5. randomly chosen
6. all teaching staff.

The decision taker will:

1. Share perceptions of the situation and decision criteria
2. Listen, encourage and absorb ideas
3. Decide after the meeting and communicate reasons and answer questions

The decision taker will not:

Suppress key information or only consult when in trouble
Deprecate suggestions
Decide in advance of the meeting or refuse to explain the reasons

The consulted will:

1. Ask questions, give views and provide facts
2. Contribute positive suggestions
3. Having had the opportunity to influence the decision try to make it work

The consulted will not:

Attack and criticise

Recriminate later
Act as if a decision had not been made

Figure 4.3 Consultation contract

The size of the group will impose some limitations on what can be expected of the group. If much interaction is expected between group members then the group must be small (about ten or less), more limited interaction is possible up to about 20, thereafter interaction is severely limited in the full group and sub-groups must be formed.

Groups, teams and decision-making

❑ Teams

The work of Meredith Belbin on successful teams and work groups has not received a lot of attention recently in education. His research examined the personal characteristics to determine the composition of an ideal team for problem-solving. He identified eight team roles which complemented one another to form an ideal team (http://www.belbin.com).

The roles are

- co-ordinator
- plant
- monitor-evaluator
- implementer
- completer-finisher
- resource investigator
- teamworker
- shaper.

He has also added a ninth role when a specialist in a particular field of knowledge has to be added to the team of generalists.

Those who have not completed the inventory in his book (Belbin, 1981) can do so on-line and receive feedback on their team role for a small fee. Knowing the strengths and weaknesses of any particular team compared with this 'ideal' team can sensitise a team to roles which need to be emphasised if they are to be more successful.

❑ Teams and groups

The word 'team' has passed into the language of school leadership and management rather uncritically. It tends to be used for any group working together and this has obscured the differences between a team and a co-operative group. Casey (1985) lists the following characteristics of a team:

- People trust each other.
- Feelings are expressed freely.
- Process issues are part of the work.
- Commitment is high.
- Objectives are common to all.
- Listening is high.
- Conflict is worked through.
- Decisions are by consensus.
- People are open.

Whereas for a co-operative group the characteristics are:

- People work together
- Commitment is high
- Process issues are worked on covertly
- People negotiate
- Information passes on a need-to-know basis
- Conflict is accommodated
- Politics are rife
- People co-operate to get the job done
- Feelings are not part of the work
- Trust and openness are measured.

Thus the mode of working expected of a team is much more intense and close than that of a co-operative group.

It follows that when a group is formed the degree of involvement and the decision-making style should either be specified by the head if the group is consultative and left to the group to decide if it is a participative team. Recent research on senior management teams in primary and secondary schools has shown how difficult it is to have a group which operates on participative principles when the members have different power positions in the school. The headteacher is deferred to even if he or she tries very hard to act as an ordinary member of the group.

For a participative group the role of the chair is to facilitate the process; to try to build consensus and to ensure that any minority views get a fair hearing.

For a consultative group, the chair who is likely to be the head, should ask each member of the group to give their own risk assessment of following a particular course of action. The head can gauge the reaction to the proposal and supply further information to reassure or rethink.

A further consideration is at what stage should the group be involved in the decision-making process? Should the group be involved all the way through or should some spadework be done beforehand and some parameters be defined at the start of the group's work?

This sort of consideration should go on with respect to formulating strategy. Who is to be involved at what stage (see p. 87)? It may be useful to draw up a network (see later) analysis to ensure that the process will work and that there are no bottle-necks.

It should not be thought from all the foregoing that the only disadvantages to working in groups are concerned with the logistics of time and resources. There are also more fundamental problems to working in groups.

❑ Group-think

Teams, and to a lesser extent groups, exert considerable pressure on their members to conform to the group norm. This tends to suppress independent critical thinking:

> Group-think occurs in highly cohesive groups when group pressures lead to reduced mental effort, poor testing of reality and careless moral judgements. (Cherrington, 1989: 626)

Group-think does not occur in all cohesive groups. Following work by Janis, Chell (1993) identifies eight main symptoms:

1. *Illusion of invulnerability* – leads to over-optimism and the ignoring of dangers.
2. *Rationalisation* – leads to poor feedback and problems being rationalised away by a series of 'convenient assumptions'.
3. *Illusion of morality* – the group does not question the moral rightness of their position.
4. *Shared stereotypes* – other groups and their leaders are viewed in an undesirable light.
5. *Pressure for conformity* – dissenting views are suppressed.
6. *Self-censorship* – individuals suppress their own doubts and anxieties.
7. *Illusion of unanimity* – as there are no dissenting opinions everyone assumes that everyone else is in full agreement.
8. *Mindguards* – individuals suppress and protect the group from bad news.

Some of the group techniques described below seek to minimise the consequences of some of these undesirable effects, however, some general advice offered by Chell (1993) based on work by Janis and Maier includes the following:

1. The leader should encourage critical evaluation of ideas including his or her own.
2. High-status members of the group should not initially indicate opinions in order to encourage a full consideration of the issues.
3. Dominant personalities should be prevented from having disproportionate influence.
4. The views of the silent should be sought.
5. Blame-oriented or critical statements should be avoided.
6. Alternative possibilities should be examined.
7. More than one group could examine the same question and involve some outsiders in each.
8. Outside experts could be invited to a meeting and encouraged to challenge the group's views.
9. After a preliminary decision has been reached, a further meeting should be held after members of the group have had time to reconsider and express any doubts.

❏ Risky shift

There is evidence that groups are more likely to take greater risks in their decisions than the same individuals would have done if working alone. This is called 'risky shift' (Chell, 1993). This appears to be one aspect of a more general effect called 'group polarisation'. This is the effect by which the average of the responses from a group tends to be more extreme and in the same direction as the average of the responses from the individuals before the group discussion. This means that whatever the overall view resulting from the sum of the views of individuals making up the group, this will be magnified when they act collectively.

Chell (1993) suggests that a manager should consider this effect before embarking on participative decision-making particularly if the group might polarise in an undesirable direction for the manager.

❏ Group ageing

> Groups, like individuals age. (Stein, 1982: 147)

Group age depends upon how long the group has been together. Creativity is at its peak after the group has been in existence for about two years, but declines after about five years. Groups can be prevented from ageing by bringing in new people of any chronological age. There is some evidence to suggest that groups that have been is existence for four to five years produce their most useful work.

❏ Conflict

Most accounts of organisations assume that there is a large degree of consensus and few serious disagreements. For many organisations, including schools, this is true for much of the time. However, in some schools for some of the time and in other schools for a large portion of the time conflict, either open or hidden, is present. In order to give a complete and relatively realistic account of organisation working we need to acknowledge the possibilities of conflict and offer sources of advice.

Turning to the literature on organisational development in schools we find that conflicts are not uncommon:

> Conflicts are ubiquitous within educational organizations; they occur continually, arise for many reasons, appear in a variety of forms, and affect the educational process both favourably and unfavourably. (Schmuck & Runkel, 1994: p. 327)

> conflict refers to a social condition in which two or more persons or groups cannot have the same thing at the same time. (p. 328)

It is precisely in the circumstances of working more closely together that conflict is likely to emerge. Conflicts are minimised when each teacher is left to work in their own way in their own classroom. It is when they meet, discuss and are required to cooperate that conflict may arise.

> To accomplish common tasks and achieve goals generally requires collaboration . . . Conflict is likely to arise when particular educational goals are perceived as being mutually exclusive . . . when activities undertaken to reach goals are regarded as interdependent . . . or when two or more parties draw on the same limited resources to accomplish their goals . . . (p. 328)

Types of conflict and their origin
Schmuck and Runkel (1994) identify three types of conflict

- factual (argument about facts in a situation)
- value (arguments over priorities either specific or generally)
- strategy (arguments about how to achieve a particular desirable state).

The sources of conflict can be categorised as

- differentiation of function among parts of the organisation (differences of perspective on the same situation – each observer sees only a partial picture and some are more acceptable than others)
- power struggle between persons and groups (there is competition between individuals or groups)
- role conflicts (differences of expectation about particular role relationships)
- differences in inter-personal style (individuals have a personal way of operating that may not be the same as others expect)
- stress imposed by external factors (third parties may impose pressure which exposes differences of opinion about how to react).

Whether to resolve conflict and to what extent
Conflict resolution is not easy and if not successful may make the situation worse so a great deal of preparatory work needs to go into deciding whether this is an issue which should be tackled. This involves an assessment of the seriousness of the conflict and its type. Conflicts are unlikely to disappear of their own accord and may either be hidden or other coping mechanisms will be created.

> Some conflicts are inevitable and may even provide a creative tension that has the effect of improving educational performance; others . . . are not so destructive as to require the services of an outside OD facilitator. Still others, however, can significantly weaken the instructional program of an educational organization and for that reason should receive a facilitator's attention. (p. 336)

Do the individuals need to work together closely? The closer they have to work the more important it is to take action on problem-solving. Everard & Morris (1996) offer general advice on preventing and managing conflicts as part of the management of schools. Managers should attempt to manage any conflicts between those whom they manage. The more intractable case is when senior managers are involved in the conflicts. More specialist advice is offered by Schmuck and Runkel (1994) but for more difficult cases they assume that an Organisational Development (OD) specialist, or other external specialist, will be needed to help.

How to use the activities as individuals and groups

❏ Learning styles

Honey and Mumford developed some early work by Kolb and Fry on how individuals learn. Their simplified learning cycle is shown in Figure 4.4. This emphasises the difference between *experience* and *learning from experience*. The stages of the cycle facilitate learning from experience.

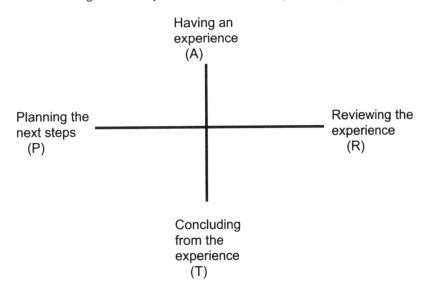

Figure 4.4 Honey and Mumford's learning styles

Honey and Mumford have developed an 80-item questionnaire which identifies an individual's predominant learning style(s) (Honey and Mumford, 1986, reproduced in Everard and Morris, 1996). These are related to particular stages of the cycle and are:

1. Activist (A) – 'What's new? I'm game for anything.'
    (a) learning features:
       (i)   are stimulated by new activities
       (ii) like being thrown in at the deep end on a difficult task.
2. Reflector (R) – 'I'd like time to think about this.'
    (a) learning features:
       (i)   like to watch and ponder
       (ii) like time to think before acting.
3. Theorist (T) – 'How does this relate to that?'
    (a) learning features:
       (i)   like structured situations with a clear purpose
       (ii) like to explore interrelationships methodically and question assumptions.
4. Pragmatist (P) – 'How can I apply this in practice?'
    (a) learning features:
       (i)   like to see a link between subject matter and their work
       (ii) like to see obvious advantages of new techniques.

A knowledge of preferred learning styles provides valuable information both about natural propensities for learning and also about the need to try to broaden the range of learning styles used in order to become a more effective learner and profit from a greater range of opportunities and situations. Honey offers ideas for developing complementary learning styles to one's natural style.

The activities at the end of the book address different parts of the cycle. Some ask for the collection of data or other active process (A), many lead to reflection on current practice (R), a number try to stimulate a search for relationships and conceptualisations (T) and a few ask for implementation plans to put the ideas into practice (P).

❏ Individuals

Most of the activities are self-contained and can be completed on their own. Many are, however, interconnected and form part of a sequence of activities. Few of the activities have direct prerequisites in terms of the completion of previous activities. Although the area of the text to which the activities refer is noted, an individual user can carry out the activities in a flexible manner depending on his or her interest, the state of preparation of an individual school and the relevance of the activity to its present needs. Thus it is possible to dip into the activities and to proceed from one to another as interest is stimulated and connections become apparent.

Each activity is intended to be capable of being undertaken by an individual manager working alone. Many of the activities consist of questions whose answers it would be worthwhile to write down. Other activities require data to be collected (some of this may involve other people) and others ask for judgements to be made.

Some of these activities are so crucial to the strategic planning process that it would be foolhardy to proceed only on the basis of one person's knowledge or judgement, however good they were, and so the process should involve others before any plans are finalised.

One way of using the activities would be to complete them sequentially and work through each section in turn. However, the activities are interactive in the sense that working on and thinking about each can influence the results of other activities. Thus the 'curriculum' is more helical than linear.

❏ Groups

Later parts of this section offer ideas on when and how to involve others in the process. Trialling of the activities has shown them to be very worthwhile in provoking group discussion of contentious and often unwritten assumptions. These activities provide a vehicle so that different perspectives and different opinions and judgements can be explored profitably. It is, however, very important that the function of such group discussion is made clear and that such sessions have some plan to move to conclusions, recommendations or decisions in some organised way, possibly over more than one session, if that is appropriate, and if they are to play a part in strategic planning.

One particular group which I see as having a critical role to play in the formulation of strategy is the senior management team of a school. I think that the use of the activities by individual members of the team before pooling their results would be particularly valuable. Some activities may also be useful to work on with governors as a way of structuring discussion about future strategy. However, given the likely extent of the time commitment which it is reasonable to expect of governors, the activities will have to be chosen very judiciously.

Where the activities are used with larger groups and particularly the whole staff of a school on a training day, then much careful planning of the composition of discussion groups and the balance between plenary and small group discussion will be required if the sessions are to be purposeful and successful. Some guidance on this is given in the next sub-section.

❏ Tailoring the activities

The activities generally are intended to provoke discussion and to provide an agenda to work through. They are intended to raise matters which may be implicit in day-to-day practice in schools but which are not generally analysed. A number contain suggestions which may bring to mind possibilities which might not otherwise be discussed. But this means that a number of the activities have become quite compendious because they have accumulated environmental factors or school performance characteristics which may be relevant to some schools. But this means that some may not be relevant to others and could be eliminated.

Herein lies a dilemma. If schools operate with the full activities, particularly S2, S3, S4, and S8, staff interest and motivation may be lost because a number of the possibilities are of little relevance. This suggests that the activities should be edited for use in a particular school to include only those parts which are relevant. However, this editing needs to be done with great care and some forethought as the sections which are deleted may be precisely those which might offer new and unthought of possibilities. My recommendation is to edit but to spend some time ensuring that the parts which are not used are really of low priority to a particular school.

❏ Generating ideas and prediction

Delphi method

This is a technique for making estimates of present unknowns or future developments. It combines the best estimates of 'experts' in a systematic way that does not require them all to be present and does not suffer the disadvantage of the behavioural effects of direct group discussion. In direct group discussion the personal attributes and behaviour of some members may cause their opinions to be accorded higher standing than others, irrespective of the 'real' value of their opinions. In the Delphi method the group does not need to meet. It uses the principle of successive approximation.

Stages of the process

1. The problem is clearly formulated.
2. Each expert is invited individually and anonymously to provide an estimate of the answer and to make any comments on other facts needed to inform the solution and to briefly outline their method of arriving at a solution.
3. These responses are summarised by the organiser and a summary of results and methods is circulated to all the participants.
4. They are invited to evaluate the methods used by others and, taking account of the results presented by others, they are given the opportunity to revise their original estimate.
5. Steps 3 and 4 are repeated until the estimates achieve a measure of convergence.

The Delphi technique was pioneered by the Rand Corporation in the USA when working on estimates of enemy resources and capabilities for military intelligence (Dalkey and Helmer, 1963). The 'actual' facts were unknown but various experts could make estimates of unknown accuracy. The technique was both used to make estimates of the facts and also to probe how the experts made their estimates.

Cherrington (1989) sees the advantages of the technique as:

1. The group decision is not swayed by a dominant individual and is reasonably free of the biases caused by individual personalities.
2. The problem of group-think is minimised.
3. The time and expense of assembling the experts for a meeting is avoided.

The disadvantage of the technique is that, unless the process is carried out expeditiously, the motivation is lost when the successive rounds of information collection and dissemination become protracted.

This technique may be of value in the strategic management activities which involve scanning the environment to predict future forces of importance to a school and also in making assessments of the school's present performance. These two areas and a number of others fit the circumstances in which the technique should be of value – the actual answer is unknown and a number of individuals have expertise in making assessments of the likely answer and it may be desirable to minimise the behavioural effects of direct group discussion.

The greater use of electronic communication particularly e-mail makes greater use of this technique more feasible and attractive.

Brainstorming

This is often misused and is properly carried out only under very strict rules (Rae, 1983).

1. Ideas are generated with no discussion or evaluation.
2. All ideas are encouraged and recorded.
3. Building of ideas on those of others is to be encouraged.

A quite separate and discrete activity, following the generation of ideas, is a reasoned discussion, evaluation and synthesis of the ideas. This can be carried out by the same group or a different group, although in the second case the ideas would need to be sufficiently developed as to be self-explanatory.

Jaques (1984) maintains that there are four rules for generating ideas:

1. Criticism is ruled out.
2. 'Free-wheeling' is welcomed – the wilder the ideas the better.
3. Quantity is wanted.
4. Combination and improvement are sought.

A member of the group should be charged with the task of monitoring the group to see that these rules are followed.

Buzz groups

As a way of generating thoughts and activity small groups (as few as two) can be asked to converse with a purpose. This can be to formulate questions or make presentations. Discussion is less inhibited because the group can be made small and the deliberations can be mediated by a spokesperson from the group thus preserving anonymity of individual ideas (Rae, 1983).

Nominal-group technique

This is an important technique which is intended to *minimise the disadvantages of group processes – the excessive influence which certain individuals may have either because of their status or because of their personality.* The process ensures that all have the opportunity of making an equal contribution to the discussion.

Based upon the description of the process by Cherrington (1989) we may identify the following steps:

1. After the problem has been clearly identified individual members develop their own response privately (this may be done in advance of any meeting).
2. At a group meeting each individual in turn is asked to contribute one of their ideas. These are not discussed but recorded on a flipchart.
3. This process is continued for a second or more round until all ideas have emerged. Ideas can be grouped but may be synthesised only by agreement.
4. The ideas are clarified, discussed and informally evaluated.
5. Each individual privately prioritises the ideas which have been generated.
6. The results are collected in and displayed.

This method can also be used to explore opinions and views in a systematic way.

Effectiveness of conventional groups, brainstorming, nominal and delphi groups

When comparing the quantity of ideas generated and the perceived satisfaction of participants in conventional interacting groups and in nominal and Delphi groups, Van de Ven and Delbecq (1974) conclude that the latter two are superior. The chart in Figure 4.5 adapted from Murnighan (1981) compares conventional groups, brainstorming, nominal and Delpi-groups.

Criteria	Ordinary	Brainstorming	NGT	Delphi
Number of ideas	Low	Moderate	High	High
Quality of ideas	Low	Moderate	High	High
Social pressure	High	Low	Moderate	Low
Time/money costs	Moderate	Low	Low	High
Task orientation	Low	High	High	High
Potential for inter-personal conflict	High	Low	Moderate	Low
Feelings of accomplishment	High to low	High	High	Moderate
Commitment to solution	High	NA*	Moderate	Low
Builds group cohesiveness	High	High	Moderate	Low
NA* = Not applicable				

Figure 4.5 Evaluating the decision processes (Murnighan, 1981)

Communicating and recording the results of discussions

Flipchart
The flipchart is easily maligned, for it has become somewhat hackneyed and can be taken to be a caricature of a certain way of organising activities which is participative but fails to achieve any definite conclusion.

The advantages of using a flipchart are

- collective memory which can later be carried away and transcribed
- aids communication
- concentration on single idea
- cuts down misunderstandings
- allows ideas to be grouped
- allows use of diagrams, charts and other pictorial representation.

For group work allowing each group to record their thoughts on a flipchart sheet:

- summarises discussion
- facilitates explanation to others
- allows quick comparison of the findings of different groups.

Thus for most group activities a flipchart or equivalent should be regarded as essential.

Computer software
Computer software is beginning to appear which allows discussion points to be summarised and connected in box diagrams, for example, Inspiration software. These need some familiarity to operate but have the obvious advantage of being able to be displayed to a large audience and also printed off for each to have a copy. As data projectors connected to laptop computers become more common this form of recording and display is likely to become more popular, for example, Inspiration software (http://www.inspiration.com/productinfo/Inspiration/index.cfm).

Snowball groups
This technique can be used as a way of gradually sharing ideas with an increasing number of others (Jaques, 1984). Groups can progressively combine, for example, 2 + 2, 4 + 4, etc. The tasks at each regrouping need to be increasingly sophisticated or involve the elimination of alternatives if there is not to be wasteful repetition. The first stage can be for individuals to write down their own thoughts on the topic before sharing them. This provides quiet contemplation before the buzz of interaction.

Crossover groups
Jaques (1984) offers this as an alternative to a plenary session for acquainting all the participants with what has been said in other groups.

Individuals are assigned a code which instructs them to move round other groups in a predetermined order. At each new group previous discussion is recapped by the new member. For this method to work the size of each group should be the square root of the total number of participants.

Reporting back or plenary session
Time needs to be reserved for reporting back but unless this is well structured and has a clear purpose it can appear a formality.

Producing written reports in as standardised a form as possible is recommended. It should be a summary made after the discussion rather than a direct recording of the discussion. Standardised headings or format are suggested. The suggestion is to get more than one person from a group involved in feedback.

As an alternative to each group giving its account of similar discussions, it is possible to structure activities such that different groups can address a different aspect of the issue in some predetermined manner rather than all address the same point.

❑ Problem-solving, prioritisation and planning change

Problem-solving

This is a complex topic. The models below offer a systematic way of thinking through problems which can be used by individuals or groups. They are heuristic devices rather than a set of rigid procedures to be followed. Probably their most significant contribution is to prevent the adoption of preconceived instinctive responses to important problems.

Jackson (1975), amongst others, offers a rational model for solving problems. The stages of the process are

- Formulation – involves detection, identification and definition.
- Interpretation – developing an understanding of the problem and its ramifications.
- Constructing alternative courses of action – a range of possible solutions to the problem are formulated.
- Decision-making – evaluating the possible solutions and choosing one of them.
- Implementation – detailed planning, implementation and evaluation of the proposed change.

A more detailed series of steps from Francis (1990) provides the TOSIDPAR model which many find helpful as a systematic framework to analyse and tackle problems:

- Tuning in
    - Categorising the problem – what sort of task is this?
    - Mystery, assignment, difficulty, opportunity, puzzle, dilemma.
    - Situation appraisal – what are the issues?
    - Significance analysis – what is important?
    - Getting organised – how can we work on this problem effectively?
    - Emotional tuning in – how can we work on this problem with energy?
- Objective setting
    - Choosing objectives depending on the category of problem.
- Success measures
    - Devising success criteria and success measures for objectives.
- Information collection.
- Decision-making.
- Planning.
- Action.
- Review to improve
    - Learn from the process of problem-solving on this occasion to improve problem-solving in future.

Collecting data

Evidence can be collected in a variety of forms:

- documents
- questionnaires
- interviews
- focus groups
- observation
- diaries.

Inevitably, data collection has to be tailored to the purpose, sources of data and availability of data. A good general book which covers each of these methods, albeit briefly, is Bell (1999) *Doing Your Research Project*. Further details and discussion of each of the data collection methods are to be found in Bennett, Glatter and Levačić (1994).

It should be remembered that any decisions will only be as good as the information on which they are based. Thus data needs to be collected in an informed way and its possible sources of bias assessed. Whilst the aim should be reliable and valid data, the appropriate criterion for assessment is not whether the data would be defensible in a research sense but its 'fitness for purpose'. Does it help sufficiently to improve management decisions? As is well known, collecting information operates on the principle of marginalism. It is relatively efficient to collect data to begin with but the search for ever more data becomes progressively more expensive and eventually the cost of collection exceeds the value of the information. Thus in management terms some information is invaluable as an aid to improved decision-making but the search for all the necessary information is, and may ultimately prove, illusory. There are, in any case, as we have seen, limits to the ability to process data and most decisions involve qualitative evidence and 'soft' data to be weighed in with more quantitative evidence. Thus ultimately judgements have to be made under conditions of uncertainty. It is only the extent of the uncertainty which can be altered.

Fishbone diagrams

Francis (1990) commends the fishbone diagram as a way of structuring information on a complex problem and providing an overview when it may have multiple and interlocking causes. The problem is placed at the head of the fishbone and the possible contributions to the problem are assigned to different fishbones. Each of these lines of contribution may have a range of possible contributions which are added as further 'bones'. Experience suggests that analysing a problem in this way should be carried out over several sessions to allow fresh ideas to develop and others to be elaborated because people have had time to reflect. What are seen as the major contributors to the problem are circled and these provide foci when solutions to the problem are developed. An example used by Murgatroyd and Morgan (1992) for examining a school based problem is shown in Figure 4.6.

Why-why diagram

This is a variation on the fishbone diagram and provides a systematic way of examining cause and effects (Majaro, 1992). A group works on a problem and causes are sought. As each is proposed it is subjected to

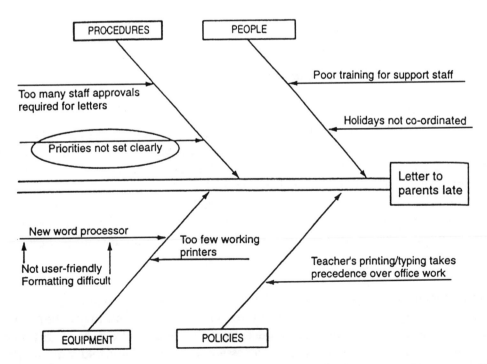

Figure 4.6   Example of fishbone diagram (reproduced from Murgatroyd and Morgan, 1993: 170, by permission of the publisher, Open University Press, Buckingham)

the question 'Why?' Answers to this are also subjected to the question 'Why?' until some fundamental reasons emerge. For complex problems there may need to be several rounds of the question 'Why?' as deeper reasons are sought. Experience suggests that this activity needs to be conducted in a good spirit where each answer to the question 'Why?' is seen as a success rather than as the butt of yet another 'Why?' The results of this activity can be drawn as a flow chart which then provides an overview of the problem so that potential areas to work on can be seen in context.

Force-field analysis

In examining the prospects of changing any situation force-field analysis (FFA) is a worthwhile exercise originally formulated by Kurt Lewin (1951). Its advantages are

- pictorial display
- attention on one part of complex situation
- structured discussion
- leads to structured further planning.

The forces tending to drive a change and those opposing it are represented pictorially. The strength of the force is represented by the length of the arrow and the number of the forces is represented by the number of arrows.

After agreeing the FFA the next step is to plan how to reduce the opposing forces and strengthen the driving ones (see the FAA example for a new teaching scheme for technology in Figure 4.7).

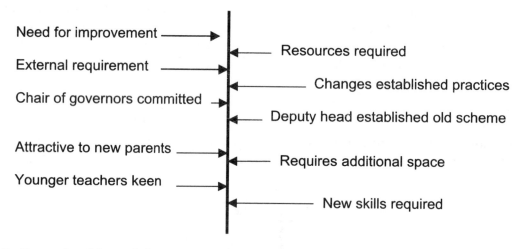

Figure 4.7   Example of force-field analysis

Capability and readiness charts

Everard and Morris (1996) point out that there are two distinct features to be considered when assessing individuals and change. One of these is their readiness for change – have they fully accepted the need for change and are they psychologically ready for change. The other is their capability for change – do they have the necessary skills to play their part in the change?

Each key individual involved in a change can be assessed for their readiness and capability on a simple scale, for example, high, medium and low. This is useful for focusing on planning how to increase the readiness and capability of key individuals (see the example of a capability and readiness chart in Figure 4.8).

Commitment charts

Another useful chart suggested by Everard and Morris (1996) is a commitment chart (Figure 4.9). This involves assessing key individuals and the stance they are required to take if any change is to be successfully implemented. Their position can be assessed on a simple fourfold scale – oppose, let, help, make. Any difference between their present stance and that required as a minimum position for the change to be successful should provide a focus for efforts.

Key individual	Readiness			Capability		
	H	M	L	H	M	L

Figure 4.8 *Example of a readiness and capability chart*

Individual	Oppose	Let	Help	Make
Headteacher				xo
Deputy/teacher governor			x	o
Chairman of governors				o
Union representative		x	o	
Parent governor A		x	o	
Parent governor B		x	xo	
x = present position				
o = desired position				

Figure 4.9 *A commitment plan for greater governor involvement*

Decision trees

This is a diagrammatic technique which permits the structured discussion of decisions and the consequences which might result from these decisions. The technique can be developed mathematically by assigning probabilities to each course of action and the resulting consequences. Thus the overall probability of any course of action and its consequences can be calculated (Gear, 1975; Ball, 1984). In practice it is very difficult to have a great deal of confidence in the estimated probabilities and, therefore, for most purposes the mathematical elaboration is not worthwhile. However, as an aid to structured discussion of possible decisions and their consequences it has much to commend it (in its non-mathematical form).

The decision tree demonstrating the Vroom and Yetton decision-making model is an example (Figure 4.10).

Decision matrix

Morrisey (1976) has provided a technique for indicating priorities when having to choose between a number of competing projects. It is a way of accomplishing a systematic pair-wise comparison of each option. It is based on the proposition that individuals can make a valid choice between any two alternatives but are less likely to be able to do so directly when confronted with a greater number of attractive alternatives. Each project is compared with each other and the preferred one of the two is noted. When this has been done for all possible comparisons then totting up the scores indicates an order of priority. The final stage of the process is to convert these scores into a rank order for the projects. Whilst each individual in a group can do this, these rankings may not subsequently be combined arithmetically.

Rankings are ordinal numbers. This means that although their order is specified there is no means of knowing how much larger one is compared to another. Numbers need to be on an interval scale before arithmetic means are valid.

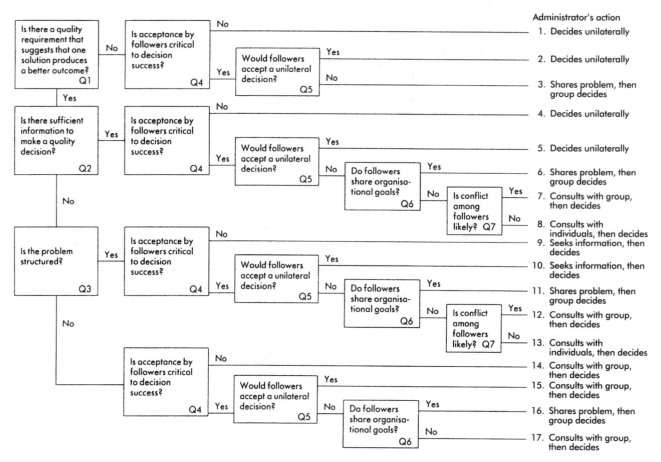

Figure 4.10   Vroom and Yetton decision tree (Hoy and Miskel, 1991)

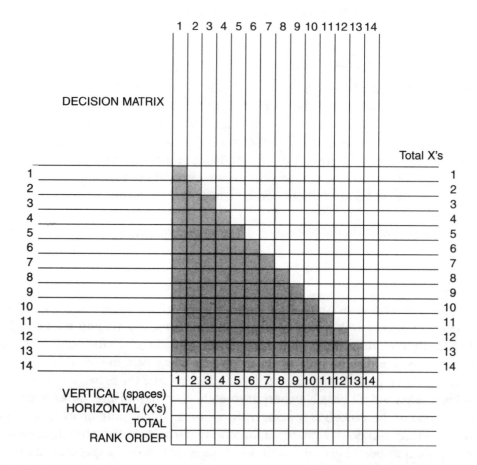

Figure 4.11   Decision matrix (copyright 1974 by George L. Morrisey, MOR Associates, Buena Park, CA 90622)

Thus to find the resulting preferences for a group of people there are two possibilities. Either the decision matrix can be completed taking a simple majority preference of the group at each pair-wise comparison. Alternatively, each individual can complete a decision matrix (Figure 4.11) and then the raw score total can be summed for each individual to find the overall group ranking.

Flow diagrams (network analysis)

If some complex operation or process is being planned then a very simple network diagram can aid both thinking and communication about the steps involved. It draws attention to prerequisites for any step in the process and also to parts of the process which may go on simultaneously. This is also a technique which can be elaborated mathematically by making estimates of the length of time required to complete each step in the process and, hence, estimates for the likely time for the overall project (Gear, 1975; Ball, 1984). Time estimates allow the identification of the critical path or minimum length of time for completing the whole project. Any delay in the critical path delays the whole project by a similar amount.

Only the simple drawing of a flow diagram showing the sequence of steps involved is probably worthwhile in most cases. For any long project the chart can be used to show current progress. Thus it could be useful to pin up a copy of the flow chart in a prominent place and colour in the stages of the project as they are completed.

In the example shown in Figure 4.12, the various component activities are drawn within boxes and arrows show how the results of one activity feed into subsequent activities. To create a flow diagram all the component activities are listed then consider the ordering of activities. For each activity list the immediately preceding activity(ies). From this try drawing a flow diagram meeting these requirements. Probably a neater final flow chart can be designed.

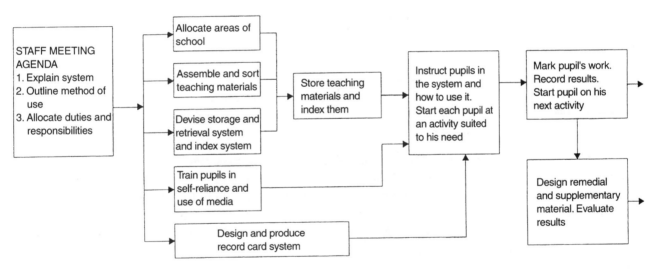

Figure 4.12 A flow diagram of the main areas to be considered when designing an integrated scheme for mathematics (Vaughan, 1978)

5 Managing School Improvement

Introduction

This chapter suggests that ideas for improvement must be related to the aims of schooling and that major questions concern what to improve and how to improve it. It is argued that school improvement has an organisational dimension in addition to being concerned with teaching and learning.

A section examines the state of knowledge of school effectiveness and school improvement. It identifies a number of routes to school improvement and differentiates between internally generated ones and those imposed from the outside. Some of the internally generated routes involve major organisational shifts of culture whilst others involve more restricted techniques. An array of such techniques is identified.

A particular concern is to identify routes to improvement for the long term. Three approaches for different time periods are presented – learning organisation, core competences and benchmarking.

What is school improvement and what do we know about it?

As has been written earlier, this book uses the definition of improvement from the International School Improvement Project of the 1980s. That is:

> A systematic, sustained effort aimed at change in learning conditions and other related internal conditions in one or more schools, with the ultimate aim of accomplishing educational goals more effectively. (Miles and Eckholm, 1985: 48)

This definition accommodates longer-term planning as it recognises that there may be preparatory changes needed before the ultimate aim of improving the attainment of educational goals. It also accepts that there are school processes and conditions which directly contribute to the attainment of educational goals and other that do so indirectly. The definition does not distinguish between the two types if they contribute to the ultimate goal. However, much of current usage of the word 'improvement' appears to concentrate only on direct contributions.

❏ Why school improvement is high profile

A visitor from overseas when hearing about the drive for school improvement in England asked the rather naive but profound question: 'Is there something wrong with the schools?' We take for granted that global competition is driving a need for higher standards but at a world level this is a zero-sum game. If all countries improve their educational system there is no competitive advantage. A further issue concerns the contribution of education to generating economic wealth compared with other sources of innovative products and higher productivity. We need to keep a sense of perspective, particularly over the drive to raise cognitive standards if this is at the expense of other components of education which contribute to happiness in adult life.

There may be a much better case for being selective about those whose examination and test performances need particular attention. There are groups who have not achieved as much as their potential indicates and there are those for whom education appears to provide one of the few means by which they might change their life chances. Thus, consonant with ideas on strategy, I am arguing for a more discriminating and judgemental approach to improvement rather than a knee-jerk one which concentrates only on test and examination results.

❏ What are the aims of schooling?

The current preoccupation appears to be with the value of education as a contribution to employability and the generation of economic wealth. Whilst this is important to individuals and to the nation, it is not the sole purpose of education and, many would argue, not its main purpose.

The range of aims of schooling from the perspective of individual students generally involve the four main types:

- personal fulfilment
- preparation for adult life
- preparation for democratic participation
- preparation for employment.

Whilst each school needs to formulate its aims, they are likely to be based on these four. Thus school improvement can involve trying to accomplish any or all of them more effectively. This leaves enormous scope for choice and this is the essence of strategy. It is concerned with long-term aims and planning how to achieve them. It should build on and use existing knowledge. Thus much of this chapter will deal with what is known about effective schools and how to improve.

Activities S10 and S11 suggest ways of analysing the current school curriculum.

❏ School effectiveness

School effectiveness research began as such in the 1970s. It started out from the recognition that some schools achieved better results than others in similar circumstances and particularly with disadvantaged students. The research has mainly been on elementary schools in the USA in the 1970s and 1980s, although there have been notable studies in Scotland in the 1980s and in London in the late 1970s and early 1980s.

The measure of effectiveness which has been used is generally very narrow. Children's test scores mainly in basic skills have been the principal measure. This has made the judgement of outcome objective but at the expense of wider aims of schooling. Indeed, there are conceptual problems in examining effectiveness where there is more than one type of outcome. Effectiveness has been defined in terms of the progress which children make whilst they are at a particular school. Schools where children make more progress than would be expected in similar schools are termed effective.

There are two distinct types of research which are generally included as school effectiveness studies:

- school effectiveness factors
- school effect or value-added studies.

School effectiveness factors

The search for the factors which are found in effective schools has mainly been carried out on elementary schools in the USA. Effectiveness was usually defined as higher test results than would be expected from the social characteristics of the children. The factors or correlates were characteristics of effective schools which were identified by questionnaires. I and others have drawn attention to the weakness of such studies and I do not want to take space rehearsing these; however, I do want to give a small number of 'health warnings' about the lists of correlates which have been promoted:

- There is no suggestion that these factors 'cause' a school to be effective. They are only associated with such schools.
- The factors are generic rather than being specific to a particular type of school.
- Factors which are not on the lists are still important. The lists are a product of their time and context. Thus processes not common is American schools or London schools at the time of the research will not be included, for example school development planning, parental partnerships, strategic planning.
- The factors are generally not sufficiently specified so that they could be used as a component of a self-evaluation schedule without a great deal of interpretation.

There are two lists which I think are worthy of note. First, there is the list of 12 factors from the Junior School Project in 50 London primary schools in the 1980s (Mortimore et al., 1988):

- purposeful leadership of the staff by the headteacher
- involvement of the deputy head
- involvement of teachers
- consistency among teachers
- structured sessions
- intellectually challenging teaching
- work-centred environment
- limited focus within sessions maximum communication between teachers and students
- record-keeping
- parental involvement
- positive climate.

A more widely known list of 11 factors appeared from a review of the literature in 1995 which was commissioned by OFSTED (Sammons, Hillman and Mortimore, 1995). The literature from which it was compiled was mainly from the USA and little post-dated the 1980s:

- professional leadership
- shared vision and goals
- a learning environment
- concentration on teaching and learning
- explicit high expectations
- positive reinforcement
- monitoring progress
- student rights and responsibilities
- purposeful teaching
- a learning organisation
- home–school partnership.

A more recent study of departments in 90 secondary schools in England in the early 1990s (Sammons, Thomas and Mortimore, 1997) identified three groups of schools – those with consistently high value-added across departments, those with mixed results and those with poor value-added. From an examination of six schools and 36 departments across these three groups the researchers identified nine major factors associated with effective departments in effective schools

- high expectations
- academic emphasis
- shared vision/goals
- clear leadership
- an effective SMT
- consistency in approach
- quality of teaching
- student-focused approach
- parental support/involvement.

School effect or value-added

The other major thrust of school effectiveness research has been an attempt to measure the size of the school effect, that is, the difference in progress which students might make in an effective school compared to an ineffective one. This has mainly been carried out in Scotland and England, and has led to a methodology for studying student academic progress from starting at a school to leaving. This provides a means for monitoring whether schools and departments are improving students' academic progress.

This methodology has yielded a number of findings which are important for school improvement

- Primary schools contribute more than secondary – when the London Junior School project children were followed through secondary schools and their performance at GCSE analysed, the contribution of their primary school to their progress at secondary school was greater than that of their secondary school.

- Most schools make similar progress – studies of groups of secondary schools show that once the random errors in the methodology are taken into account most schools are indistinguishable from the point of view of the progress which their students make. There are about 20 per cent of schools which clearly make more progress than expected and about 20 per cent which make less progress, but 60 per cent make similar progress.

- Few schools have a consistent profile of progress over a number of years – studies of schools over three years show that only about one in seven have a consistent profile of increasing student progress. Three years is the minimum period for a trend to be demonstrated.

- Not equally effective for all students – studies which have examined the progress of students of different ability show that schools are not equally effective for different abilities. Some allow more able students to make greater progress and others allow the less able to make greater relative progress.

- The composition of the student body has an effect on progress beyond that due to the social background of each individual student – the social background of each student typically has a contribution to his or her progress beyond that indicated by measured ability. Surprisingly, it is found that the average social background of all students has a further residual effect, with schools with more middle-class students making greater progress than their measured ability, and individual social class, would suggest.

- The largest source of variation is between departments and classrooms – when the results from effective schools are analysed further it is found that there are differences in effectiveness of departments in the same school and between different teachers. Further analysis of the teachers in the London Junior School project showed that the same teachers were not equally effective at teaching language and mathematics. Looked at another way, although there are differences between the effectiveness of teachers in individual classrooms, there is still an overall school effect (although this is much smaller than the apparent effect before taking within school differences into account).

Although many of these studies have not been replicated to give added confidence in the results, the actual results are valid for substantial numbers of schools and students.

❏ School improvement

The knowledge base of school improvement is much more diffuse. Partly this is due to the different style of research and partly it is due to the nature of the area of endeavour. The later section – Routes to School Improvement (p. 75) – poses the questions – how do we know what to improve? and how do we go about it? This and Managing Strategic Change in Chapter 6 (p. 92) bring together much accumulated knowledge of how to develop schools.

This knowledge has come from curriculum development projects particularly in the UK and North America in the 1960s, 1970s and 1980s and, more recently, from school development and school improvement projects. Mainly such projects involved external interventions by government, charitable foundations, universities or local authorities. Generally these proposed new curriculum materials or new teaching methods and sought to interest schools in taking them on. In this respect a number which originated in England were different.

These projects presented a means for schools to diagnose their own need for improvement. This contingent view was in contrast to other projects which had a ready-made solution. Such diagnostic projects were school self-evaluation schemes from local authorities in the 1970s and early 1980s, Guidelines for Review and Internal Development in Schools (GRIDS) project of the 1980s, school development planning of the 1990s and the Improving the Quality of Education of All (IQEA) project of the 1990s. The latter two also had a framework for planning and implementing developments following the diagnostic phase.

As a consequence of most research being on external initiatives, the knowledge of how to bring about the success of an external innovation is greater than that of diagnosing a need for change and identifying an appropriate form of improvement at school level. However, there are general findings on the change process which can inform the improvement process:

- Change is a process not a single event.
- More is required than just identifying the appropriate innovation and assuming that it will work. In addition to the innovation and its attributes and requirements, there is a change process which needs to be separately considered.
- The support and encouragement of the headteacher or principal is essential.
- It is possible to anticipate much that will occur during the change process.
- There are three stages to the change process – initiation, implementation (mutual adaptation of the innovation and the school) and institutionalisation or making the change permanent.
- A change facilitator is needed, either within the school or outside, to diagnose attitudes to the change and skills needed to implement the change and respond accordingly.
- Understanding the change from the point of view of *participants* is critical.
- More than one person in the school needs to be committed and a driver of the change. There can be complementary styles and roles of the main change facilitator and a second change facilitator.
- Ready–fire–aim is a more apt description of progress on complex innovations rather than the more rational ready–aim–fire. This recognises the difficulties of planning very complex innovations and acknowledges that often participants become clearer about the deeper implications of a change as they proceed with it.
- Pressure and support. There is a simultaneous need for pressure and support. This need is present at all levels. The institution needs pressure and support from outside just as individuals and groups internally also need pressure and support. The pressure is to legitimate and demand, when progress is in peril, whilst the support is to encourage and make possible. Increasingly support is being referred to as capacity building.
- Staff development to support innovation is a complex process. The timing and follow-up of training to ensure that participants have skills and confidence to change their practice are important.
- Familiarisation, training and coaching (and other forms of support) need to be sequenced throughout the project rather than being concentrated at the start. People recognise new needs for training and development as they appreciate the requirements on themselves more clearly through experience of trying to implement the innovation.

Two main constraints on change are likely to be:

- the reluctance of many staff to change their practices and acquire new skills
- how to find ways of working together on change whilst also maintaining most current activities.

Although a number of ingredients of school improvement are known and conditions for their success have been discovered, there is a lack of any overall theory of school improvement. What are the best starting points, in what order should activities be attempted, at what pace and in what circumstances are crucial and unanswered questions.

School improvement needs to be managed strategically

It is clear from the definition of school improvement from the ISIP project that school improvement involves more than what goes on in classrooms. Changes in learning conditions can be a whole-school activity and I want to argue that school improvement involves the health of the organisation in addition to the teaching and learning that goes on within it.

I want to contrast two approaches to improvement:

- collection of teachers' approach
- organisational approach.

Much of what is written on school improvement concentrates on the classroom which assumes that schools are collections of teachers rather than organisations with teaching (or, rather, learning) as their main purpose. An organisational approach assumes corporate goals and the need of an infrastructure to help deliver them. One approach takes teachers as central and rather ignores the organisation in which they work, whilst the other takes purpose as the main determinant and makes teachers secondary to it (although they may have played a part in formulating the purpose). This will be more difficult in a professional context.

If the organisation is failing, then it is highly unlikely that much successful teaching can be going on in such conditions. Thus an organisation which is properly staffed, financed and organised is a prerequisite for the conditions in which teaching can be improved. Unless the atmosphere within a school is conducive to learning and students come to school prepared to learn, conditions in individual classrooms will be very difficult. At a more subtle level the composition of the student body has an effect on what is possible within a school. If there are too many who are not willing to go along with what the school offers, they can make it very difficult for the rest. Bringing in more able and motivated students may be the only viable way of substantially raising achievement. Accepting the present student body and working on improvement of teaching may be relatively ineffective.

In addition to an organisational dimension I also want to make the case that this process needs to be managed strategically. That is, it needs to view the process as long term, needing co-ordination and co-operation between staff and to be appropriate for the context in which the school finds itself. What is successful in one context may not be so in a different set of external circumstances.

A further element which needs to be considered strategically is the degree and pace of any developments. The challenge is how to combine high-quality ongoing processes with an appropriate degree of innovation. An important consideration is – how much development is possible and how should it proceed? An implicit view from many quarters is that it should be continuous, but based upon the experience of other organisations this must be viewed as unrealistic. A more strategic view is to recognise that following a period of innovation there needs to be a period of consolidation before the next development.

For these reasons I believe that the future of the whole school has to be considered as integral to the improvement of teaching and learning within the school. Whilst the strategic planning model deals with the future of the organisation and recognises that this needs to be contingent on its purpose, it does not deal directly with how to improve teaching and learning from a professional perspective. Ways of applying professional knowledge to this, need to operate within a strategic planning framework. Thus the next section presents ideas on how to identify what to improve and how to improve.

Routes to school improvement

Whilst strategic planning is the overarching activity to plan for the longer term, it does not prescribe particular ways of improving nor how staff should work together to bring about improvement. This section looks at other more restricted contributions to particular aspects of school improvement, particularly those concerned with teaching and learning. They may form part of the strategy.

These improvement approaches may contribute directly to improvement of the student experience and outcome or they may contribute indirectly including those which are directed at organisational survival and success. To assemble this typology I have drawn on approaches from the commercial and business world in addition to those from education.

They are intended to help in the process of deciding:

> **what to improve**
> **how to improve.**

There are a number of types of route to school improvement or ways of bringing about school improvement. These are either

- internal interventions or proactive choices
- external interventions or reactive choices.

I distinguish between choices which a school can initiate and choices which involve reaction to events outside the school. Although these are not quite synonymous with internal and external interventions, that is the basis on which I have chosen to categorise improvement initiatives.

❑ Internal interventions

There are two types of internal intervention:

- organisational change philosophies
- Management techniques.

Organisational change philosophies involve members of an organisation operating to certain principles during their work. These are not principles which operate only for certain aspects of their work but an underlying philosophy which underpins their whole work. When stated so baldly the scale of a change to introduce such philosophies should be clear – it is massive. It is not only those who are in management who have to be convinced by these schemes it is all the workers who have to 'buy in' and operate in this way. Undoubtedly a failure to recognise the scale and viability of such a change has contributed to the failure of many of these improvement schemes when they have been attempted in commercial and other organisations.

Management techniques are more limited in the scale and scope of the changes which are required to integrate them into working practices. They are generally techniques which are chosen by the leadership and management of a school; thus those who choose to implement them need to understand their strengths and limitations. They can be applied to parts of the organisation's work rather than the whole and they involve only more surface-level changes to the work practices of individual staff. This is not to say that they are easy to institute effectively but that they are more feasible for most organisations and, if their introduction is properly thought through and implemented, there is a high expectation of successful operation. The management techniques are not generally mutually exclusive and a degree of 'pick and mix' is possible for particular circumstances.

Organisational change philosophies

Within the type organisational change philosophies I have included the following in order of their chronology in terms of impact on Western commercial organisations:

- organisational development (OD)
- cultural change programmes
- total quality management (TQM)
- learning organisation.

Organisational development

Organisational development assumes that organisational functioning can be improved by using behavioural science knowledge to change working practices. The main impetus to do this comes from within the organisation rather than from outside. How people work together and other organisational processes are scrutinised to spot and improve malfunctioning. There is a process awareness which is explicit rather than implicit. This awareness is the responsibility of management whose own processes also need to be scrutinised. In any change process the behavioural effects are taken into account at the planning stage and monitored as the change is implemented. A range of planning techniques for organisational change is used, process consultants may be used and there are explicit ways of working through disagreements and conflict.

Although I have classified this as an organisational change philosophy (which it is), it is more a philosophy of management than of the whole organisation. It takes the organisation as the locus of activity rather than waiting for external intervention. However, some of the techniques associated with OD are more widespread in planning change within organisations, for example force-field analysis, commitment charts, readiness and capability analysis, and process consultants. These assume a management responsibility for planning change which takes account of behavioural influences even if there is not a total commitment to OD.

Cultural change programmes

The vogue in the 1980s for cultural change programmes in commercial organisations resulted from the influential book by Peters and Waterman, *In Search of Excellence* (1982) which suggested that they had identified eight attributes of the culture of successful organisations. (This was the commercial analogue of the school effectiveness research which yielded the school effectiveness factors, although the empirical work was not so public on the grounds of commercial sensitivity.) This was based on the management consultants McKinsey's Seven S Framework of organisational effectiveness – strategy, structure, systems, staff, style, shared values, skills. Although organisational culture remains a key variable in current thinking about organisational success, any idea that there might be one successful culture has been abandoned, particularly in the light of the rapid decline of so many of the 'excellent' companies on which Peters and Waterman had based their findings. In any case, an enduring problem to which I shall return is the difficulty of trying to change the culture of an organisation.

Total quality management

The rationale for TQM is that an organisation will prosper if it meets and surpasses clients' expectations. Thus, ensuring that client needs are met and that some of their expectations will be exceeded are integral to the operation of TQM. Total quality management requires a commitment to continuous improvement. This is improvement to the quality required by the consumer or client. Total quality management makes the concept of client more complex since it identifies both external clients and internal clients. One of the clients for the teaching of students this year is the teacher who will take over their teaching next year. Although the concept of client becomes more complex, this kind of thinking does identify many more interconnections between activities which can contribute to a more comprehensive overview of the work of a school and its teachers. Total quality management requires total commitment to the needs of the beneficiary of the service which is being provided. This commitment is both individual and collective, so there need to be ways of discussing possible improvements by all staff and agreement on which are to be instituted. In the ultimate, this is a selfless activity dedicated to others.

Learning organisation

The rationale for a learning organisation is that, if the future is unknown and change is unavoidable and continuous, organisations need to be able to adapt continuously to client needs and external circumstances. This can only be achieved if individuals are flexible and can adapt by learning from their past experience and acquire new skills. Whilst there are different interpretations of organisational learning, the concept implies more than each member of staff learning individually. There is a notion of collective learning. It is in trying to operationalise this that interpretations differ

Although the choice of one of these philosophical change strategies is a major one, it is not the only choice to be made. Within any of these organisational change approaches, individual management techniques may be used. However, these need to be consistent with the underlying principles of the particular change philosophy.

Management techniques

The range of more limited management techniques which can be used as part of a strategy for school improvement includes the following:

- school development planning
- benchmarking
- school self-evaluation and self-review
  - quality schemes
    - school effectiveness factors
    - European Business Excellence Model (EFQM)
    - Investors in People
    - ISO 9000 (BS5750)
  - comparative data
  - materials
  - quality circles
  - other
- performance management, individual staff reviews and target setting
- staff development
- feedback from stakeholders (parents and students)
- consultancy advice (process/content).

Although these have been classified as internal initiatives, in some countries a number of them may have been required to be implemented by external authorities. However, where they were required or recommended they were intended to fulfil a number of functions and their potential for school improvement is largely a school-level decision.

School development planning

In a number of countries school development planning using a four- or five-stage cycle has been used for a number of years. This cycle provides for analysis of current operations, planning of improvement, implementation of improvement and evaluation. As schools have become familiar with this technique, they have begun to cost and prioritise developments.

The range of developments covered by school development planning have extended up to three years but have mainly involved curricular and teaching developments.

Benchmarking

Benchmarking is a technique for identifying good practice in other organisations and taking action to understand and adapt it so that it can be replicated elsewhere. This is described in more detail in a later section of this chapter as a valuable technique for improvement which can be applied to student-level improvement efforts or at the organisational level.

School self-evaluation

School self-evaluation can play a part in identifying areas of work within a school which need improvement. Self-evaluation has a number of forms and has been in operation in a number of countries for some years. There are a number of issues which have to be addressed if the process is to progress from the criticisms of earlier experience:

- Which areas are to be covered?
- What evidence is to be introduced?
- Who is to make judgements?
- What criteria are to be used to make judgements?
- How are these judgements to be validated?

Any guidance on answers to these questions will make the process more systematic and more rigorous. Thus ready-made schemes to be followed will have some appeal. It should be remembered, however, any such scheme has an implicit model of organisational functioning within it. Where this is made explicit, is well-argued, based upon theorisation and research, and has been critically evaluated, such a scheme has much to commend it. I leave it to readers to decide how far the schemes below meet these tests. My warning is that where they do not, their authority rests only on face validity. In which case any results from the process need to be interpreted and evaluated rather than taken as definitive.

The various forms which are categorised below have different responses to the above questions.

Quality schemes
There are a number of quality schemes. These are essentially prescriptive models to which an organisation should aspire. An organisation is analysed against the prescriptions of the particular model and the discrepancies are points for improvement. The differences stem from the different bases for the prescriptive models

School effectiveness factors
Research on effective schools mainly on elementary schools in the USA have identified a number of factors which are generally present in such schools. There are various analyses of the literature but a recent one in England identified 11 such factors as discussed previously. These could be used as the template against which to compare school practice. The weaknesses of such an approach have been increasingly pointed out.

The next three schemes are promoted by organisations concerned with quality and I have provided web site URLs for those who wish to follow them up.

European Business Excellence Model from the European Forum for Quality Management (EFQM)
This prescriptive model based on a number of the principles of TQM rather disingenuously claims to be 'non-prescriptive' by casting its assertions as facts rather than as normative statements. It started life as the Business Excellence Model. The Scottish Office has applied the model to schools and compared its elements and criteria with a self-evaluation schedule drawn up for schools called 'How Good is Our School?'. (http://www.efqm.org/), (http://www.standards.dfes.gov.uk/schoolimprovement/efqm.html), (http://www.scotland.gov.uk/library/documents-w10/qis-01.htm)

The next two schemes are somewhat different in that they lead to a quality award when internal organisational processes have been checked by an external assessor. Such awards last for a specified period before needing to be renewed.

Investors in People (IIP)
This is a scheme in England which has 16 areas where good practice is prescribed. Many of these are concerned with the actions and development of staff. This involves all staff in the school both teaching staff and teaching support staff. To lead to a quality mark an external assessor assesses these in accordance with the IIP requirements. (http://www.iipuk.co.uk/), (http://www.standards.dfes.gov.uk/schoolimprovement/iip)

ISO 9000
Organisational standards of operation were drawn up by the British Standards Institute (BS5750) and these have been incorporated into those of the International Organization for Standards (ISO 9000). This is a scheme which is assessed against criteria and a quality standard awarded for successful completion. (http://www.iso.ch/iso/en/ISOOnline.frontpage)

Comparative data
Comparative data from other schools can be used to compare the performance of a school against one or more others. This is dealt with in greater detail under strategic analysis in Chapter 7.

Self-evaluation materials
A number of organisations have produced self-evaluation materials. Recent ones emanate from OFSTED in England and the Scottish project funded by the Scottish Office, Improving School Effectiveness project (ISEP). (http://www.ofsted.gov.uk/public/docs00/schseleval.pdf) (http://www.scotland.gov.uk/library/documents-w/hmi3–00.htm)

Quality circles
One feature of TQM which could be used for systematic self-evaluation and improvement is the concept of a quality circle. This has been reported from schools and community colleges in the USA. (http://www.ed.gov/databases/ERICDigests/ed353008.html)

Other

Finally, school self-evaluation can be carried out on a more intuitive basis that does not involve following any systematic scheme. This uses professional experience and may use some instruments as they are considered necessary.

Performance management

Performance management which involves individual staff reviews and individual target setting has been required in schools in England since the year 2000. Such reviews are intended to identify areas for personal individual improvement and may also contribute to formulating group and school improvement programmes. The sequencing of institutional development plans and individual development plans should mean that areas identified in one feed through into the other. Since each member of the teaching staff is subject to performance management each year, this should contribute to knowledge of performance across the range of work in a school.

Staff development

Personal development plans originating from performance management should involve targets for each member of the teaching staff. Such development should involve training and also learning from experience. Institutional development plans should lead to staff development needs. Teaching support staff will also need personal development plans.

Feedback from parents and students

Although systematic feedback from parents and students contributes to the development of strategy in other ways, such feedback can be used to obtain a fuller picture of teaching and learning. Students' experiences can be particularly illuminating in terms of how they perceive their education. Parents' views can both provide another perspective on what happens in schools and also the extent to which they work in partnership with a school.

Consultancy advice

External consultants can both contribute to identifying areas for development, suggesting what should be developed and how it should be developed. Generally they provide:

- an external perspective which can highlight 'taken for granted' actions at a school
- knowledge of practice in other schools (both to assess the current level of work and to suggest better practice which works elsewhere)
- experience of how other schools have developed.

The role of process consultants is developed elsewhere in Chapter 9.

❑ External interventions

External interventions are those which are 'imposed' from outside a school and to which a school must respond in some way. I have used 'imposed' although, in some cases, there may only be strong pressure to follow the practice of other schools rather than a direct requirement to do so. Such impositions in the future may be anticipated if they are spotted as part of a strategic analysis, in which case, a school may be able to choose the timing of the implementation of the requirement – such decisions are essentially reactive. Only in the case of a voluntary improvement project could a school make a decision not to take part.

Market mechanisms which require a school to respond to attract students are included in strategic considerations elsewhere in Chapter 2, as they provide an indirect requirement to change rather than the more direct effects included here.

I have included the following external interventions in the order to which they can be increasingly resisted:

- official mandate
- inspection
- improvement projects.

Official mandate

An official mandate is one of a number of types of external requirement. This may be a legal requirement such as a national curriculum or a widely commended, officially sponsored initiative. It is difficult for an individual institution to refuse to implement such a sponsored improvement. There are two kinds of intervention:

- curricular
- organisational.

In England the national literacy and numeracy strategies in primary schools are of the first kind. The requirement to implement performance management for teaching staff is of the second kind. It does not directly influence teaching and learning but provides a mechanism by which they can be influenced.

School inspection

If schools are inspected and an inspection report based upon the inspection identifies weaknesses, a school will need to respond to the report in some way. This may be by defending its current practices and suggesting that these have been misunderstood, or by proposing to make changes to improve the areas of weakness. Inspection is likely to report on the curriculum and also organisational processes in a school.

School improvement projects

Over the last few years in many countries there has been a number of improvement projects run by outside bodies, for example charities, local authorities and universities, which offer assistance and possibly finance to schools which opt to take part. Whilst the ones in this category are voluntary there may be a good deal of pressure to take part. Some projects may be more prescriptive than others. The degree of prescription may include:

- curriculum covered
- teaching programme
- ways in which staff work together
- equipment which can be purchased
- training to be undertaken
- format of research undertaken.

Examples in England of some of these are Education/Business partnerships, National Grid for Learning, New Opportunities Fund of the National Lottery, Best Practice Research Scholarships, headship and other training programmes.

Organisational strategies for improving schools

From the range of ideas in the previous section and particularly bearing in mind the difficulties of predicting the future, I want to select a small number of ideas for further discussion.

❏ Learning organisation (for the very long term)

If the future is uncertain, then a capacity to learn and reapply learning will be particularly worthwhile. However, despite the rhetoric, what this means is really rather unclear. It should mean rather more than an organisation with individuals who learn. In addition to that, it should mean that there are corporate ways of learning. A number of elements which could make up a learning organisation have been put forward:

- routines which incorporate facets of learning
- monitoring and reporting on current practice
- records of current practice
- reflecting on data on current practice
- having a problem solving routine to deal with non-standard problems
- memory of how previous problems were solved.

One key issue concerns how learning is passed on from one organisation member or group of organisation members either to other members of the organisation or their successors. A strong organisational culture has been offered as one solution to this issue of communication and succession, but this would only represent a habituation of past practice rather than a capacity to learn and improve on past practice. Thus, whilst organisational learning is an intuitively appealing idea, so far suggested practice falls well short of this ideal.

❏ Core competences (for the long term)

If the future is unclear there may be certain attributes which can be recognised as important for the future of education and, in particular, for the future of a particular school. A capacity to identify these and to develop them will help in the middle to long term.

For core competences and for other key activities this suggests that there should be a basis of expertise which involves more than one person. Any key activity should have a minimum of two people involved. This provides:

- protection in case a key member leaves
- succession planning
- stimulation as two sets of expertise interact
- sharing of workload and easing pressure points in time
- improved communication with others.

Sometimes a requirement for people with technical expertise may limit the possibilities for forming these key teams. However, when there is some degree of flexibility, the above set of advantages may suggest a number of possible team members. There may be advantages in having two people who are unalike working on an issue, providing they can co-operate to a minimum level. In this way there is more likely to be intense discussion of a range of possibilities rather than two people who tend to think alike working together. This is likely to be particularly effective when the issue is complex and contentious.

In primary schools, for example, the co-ordination of English, the co-ordination of mathematics and the co-ordination of assessment are areas of work for forming such teams because they are vitally important activities for the long term future of a school.

In secondary schools having deputy heads of department and deputy heads of year can form a similar team to undertake important tasks for the organisation.

A capacity to improve may be a core competence in the future for schools.

❏ Benchmarking (for the medium term)

In the medium term a useful technique is that of comparing with the best of current practice and seeking to integrate this into future activities.

Benchmarking has a number of facets:

- identifying and copying general practice in another school
- identifying and copying one or more features of another school
- identifying another organisation – educational or non-educational – which is successful in one particular aspect of management and discovering how it obtains its results. This involves both understanding what the organisation does but, just as importantly, understanding how it thinks about that aspect of its work.

The final one offers the prospect of new thinking. It involves taking ideas from one sphere and incorporating them in another, for example, in boarding schools, particularly where there is an intention to offer flexible accommodation, benchmarking with a hotel with a good reputation for service and a high occupancy rate may offer insights into how to deal with such a problem which does not arise using standard operating procedures in existing boarding schools.

Although potentially benchmarking offers a great deal, there are a number of provisos. Whatever the practice it will be incorporated in the culture of the existing organisation and not easily transportable, and the priorities it represents may be at variance with the major aims of an educational organisation such as a school (not throwing the baby out with the bath water). Looking for examples in the not-for-profit sector will involve less translation into a school setting than examples from the commercial sector.

Recently in England, Beacon schools have been established on the basis that they have high performance in particular areas of their operation. Investigating such schools to discover ones which provide particular examples of good practice should be facilitated.

Stages in benchmarking

There are a number of discrete stages in benchmarking:

1. *Identifying the area of interest.* This may arise from an explicit problem, an area for expansion or a possible improvement.
2. *Identifying a sector and an organisation with which to benchmark.* The first decision is to identify a sector. Is there a school or other educational source which might provide a benchmark organisation? If not, what kind of organisation might engage in the particular practice? Having identified the sector, the next decision is to identify the other organisation with which to benchmark. There are a number of sources for this:
    (a) data in the public domain
    (b) expert recommendation
    (c) personal recommendation
    (d) Snowballing – being passed on from potential sources.

    Any one of these sources may provide a number of leads. To help decide on a particular one, a matrix can be set up which displays which sources have provided examples. What is known from each of the sources can help decide which looks the best example to pursue.
3. *Making contact and agreeing the benchmarking contract.* The previous stage of identifying an organisation may have opened up avenues of approach but before making the final choice of organisation it is worth considering what is the advantage of benchmarking from the other organisation's point of view. If it is to give generously of its time and effort there should be mutual advantage of some kind, otherwise its input is likely to be limited and might stop whenever any other priority intercedes. Compiling a list of possible advantages from its perspective might include:
    (a) reflection (from having to explain and questioning)
    (b) evaluation report (there could be an offer to write a short report appraising the working of that aspect from the standpoint of an outsider)
    (c) sharing this or other practice
    (d) writing documentation where is does not already exist
    (e) providing some specific benefit in return.

    The 'contract' should include some brief explicit statement of what both sides are contributing and gaining from the benchmarking exercise. This both codifies and also reassures sceptics about the extent of any possible commitment particularly if there are concerns about the extent of the commitment. Such an agreement should also have the effect of making the withdrawal of one partner during the enterprise less likely. If some investment of time and effort is needed to gain a deep understanding of how some process works, it is deeply frustrating if the conditions to do this are withdrawn before completion.
4. *Visiting and achieving understanding of how results are achieved in the other organisation.* This is the most obvious source of activity in connection with the project, although it might not be so much larger than the other stages if those have been particularly tricky. Here documentation needs to be studied first. This prevents time being wasted asking questions which can be more efficiently answered from documentation. Where there is no documentation then an offer to produce operating procedures may be a potential benefit to the host organisation. Documentation will describe how the process is intended to work or worked at some time in the past. Verification

procedures will still be needed to ensure that this gives an accurate view of how the process currently works.

Such documentation should provide an overview of the process but may not give sufficient detail and also probably does not provide the philosophy and thinking behind the work practices. After the study of documentation a whole host of more relevant questions can be formulated to test accuracy and understanding. What is to be achieved from any visit or other fact-finding operation needs to be formulated in advance.

My own firm conviction is that, however well formulated such a visit schedule is, all questions cannot be formulated in advance and that a minimum of two visits or other means of obtaining further information should be agreed in advance. In this way, when the initial information is studied, any gaps which emerge will need to be pursued. This may take several iterations before being competed.

5. *Translating this understanding into a workable plan for the school.*
6. *Implementing the plan.*

Sources of future school improvement

There are a range of sources of contributions to school improvement. These are mainly concerned with doing the job better rather than solving problems and, as such, a school should be selective about which to take up at any point in time.

❑ Educational advances

It is sometimes quite difficult to differentiate genuine educational advances from trends which become fashionable but then fade. Few advances are discovered as a result of valid research and few appear to build explicitly on previous developments. However, there are a range of areas where advances should be considered if there are indications of a researched base and an evaluation of practice:

- increased understanding of how children learn and particularly how particular groups of individuals learn
- new ways of teaching children and organising instruction as well as curricular and content development
- grouping children for teaching
- behaviour management techniques and underpinning psychology
- involving parents to a greater extent
- the developing role of technology for new teaching materials and techniques. Advances in the education of children with particular learning difficulties, e.g. success maker for children with reading difficulties.

What I am advocating is a sceptical approach to news of improvement initiatives. This involves such questions as: what is the evidence that it works? How long has it been working? In what circumstances does it work? What similarities do these have to our circumstances? Were there special reasons why it worked?

❑ Managerial advances

New managerial and leadership practices appear often from the commercial sector. Some of these are relabelling of previous techniques which did not quite fulfil their original promise and so here again some scepticism is needed before being convinced that such solutions should be taken up. It has been observed that the greatest need and source of new management initiatives is from management consultants who are desperate to have new services to sell. This is not to suggest that worthwhile and lasting improvements in thinking and practice do not appear from time to time, but rather to suggest that many more are heralded than survive.

New insights may be helpful but, unless there is an immediate problem to be solved, any desirable development can wait for an appropriate timing before it is introduced.

A need in many schools may be to get all those in management and leadership positions to recognise their function and to provide them with the necessary skills of thought and action to allow them to succeed in the revised role.

6 A Strategic Planning Model for Schools

Introduction

The development of theory in strategic planning was intended to allow organisations to take stock of their present position and to decide on a direction for the future. As the study of strategic planning in commercial organisations has shown, the process is much more complicated that just setting up a plan and then implementing it. It is a much more interactive and iterative process than that description would suggest. However, even though the process is more complicated, strategic planning models have their value in:

- conceptualising the process
- providing an overview of stages in the complete process
- keeping track of progress
- communicating with others.

Thus a model has value as a heuristic or explanatory aid but should not be taken to be a literal description of what is to happen. Like so many other facets of school leadership it requires understanding and interpretation. This chapter concentrates on the operational stages of the strategic planning model. It also briefly discusses strategic change.

Strategic and school development planning

Since 1989 schools in England and Wales have increasingly been engaged in a process called school development planning. A process for this was proposed and schools have followed this with some requirements from their LEA. Initially these plans were to help formulate staff development needs for school improvement and for LEAs to summarise from the plans for each school the aggregate staff training needs for the LEA. Individual schools used this planning process to deal with the introduction of the National Curriculum in the early 1990s and subsequent government and local initiatives since then. Whilst individual school needs have always played some part in the plan, these have generally been short-term needs and anything more fundamental such as the future of the school operated outside the school development planning process which was mainly concerned with curriculum developments.

Some schools have taken a longer-term perspective and deal in plans for a three-year period and have begun to undertake client surveys as a form of input into the planning process. However, school development plans (SDPs) have been

- internally generated plans
- almost exclusively generated by teachers
- concerned mainly with teaching and learning
- an internal school document approved by governors.

Whilst these are generalisations and some schools have gone further in a strategic direction, it is important to understand the differences between the concepts of strategic planning and school development planning. Whether school development planning and strategic planning have become more alike is rather academic unless the critical components of strategic planning are present. Strategic planning involves more than just a longer timescale. Three components, in addition to its longer-term horizon, which mark out strategy are market research, environmental intelligence gathering and processing, and incorporation of a 'vision of the future'.

The more short term and operational nature of school development planning can be incorporated into the implementation of strategic planning. Thus staff expertise which has been gained from school development planning can make a valuable contribution to strategic planing and its implementation. However, research has shown that school development planning has not always involved teaching staff in a holistic way. In some cases the plan is little more than the private document of the headteacher. In cases such as this the experience of school development planning is very far removed from what is needed for effective strategic planning.

A strategic planning model for schools

The strategic management model has:

- three conceptual stages
- three action steps.

❏ Three conceptual stages

The three conceptual stages introduced in Chapter 2 are the following:

- strategic analysis
- strategic choice
- strategic implementation.

The conceptual stages have a logical order of precedence. At each stage there is use of the findings from the previous stage and an anticipation and preparation for what will happen at the next stage. However, in practice there may be some movement backwards and forwards through aspects of each stage.

Strategic analysis
Strategic analysis investigates the questions: how are we doing? What might be needed in the future? What could we do better? It also raises the crucial question: what do we take for granted? This involves collecting data both inside and outside a school. It involves an assessment of the present state of the school and its context but also, crucially, asks: what developments and changes outside the school may have implications for school activities in the future?

Strategic choice
This involves combining the results of analysis with a positive vision of the future and formulating strategic options. These are then evaluated before one is chosen.

Strategic implementation
This stage extends over several years as the plan is implemented. Broad intentions are gradually translated into more specific plans as more and more of the plan is implemented. Specific components are changes to structures and systems, staff and deployment of resources.

❏ Three action steps
To carry out the three conceptual stages there are three action steps:

- deciding how to plan
- deciding how to choose
- deciding how to plan and implement.

There needs to be a plan of how to plan. This may need to be modified subsequently as events progress and unexpected information and incidents occur. Without an initial plan there will be no template to follow to steer progress and chart stages of its completion. Although the initial work on each of these stages and steps will need to be considered by the school leader, the extent to which there should be consultation with others and their participation will need to be considered for each stage.

A plan is needed of how to plan.

A composite model which incorporates the three conceptual stages and the three action steps is given in Figure 6.1.

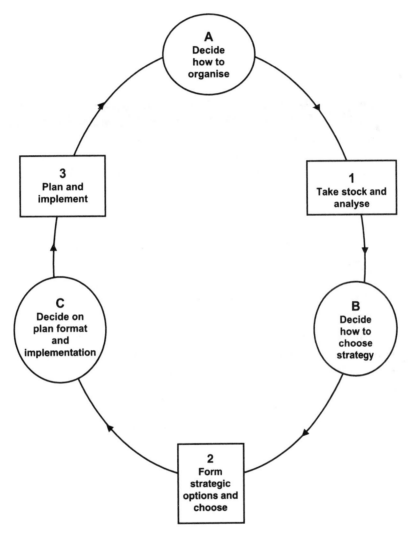

Figure 6.1   *Composite model of the strategic leadership process in schools*

Operating the planning model: the action steps

The action stages of the planning model involve a series of decisions about how to carry out strategic planning in a particular organisation.

❑ Deciding how to plan

Whether to engage in formal strategic planning

The first and major decision is whether to engage in formal strategic planning. This is not a light decision to take. When the process is announced there will be high expectations of what is to be accomplished. There can be expected to be some disillusionment if the process does not come to a successful conclusion.

For the reasons previously cited, although implicit strategic planning is better than no such planning at all, it has a number of disadvantages (see Chapter 2, p. 24).

There are some occasions when to embark on formal strategic planning might be the obvious course of action. These include:

- arrival of a new headteacher
- schools facing obvious problems (e.g. recruitment of students or staff; students' results; students behaviour; poor inspection report)
- the inauguration of a new school
- the formation of a new governing body
- competition from another school.

Who to involve?

More explicitly – who to involve at each stage? There are many advantages to wide involvement, however the logistics of a complex and time-consuming process with the involvement of a lot of people at all stages should be questioned. The practical as well as the ideal need to be borne in mind. The way in which they are to be involved will affect the numbers who could be involved. This is considered further later.

There are some obvious parameters – such as the number of people who could possibly be involved. If this is not large as in many small primary schools, there is the possibility of most of them being involved at some stage. Whilst in a large secondary school, for much of the process, only representatives could be heavily involved for most of the process for the whole school.

There will be expectations of involvement following the customary way of operating in any individual school. This provides an opportunity to follow these or to change them. Where there has historically been little involvement, this provides a seminal opportunity to change that practice. Three things should be borne in mind however. For those unused to involvement, a contribution to a new and complex process may appear very daunting. So the level of involvement should be chosen so that participants gain confidence and build on this successful experience for further involvement. Secondly, if there is to be a new pattern of greater involvement then there will need to be consistency and it will need to be continued in other school processes in addition to strategic planning. Finally, if the time requirements for involvement are not to become prohibitive, there will need to be consideration of different ways of involving people and the time involved in using different methods.

From the previous discussion of involvement in Chapter 4, p. 53 where there are choices to be made about involvement there are tests which can be used such as the tests of

- expertise
- relevance
- acceptance.

A slightly different view of acceptance may be helpful in considering the collection of data. Where data is presented which is rather negative there may be a degree of rejection and denial. This will be at its most acute when the data takes the form of judgements from outsiders, as is the case for school inspections. A way of trying to ensure acceptance of data is to involve sceptics in its collection. They are likely to develop a sense of ownership when they have played a part in its collection and have had cause to reflect on the evidence as it has come in rather than being faced with a *fait accompli*.

Finally, here as in later planning for implementation of the plan, there needs to be a consideration of the extent of involvement of particular individuals. There may be some who are involved at each stage in a major way and are in danger of being overloaded. Drawing a matrix which records individuals and their involvement in different aspects of the process should reveal those individuals in danger of becoming over-committed.

In addition to customary expectations there are likely to be formal if not statutory expectations of the involvement of the governing body of a school and perhaps representatives of its local authority – depending on the nature of relationships between the school and its LEA. In England there is no statutory requirement to involve an LEA in school-level strategic planning.

How to involve others – top down vs bottom up
There are three aspects.

Methods of involvement
There is an almost inevitable assumption that involvement means attending meetings but there are also other possibilities. As Chapter 4, p. 52 has suggested there are other ways and these should be considered in line with the amount of time which other staff wish to commit. More possibilities emerge as electronic communication becomes easier in schools. New ways of communicating that might particularly be relevant to strategy processes and the communication of progress are

- publication of details on web pages
- e-mails of progress reports.

E-mail also offers an efficient process by which individuals can contribute a swift response to strategy-making either by providing additional information or by giving reaction to data or proposals.

Consultation and participation
The differences between the two have been discussed in Chapter 4, p. 51. As has been emphasised, it is important that individuals should know whether they are being consulted or whether they are participating in decision-making if serious misunderstandings are not to occur. I have previously suggested two scenarios, one involving strategic planning by consultation and one by participation. These are illustrated in Figure 6.2.

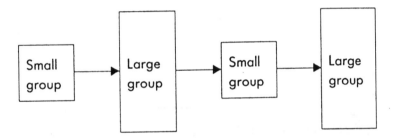

Figure 6.2   *A small working group consulting a larger group at various stages in the process*

A large participative group divides tasks to be performed by smaller participative groups before they are fed back to the larger group (Figure 6.3).

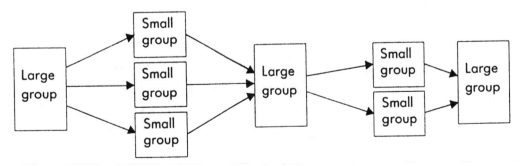

Figure 6.3   *A large participative group divides*

These two are intended to be illustrative of how to envisage the process proceeding and as starters for discussion to produce a way of involving staff and others in the process.

Top down and bottom up
In large primary schools and secondary schools there may be strong sections within the school which feel that they have an identity and are the unit for action at an intermediate level below the level of the whole

school. These may be based on year teams, subject departments or pastoral units. If these are units for action in terms of curriculum or student performance, then they may be organic units which should consider their own strategic priorities and their own mini-strategic plans. These are styled mini-plans since they will need to be consistent with the strategic plan for the entire school if the entire process is not to be dysfunctional.

As Figure 6.4 indicates the major issue concerns how to incorporate whole-school priorities if the bottom-up route is taken, by which individual units develop their mini-plans. The implications of all the mini-plans will need to be considered in terms of resources, time required and acceptability to the majority of the stakeholders. Finally, it should be borne in mind that the ultimate recipients of the results of strategic planning are the students and their education. Just what would be the impact on students of the totality of these mini-plans? These questions need consideration and much negotiation when incompatibilities and clashes of priority are recognised. This may be a time-consuming and very delicate task. The strategic priorities which do not emerge from any of the sections but are vital to the whole school as an organisation will also need to be added. There is a great tendency for sections to fail to recognise the importance of central services and whole-school priorities unless these are absent – by which time it is too late. The

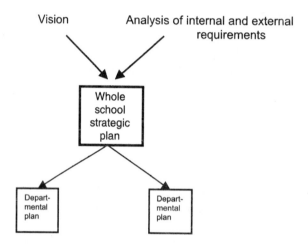

Figure 6.4(a)   Strategy formation by grand design

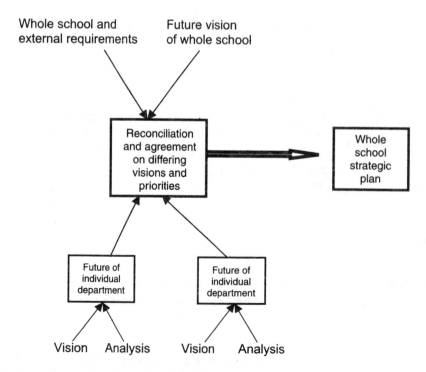

Figure 6.4(b)   Strategy formation by sum of parts

greatest danger of assembling mini-plans in this way is of 'co-ordination by stapler' rather than a more organic combination of priorities.

Timescale

An estimate of the timescale for the whole process of planning and each of its stages needs to be made to see how that fits with logistics of the school year and the time required to carry out effectively each stage of the conceptual and action steps. All my experience based on schools which have engaged in the process is that the time tends to be underestimated. There is a dilemma which should be recognised between allowing sufficient time for each stage whilst keeping up a sense of momentum and progress. Once this dilemma is recognised much can be accomplished by devising forms of communicating progress on some proforma which gives an overview of the whole process. As has been continually emphasised, at the start there can be best estimates of such timescales but these will need some adjustment in the light of experience. It is essential that any agreed adjustments are communicated to all involved so that an impression of stagnation is not unintentionally created.

Drawing a simple network of activities (see Chapter 4, p. 64) will demonstrate activities which can go on in parallel or simultaneously with other activities and should also reveal the critical path, that is, the critical set of activities which limit the time to complete the whole operation. Any delay in one of the activities on the critical path will delay the whole process by the same amount of time. To draw a network the whole process needs to be analysed to identify each separate activity. Each activity needs to identify its preceding activity or activities and an approximate timescale for its completion. This information is sufficient to draw a simple network and work out an estimated timing of each activity. This will reveal the critical path.

❏ Deciding how to choose

Deciding how to choose involves formulating a process by which ideas will be considered, synthesised, options formulated and one chosen. The two sets of contributions to the choice process are the results of the strategic analysis and one or more visions of the future. Each of these two sets of inputs will need to be discussed and interpreted for their implications. Following this, a number of options will need to the formulated to give a direction for the next five to ten years and associated actions to make substantial progress in that direction. The final element of choice is to decide on one of these.

If strategic issues have been formulated as part of the analysis process, then the results will need to be assessed for their implications for future strategy. Also, any proposed strategy will need to demonstrate how it has resolved each of the strategic issues. Each of the options which are put forward will need to be assessed for their value for money, that is, are the benefits achieved at least cost?

The choice process needs to identify who will be involved in discussing the results of analysis and the vision and formulating the options for the future and, then, how one will be chosen. If it is the school governing body which makes the decision, there will need to be consultative processes so that the views of the school staff and, probably, parents are known before the final decision is taken.

The criteria for judging the strategic options will need to be operationalised so that it is clear how they are to be assessed. The criteria are (Chapter 2, p. 18)

- consistency
- suitability
- feasibility
- acceptability.

❏ Deciding how to plan and implement

Some forethought needs to be given about the final form of the strategic plan. It will contain the strategic aim and the means for achieving the aim. Not all the means will need the same degree of detail. Initial steps may be quite detailed but beyond the short-term planning cycle the route will be less detailed. This may take the form of actions (each of which is quite complex) in some predetermined or conditional ordering. This suggests that some form of simple network analysis with a provisional timetable would give an overview and allow the implications of progress on the early stages to be foreseen.

So the plan is likely to contain:

- an analysis of the context and situation which brings out the key planning assumptions
- the strategic aim
- a route map of intended progress towards the aim
- some detail of broad courses of action to be followed
- detailed operational plans of short term actions.

This will comprise the initial documentation. Each year this will be consulted to check that the key planning assumptions still hold good and to check on progress in the last year, to consult the route map to formulate detailed plans for the next year with some provisional plans for the following year. I assume that the detailed plans will be the substantial part of the school development plan. I say substantial since there will be new requirements which have arisen in the year, from inside the school and outside, which need to be incorporated into the school development plan.

As with all plans so with plans of plans. Formulating ideas of outcome and format at the start of the process will help focus on where actions are leading but if the original expectations cannot be met, then the plans need to change. This should be a conscious choice rather than happen by default.

Managing strategic change

A number of techniques for managing change have been presented in Chapter 4. This section considers the case of major change or strategic change. This involves changes to the basic ways of working in an organisation. In other words it requires a change of culture. The stabilising force which organisational culture exerts makes it very difficult to change. Kurt Lewin (1951) characterised change as consisting of three stages:

- unfreezing
- movement
- refreezing.

For cultural change a great deal of effort will need to be expended on the 'unfreezing' process.
Scholars have suggested that the situations in which cultural change is most likely are

- *evident crisis*: where an organisation is evidently in trouble or heading for trouble, there is a greater willingness to consider deep-seated change
- *attractiveness of change*: the proposed change needs to have all its highly desirable features emphasised
- *strength of present culture*: the stronger the present culture the more difficult it is to change.

There are two cases which may affect schools and which need rather different treatment:

1. *Evolving the present culture*: this would be the case where some features of the present culture are being emphasised and others de-emphasised, e.g. teachers working in each others' classrooms goes on to a limited degree but is to be encouraged to encompass more people on more occasions.
2. *Radical change to the present culture*: this would be the case where major features of the present culture need to be overturned, e.g. an academic sixth form broadened to give equal status to a vocational sixth form (the radical change is in giving parity to both types not in introducing a clearly lower status sixth form).

Bate (1994) has a five-stage model of cultural change. His thesis is that organisational cultures have a lifespan. The early stages of a culture are very developmental for an organisation as it explores the potential offered by the new culture. This is followed by a very productive period after new ways of working have been established. However, he sees a period of decline beginning to set in when thinking has ossified and people have slipped into routines. Thus his view is that leaders need to engineer a change of culture when they sense that the current culture is becoming stale

The five stages help amplify the three steps of Lewin and give more suggestions about how to create movement between the old and the new (see Figure 6.5).

Lewin	Bate	Description	Processes
Unfreezing	Deformative	Current certainties need to be undermined if people are too comfortable with the 'recipe'. One aspect of this is 'induced crisis'.	
Moving	Reconciliative	Culture cannot be imposed. This stage is concerned with interaction and accommodation	Dialogue, argument and debate
Moving	Acculturative	Emerging ideas must be tidied up and made assimilable	Socialisation and learning the new ideas
Moving	Enactive	The new culture must be put into practice	Adapting new practices to make them fit and be workable
Refreezing	Formative	The new culture is made permanent	Embedding of the culture to reproduce itself

Figure 6.5 Comparison of cultural change stages of Lewin and Bate

Whilst the previous culture must be made untenable, Bate is clear that a new culture cannot be imposed but must emerge. Some new ideas have to be fed into the debate which are capable of stimulating new thinking. An understanding of these has to emerge in a form which people can come to terms with. New practices need to be tried which follow from the new thinking, but these may need to be adapted to be made to work. Finally, the new has to be so embedded that it will continue and generate a new momentum for the organisation.

My contribution to thinking about cultural change involves the human relations perspective. Within any school staff there will be different groups with different motivations and attitudes to major change. An essential initial step is to assess how many members there might be in each group. Some change may not be possible until the results of such an exercise appear more promising. The groups I have identified are

- change drivers
- careerists
- co-operative
- ambivalent
- sceptical
- resisters
- luddites.

❏ Change drivers
There are two types of members of this group. First, there are those who are temperamentally keen on change – any change – they like the stimulation and challenge. Secondly, there are those who are keen on a particular change. For this second group it may be that the change is supported on principle or because there are personal advantages. In seeking to harness members of this second group it is important to identify which of the types an individual belongs to. They are likely to need different treatment. The final type may be quite calculative and may need to see that his or her interests have been noted.

❏ Careerists
This group comprises the ambitious who wish to progress their careers and see developments as advantageous. For this group the advantages may need to be brought to their attention – personal learning

about change, experience of this particular development and association with a successful change. Members may be hoping for advancement in their current school or as a way of moving on to promotion in another school. Beware of too great a dependence on an individual who moves on prematurely and leaves a floundering development.

❑ Co-operative

Most staff are likely to be of this kind. They can be persuaded to go along with what appear to be sound proposals. A fund of goodwill can be anticipated if it has not previously been squandered by too much change or unsuccessful change. They will be susceptible to various forms of active leadership. They will need persuasion that the change will be beneficial to the school and for the general good. They may need reassurance about their own personal positions.

❑ Ambivalent

There may be a small number of staff who are genuinely unsure about the value of the proposed change. They see some advantages but also have some doubts about it. This may be because they do not understand the proposed change or because they have a particular perspective on the change where some negative features are clearer. Distinguishing between the two is necessary in order to then consider the reasons for the doubts.

❑ Sceptical

This is generally a small group who are genuinely concerned about the change, either because they are unsure about it in principle or they are worried about their own personal interests. This group may have reservations which should be taken into account, particularly where there has been little formal critical appraisal of the development because most staff have been in favour. Those who are sceptical and analytical may be useful early warning signals if the change is not delivering the improvements that were expected.

❑ Resisters

I have distinguished this group from the final one on the basis of their opposition. This group are people who oppose this particular change. They would almost certainly be in a different grouping for some other changes. Their opposition may be more or less active and open – active and passive resisters. Those who are less open may be difficult to distinguish from the two previous groups. Any opposition may be principled or because their own interests are threatened by this particular change. It may not always to possible to distinguish between the two reasons if proxy reasons are being given to disguise personal interests. Where they can be distinguished principled reasons should be analysed to ensure that they have been taken account of in the decision-making.

❑ Luddites

By this group I intend the usually small number of staff who will oppose any change. It may be quite difficult to distinguish valid criticisms of any particular change from this group because they are viewed as synonymous with preservation of the status quo. Their views may reflect a genuine conviction that much change does not necessarily lead to improvement or because it will mean extra work, disruption and feelings of uncertainty for them personally.

In addition to the numbers in the different groups it is also important to identify leaders of the groups. These may be in management posts, those with particular expertise or personal power. Opinion formers and those who follow them should be identified to predict how the groups might work. Although the descriptions above are intended to represent the 'true' positions of the groups, there may be more superficial characteristics of 'whinging', 'huffs and puffs', 'yes, buts' and 'no, but maybe'.

The three basic approaches to change outlined by Chinn and Benne (1976) are

- power-coercive
- empirical-rational
- normative-re-educative.

These are useful heuristic devices to consider how others are to be influenced. Although there is a natural reaction against the power-coercive, it should not be underestimated as of value in combination with other approaches at particular times. Too much reliance would clearly be counter-productive. The empirical-rational approach should not be underestimated. Everyone is aware of the limitations of 'pure brute sanity', to quote George Bernard Shaw, but the rationale for a change and the clinching arguments do need to be rehearsed. However, as so many observers have shown, a cognitive acceptance of change does not alone bring it about. Working on attitudinal change or the normative-re-educative approach is likely to be particularly effective. This is particularly associated with changing the culture of an organisation.

The starting point of change is 'unfreezing' or initiation. This is the process of making people uncomfortable with the present state of affairs. For very large changes this may be a very substantial and time-consuming task. It should not be rushed. Change is more likely to be successful if people are ready for it rather than still committed to existing ways of doing things.

A commitment chart (see Chapter 4, p. 67) is worth drawing up for key players in the change, in terms of identifying their current position and their desired position. This provides an indication of those for whom 'unfreezing' will be particularly productive. A further device to concentrate efforts where they are most needed is a force-field analysis (see Chapter 4, p. 64). From this weakening resisting forces and strengthening the driving forces (in that order) is required.

Role of consultancy

In carrying out such a fundamental change as to set up and operate a strategy there are many advantages in enlisting external support from a consultant.

Conceptually there are two types of consultant although occasionally they may be combined in the same person:

- subject consultant
- process consultant.

Schools are more accustomed to consultants who have particular subject expertise within education (see Chapter 5, p. 77). In that case it is specialist educational knowledge which is being sought. Here I want to examine the advantages of the process consultant. Such a consultant can provide:

- an external view
- experience of similar processes in other schools
- a sounding board
- knowledge of how organisations work
- a neutral collector of data.

This presupposes a consultant who has particular skills and experience. These specifically include organisational diagnosis and organisational change. In addition, there is the relationship between the school leader and the consultant to consider. I assume that it is the leader who has made a choice to employ a consultant and thus the consultant is providing a service to the leader. This may mean that staff are more guarded in their discussions with the consultant. This still provides for a neutral go-between. He or she is there to provide advice, guidance and support, but not to control or manage the activity. As a freely employed consultant he or she can be dismissed if the professional service or the relationship is not working.

It is important to clarify whether the consultant works for the school or the school leader. If the consultant is in some way chosen by the school this changes the relationship between consultant and staff and the consultant and the school leader. The role of the consultant is much more difficult as he or she has to interpret the school's interest in what may be challenging circumstances. The relationship between the consultant and the school leader will be a crucial one.

7 Strategic Analysis: Where Are We Now and What Might the Future Hold?

Introduction

This chapter goes though the practical steps in a strategic analysis. It examines the kind of data which might be available and that which would be needed for the three components of

- internal resource audit
- environmental scanning
- school culture and values.

The first two build up a picture of strengths, weaknesses, opportunities and threats (SWOT). The third examines existing priorities to see how they might have distorted the judgements required by the SWOT.

The strategic analysis process

The initial stage of strategy formation is to take stock of the present. There are three components:

- assessment of internal resources of the school and their use
- assessing external influences on the school
- recognition of the prevailing internal school culture.

Such an analysis could include the evaluation of the working of a previous strategy or, if there was no explicit previous strategy, identifying the strategy in retrospect could be a starting point. If good decisions are to be made about which direction to head in the future, then they need to be well informed and any judgements about the present state of the school need to be as accurate as possible. Such a requirement as this means that the process will take some time and needs to be wide-ranging in its use of data and as objective as possible in the interpretation of that data. A superficial analysis which is predestined to find only positive results will give a distorted picture of the present and merely confirm the current course of action. As we have seen earlier, this runs the risk of missing a turning point where a new course of action could stop the drift into complacency from which it is hard to recover.

The general procedure for carrying out the analysis should involve collecting data from a variety of sources and then quite separately examining and assessing the meaning of the data. Collecting the data should use well-informed social science practice where representative data is required (see Chapter 4, p. 64). Sampling procedures need to be carefully chosen. Although collecting data poses many problems and particularly the qualitative more impressionistic material, it is in the assessment of this data and its meaning that substantial issues lie. The data needs to be assessed in an unbiased way. Whilst each individual might try to do this, each brings his or her own preferences and values to bear in making judgements. If a number of people all do this and compare and discuss their conclusions it is possible for some of these filters and presuppositions to be exposed. The explicit consideration of culture should sensitise everyone to the norms of the school and hence the priorities which are likely to be implicitly applied to judgements.

Although some of the data may be quantitative, where it arises from school records or from surveys, there will also be invaluable 'intelligence' and judgement which is qualitative and subjective. A particular danger for qualitative data of this kind is that the data and the judgement based on it can easily become intertwined and thus it is not possible for those not originating the data to make an independent judgement. As a safeguard, therefore, wherever possible, the qualitative data should initially contain as many factual statements as possible. Any inferences which arise from the data can then be more independently assessed.

The range of sources of data include:

- school records
- surveys
- focus groups
- impressions and personal opinions
- personal knowledge.

❏ School records

As more school records are stored on computer, and particularly where the data for more than one year is stored, then this is a valuable source of data which already exists but may need analysing. Where this is not done routinely at the moment, there may be a prior stage. This will involve examining what software packages and analytical tools are available to interrogate the data. If the computerised administrative system is made up of modules, then it may be worthwhile checking whether the appropriate ones have been installed. Vital modules are those which can analyse student progress between key stages or between years and those which contain analysis software which allows data stored anywhere on the system to be brought together for analysis. Where there is comparative data from other schools this is particularly valuable.

❏ Surveys

Where there are already regular surveys of parental, student and staff opinions these can be used for strategic analysis, however, where such data is not readily available, individual surveys will need to be conducted. There are some principles which should be applied to all such surveys:

- Instruments need to be thoughtfully designed and produced.
- They should have a mixture of closed and open-ended questions.
- Groups to whom they are sent should be the whole population or be sampled systematically.
- They need a good response rate, i.e. the proportion of those who respond should be high.
- The general results need to be communicated to respondents afterwards.
- Action needs to follow or there needs to be an explanation of why no action is needed or can be taken.

Regular surveys of parental, student and staff satisfaction within a school are needed. Then any one year's results have some comparative basis. Such surveys are more likely to give a worthwhile indication of current satisfaction rather than to make major suggestions for improvement (unless current conditions are pretty bad).

❏ Focus groups

For many purposes what is needed is a combination of individual and group responses. Focus groups are likely to be effective in teasing out complex problems or exploring reactions to future scenarios. It is not a question of either/or but of both individuals and groups in appropriate circumstances. It is interaction in focus groups which is their advantage. One person may spark off a thought in someone else's mind that would not have happened without such a group effect. Groups have to be structured and conducted carefully if certain members are not to dominate and if the experience is to be a positive one.

❏ Intelligence and opinions

Much valuable data will be of the more 'soft' and qualitative kind, particularly that concerned with environmental scanning. In most areas whilst there may be some hard or quantitative data there will also be qualitative data. This is less easy to summarise and assimilate but is not less valuable.

❏ Collecting data

The primary aim of strategic analysis is to diagnose the initial state of the school and the forces acting upon it and those likely to be influential in the future. However, how the data is collected may also serve other purposes. If greater involvement is one aim of strategy then this can be exemplified in the collection of data. This can be a process in which a large number of people are engaged. A further consideration is of who should collect particular data and on whom it might have great impact. Those who collect data are likely to feel a greater sense of ownership of the data and are much less likely to reject it as invalid. Thus getting individuals to compile data which they may know nothing about and which they may find surprising has particular benefits. Discovering data which is not particularly palatable is a way of ensuring that such data has an impact on those who ordinarily would be unaware of such findings.

Internal resources and pressures

❑ Professional assessment

The range of areas of strength and weakness is a huge one as is the range of data which should be collected and analysed.

School records

There may be statistics on student performance, data on staff expertise and qualifications, an assessment of school facilities and its buildings but other more intangible assets should also be included (**Activities S12 and S13**).

Judgements on performance

There are activities which call for a staff assessment of school performance on a range of criteria (**Activities S2 and S8**). Staff responses may pick out areas of disagreement or some surprising results; these help prioritise any follow-up to see if there is evidence which validates the views. The school may have a strong sporting reputation or one for some other facet of performance. It may have a reputation for training staff who move on for promotion in other schools. On the other hand, it may have a reputation for poor student behaviour. In such cases, if possible there should be an assessment of any factual data and a separate assessment of external perceptions. This is important because, if the data paints a better picture than current external perception, it indicates an area where communication and promotion of a more favourable school image is possible.

Staff survey

A survey of staff satisfaction can provide a benchmark against which future changes can be compared and provides an outlet for staff who are not happy with current ways of operating. Such a staff survey can be made very sophisticated as illustrated in the approach as part of the school review process in the State of Victoria in Australia. The instrument used has 16 sections which examine different aspects of staff commitment and morale as well as factual information on staff development activities undertaken etc. (http://www.sofweb.vic.edu.au/standards/pdf/opinion.pdf)

❑ Client and stakeholder assessment

- Current parents
- Current students.
- Other stakeholders

Current parents

Parents are an important group from whom an assessment of school performance is needed. They will be partners in the education of their children and, in the case of a market environment, they will be active choosers of their children's school. They have originally chosen the school but they could decide to move their children elsewhere.

A knowledge of how current parents view a school is important in two ways:

- individual experience
- contribution to the 'grapevine'.

Parents' individual experiences gives an indication of how they are treated by the school and whether they are satisfied with it. These are important both from the point of view of parents as clients of the school's services and also as partners in the education of their children. The views and experiences of parents can contribute feedback on the working of school policies.

The other important aspect of parental perceptions is their contribution to general conversations about the school within the community. An important determinant of parents' choice of school for their children is the 'grapevine' or the general way in which the school is viewed in the community (see Chapter 2, p. 27). How this is formed has been little researched. The general feeling is that school reputations are more easily damaged than built up, but there appears to be a general reservoir of goodwill for schools which have a good reputation. Although press comment and official school documentation has some impact on public perceptions, much more pervasive is the widespread uncontradicted assertions which are made about the school in the course of conversations in the local community. This will be based on experiences from the past, current experience and much hearsay. It is likely that the experiences of present parents will contribute to the grapevine in some way and these may be positive or negative. There will undoubtedly be opinion formers who are particularly influential, but each contribution will add to the current image. It is obvious that negative experiences should be minimised, but they also need assessing both for their number and severity.

A regular parental survey of satisfaction with a school has much to commend it. This should have some general features which are constant each year so that trends can be detected on comparable data, but it is desirable that the instrument should not be too unchanging. If there are some differences each year, they provide interest for those completing the questionnaire and such sections which change from year to year provide an opportunity for a school to investigate in more detail a different feature of its operation each year.

In addition to the data generated by parental questionnaires there may be other data which could be assembled which provides another perspective on the school's relations with parents, for example, attendance at parental consultation evenings, numbers of parental complaints, issues referred to parent governors, etc.

Current students

As has been noted earlier, schools are unusual in having two-part main clients – parents and students. Whilst parents may play the larger part in choosing the school for their offspring it is the student who is the direct recipient of its services. Although the previous section's satisfaction survey of existing parents indicates their perception of the work of the school, the students' perception will inevitably be different. Thus there is great merit in carrying out regular surveys of student opinion. The content of this and how they are conducted will obviously depend on the age of the students. For young children it may be selected interviews with a teacher or other helper or, for older primary children, it may be a very simple questionnaire and class discussion. For secondary age students, questionnaires, class discussion and selected interviews should be used. Questionnaire data needs to be anonymous so that students are not inhibited. Class discussion and interviews need to be with someone who students trust and who can collect data impartially.

Surveys that are conducted on a regular basis provide data which can be compared from year to year. The results may indicate changing attitudes from students of different cohorts or they may indicate changing satisfaction because of efforts by the school to become more client oriented. Surveys of different age groups have the advantage of showing trends as students move through a school. A number of surveys in England have shown a rising antagonism to school as students grow older predominantly among boys. Knowledge of such trends makes the targeting of action more efficient.

Other stakeholders

Activity S1 will reveal other key stakeholders and their criteria for success.

❑ Market assessment – potential parents

A market assessment indicates how parents of potential students perceive the strengths and weaknesses of a school. Obtaining the perceptions of the school from potential parents is very difficult and usually only a number of very partial scraps of data are available:

- new parents
- grapevine
- previous schools
- parental visitors.

A survey of new parents may give a good indication of how they perceived the school but once they have experience of the school their perceptions may have changed. And those parents who have chosen the school may have a perception of its strengths and weaknesses which is not shared by other parents who rejected the school and chose an alternative.

As has already been mentioned, the grapevine will be very influential and members of the community including those on the governing body can relate their knowledge of what is being said on the grapevine. Any such account needs to be warts and all not an edited account which mentions only the good points.

Staff in schools from which children move on may have useful intelligence to contribute about the reported bases for school choice and the prevailing impressions informing such choices. Both the teachers of such children and their headteachers may be useful sources of information. Headteachers may be consulted by some parents before they make their choice of the next school for their child.

Where staff from a receiving school carry out liaison activities with the previous schools, including school visits, they may be able to pick up intelligence and trends in student recruitment in local schools. They may have the opportunity of asking all children about their next school and why they are going there.

Schools have open days or evenings for prospective parents, which can be occasions for intelligence gathering. The questions which parents ask, their conversation and their general attitude can give clues about their priorities and their perceptions.

In trying to evaluate this intelligence and its implications for the school there are a number of reservations. First, such snippets are partial. They give some limited accounts from a small number of parents. Secondly, unless the accounts are in some sense representative, they are likely to contain a higher proportion of unusual events and occurrences, which for some reason have had a larger impact on the respondent. Thus such data is most likely to be of value either to corroborate other accounts or as the source of hunches which need further investigation.

Environmental scanning

Environmental scanning involves examining influences outside an organisation and identifying the nature of their current level of influence and, more importantly, trying to assess the level and nature of future influences. Although this is a skill which inspired strategists acquire by experience, individuals have differing abilities at this. This section tries to offer some general guidelines for areas which need assessing and some means of acquiring data to make such an assessment.

What is needed is a rapid cursory assessment of the very many potential influences to identify a smaller number of promising ones to investigate more thoroughly. The net for the original trawl needs to be set fairly wide so that the smaller list for further study includes all the important ones and to reduce the chances of any having been missed. One of the intentions of a number of the activities related to environmental scanning is to suggest a range of influences from which to select the smaller number. It may also be that ones in the activities bring to mind others that are likely to be important to particular schools (**Activities S3 and S4**).

❏ Futurology

It is worth keeping an eye on futuristic developments which are predicted for more than 10–15 years in the future. Only some of these will come to fruition but having logged them as ideas to watch makes it much more likely that, as their potential waxes and wanes, they will be noticed. Some ideas which will take off in the future could influence some current decisions. This is very speculative but could be very promising.

It is ideas concerned with lifestyles and education and training which are the areas to watch. Life styles influence the lives of parents and how the education of children fits into this. Developments in education and training are of more obvious relevance. It is both the organisation of these activities as well as any new breakthroughs in learning which will be of interest.

❑ Socio-technical trends – national and local

This involves keeping abreast of developments in PESTEd spheres.

- political
- economic
- social
- technological
- educational.

This represents the general range of developments which affect the future in one form or another. Their importance was discussed in Chapter 2, p. 14 and so here the issue is – how are they monitored and information pooled? Each of these has a national and a more local dimension. For example, whilst national politics has an influence on all schools, it is local politics which also has an influence which, in the case of school reorganisation for example, may have the most dramatic effect. Early warning of such events can make pre-emptive action possible rather than only reaction afterwards.

All staff can be expected to spot educational developments and practices which are reported from other schools. There will be developments which are relevant to some sections or departments and some which are whole-school issues. Such intelligence can be gained from the educational press, conferences, courses and television and radio programmes. The challenge is to find ways of recording such developments for later study and follow-up.

Locating and organising expertise

This is where the interests and contacts of other staff and networks of supporters of the school become important. For example, those with an interest in politics will be avidly reading, digesting, interpreting and reformulating political trends as a matter of course. Such expertise has to be located and then harnessed, for what is important is how these political trends will affect schools and particularly this school.

When sources of expertise have been located and briefed, it remains to arrange how they report the developments and trends that they have become aware of. This probably requires a regular reporting cycle with possibilities of passing on urgent items more quickly. Individual debriefings with the headteacher or other repository of central intelligence can be the main vehicle for passing on knowledge, although there may be occasions when discussion between some of the sources collectively is more productive.

❑ Local environment

Although a number of influences will also be included in the local PESTEd spheres, this category is specifically intended to pick up developments in the local geographical environment. In addition to new housing and other influences on demographics, such features as changes to local transport patterns should be noted. Schools have closed because of the changing patterns of bus routes.

A major area of investigation concerns the number of children in the locality to be educated and the current pattern of choices. These are the factors that local authorities use to make predictions of future numbers of children in each school. Examination of past predictions with the actual numbers of children who have entered the school will indicate the extent to which the current predictions can be trusted. The comparison needs to be a sophisticated one if it is to be valid. Where there are established trends in a stable population, the predictions can be expected to be accurate, but where there are fluctuations in either, there will be difficulties in principle which will trouble the best of forecasters.

In addition to the numbers of children who come to a school there should be interest in where they come from and how many children a school would expect to enrol. What is the pattern of choices from the parents of children who the school would expect to enrol on a geographical bases? Even if a school fills all its places, if many of these children are not from its neighbourhood because these children go elsewhere, this has implications for the future of the school. If the total number of children in the neighbourhood declines or if other schools increase their attractiveness this will make for an unstable situation which the school is not well prepared to survive.

Such influences as changing employment patterns and the appearance of local commercial enterprises that might be sources of support and funding are intended to be noted under this heading.

❑ Other schools and educational institutions

There are two separate groups which are both significant:

- competitor schools
- feeder schools and receptor schools.

Although competitor schools might sound as if there is expected to be intense competition, this is really meant to signal other schools which parents may compare. This could be when they are selecting a school for their child's education or it may be later when this school's performance is being compared to others on the grapevine. Knowledge of what is happening elsewhere is indispensable as this may have implications for educational practice or for promoting the image of the school.

There will be published documents and news in the media but these will tend to cover past and current events rather than future plans. There are a range of low-profile ways of keeping abreast of developments in other schools but these will need to be identified and set up if regular intelligence is to be contributed, rather than news only being available at times of crisis.

A less obvious source of well-being for a school is the reputation and popularity of schools from which children come before attending the current school and also those of the school to which they move on. Parents increasingly study transfer patterns through the school system and make their decisions with these in mind. Often it is a particular choice of secondary school which guides a choice of primary school and, so, for primary schools the popularity of the secondary schools to which their children go will be important. Infant schools may experience a similar effect depending on the popularity of the junior school afterwards. The reverse effect also operates but in a more obvious way. If the feeder school is unpopular and takes only small numbers of children, this limits the number of children who can move on at transfer.

In cases where feeder schools or the schools to which children go on are unpopular, this may mean arranging to work in conjunction with those schools to improve the situation. Needless to say, this is easier if the problem has been recognised. Even then there may be difficult structural problems to be overcome.

Emergence of opportunities and threats

As a result of environmental scanning, opportunities and threats should be recognisable. Opportunities are those potential eventualities in the external world which would prove advantageous to the institution in its present state. There may be more opportunities than could be taken up and, so, at a later stage some prioritisation will be necessary. On the other hand, threats from outside, if they materialise and no action is taken, could place future success in jeopardy.

SWOT

From internal strengths and weaknesses and external opportunities and threats the SWOT analysis emerges (**Activity S14**). If this were acted upon without the next step of examining the organisational culture, it would have the effect of reinforcing the current strategy since the aims and values of the organisation have permeated all the judgements which have been made to produce the SWOT. This would not be disastrous if the organisation was already successful in an external environment to which it was well suited. However, if either of these two conditions are not satisfied, acting on the SWOT would compound problems rather than deal with them.

The next step, therefore, is to try to bring out the key hidden assumptions which are subsumed within the organisational culture.

School culture

Some knowledge of the current school culture is important for a number of reasons:

- It indicates prevailing attitudes and values.
- It will affect current perceptions of threats, opportunities, strengths and weaknesses.
- Deviations between rhetoric and reality or between 'espoused theories' and 'theories-in-use' are more likely to be noticed.
- Future changes can be considered.

As the culture is so all-pervasive it is quite hard to try to stand back and ask what are the prevailing norms and priorities in a particular school. A further difficulty in an organisation like a school is that there are two groups which will have a predominant culture – staff and students. Little investigative work has been carried out to examine the way each affects the other.

There are differences of view between organisational theorists about the nature of culture, how it can be investigated and how deep-seated it is.

❑ What is the aim of education? What is the school trying to achieve? What are the implicit answers to these questions and when these are made explicit are the answers appropriate?

Each school will have different priorities in terms of what it is trying to achieve for children during their time at the school. Different years in the schools may contribute differentially to these aims. Although there is a tendency to concentrate on the later years of schooling, important attitudes and work practices are built up in earlier years in the same school or in a previous school. Many problems which are manifest in the later years of schooling began to germinate at an earlier stage. Thus a more sophisticated look at aims will begin to identify how overall aims are to be achieved over the school career of a student and how each year contributes to this.

For some schools these aims may be different for different groups of children within the school. Questioning why these aims are different may help indicate what priorities the school has and what it prizes. It is likely to indicate expectations of students and limitations on these which the school imposes.

In addition to the aims of the school it is instructive to analyse how the school achieves its aims (**Activity S9**). This will reveal further assumptions about how children learn. 'Are they to be filled with information?' 'Is education to be drawn out of them?' 'Will they learn some skills by imitation?' 'To what extent are they being prepared to be independent learners?' Answers to these questions will reveal some more deep-seated assumptions about the nature of learning and basic human nature.

❑ To what extent are the aims shared across the school?

If the school's aims are widely shared across the school this probably means that the school's culture is a strong one. Whilst this has advantages in terms of operating in unison without much supervision, it has its downside in terms of being able to make changes, particularly any changes which are outside the envelope of the current culture. The more successful the current culture, the greater the chances are that it will become deeply entrenched and fail to recognise external changes to which the school needs to respond.

Where different parts of the school have some differences in terms of priorities, this can be a strength if the differences are not too pronounced. I have likened this to using the same language but with different dialects. There is the possibility of some harmonisation around what appear to be growing points for the future and if some differences persist these provide further possibilities for the future.

The final possibilities are that there are large differences in culture in different sections of the school or there are no pronounced principles for which the school stands. Either of these cases is dysfunctional. If there are large differences, concerted and united action will be difficult and, if there are no clear values, it is unlikely that there is much that people care about and are willing to strive for.

❑ Some further criteria offered for dimensions of culture

The essence of the culture of any organisation is very difficult to capture. There have been attempts to create instruments which gauge values and practices. These tend to emphasise particular processes within an organisation or particularly how its management operates. These give a rather incomplete account of organisational culture. There is a trade-off between having a very full description of what goes on and the accuracy that this can give and the need for parsimony if the description is to be an economical one which allows rapid comparison of one culture with another.

As one of the activities I have devised an instrument which has nine dimensions (**Activity S6**). Three are concerned with the internal working of the school – how staff interact and how staff and students interact. Six are external in the sense that they indicate the school as seen from the outside although they will also reflect what happens inside. The nine provide a broad range of criteria which can reflect differences between schools.

Other activities try to probe in more detail practices in school which capture distinctive practices and are indicative of underlying priorities (**Activities S5 and S7**).

❏ The aims of schools are multidimensional – social, cultural, moral, spiritual, physical and academic

Although the aims of schools have been polarised as either social or academic and cultural or academic there are clearly more possibilities. One of the activities requires an assessment of what the school is trying to achieve for students in terms of the proportion of effort which is devoted to the different aims. Another activity requires an assessment of contributions from the home and the school to each component. These assessments are generalisations and may be different for different groups of students (**Activities S10 and S11**).

Activities on culture

The activities on culture offer a number of ways of examining aspects of culture. Whilst those who have been in the school for a long time will find them most revealing, they are the ones who are least likely to recognise them. Newcomers to the school and outsiders are most likely to recognise distinctive practices and be in a position to ask why they are carried out like that. In some cases the reasons which brought them into existence might have been quite pragmatic. In this case the way in which different priorities or values were balanced might be quite revealing.

The assumption about culture is that it is the resolution of an accommodation between underlying values held by powerful leaders in the past and past environmental conditions. Whilst the culture may have been well adapted in the past, it may be less well suited to the present or future. Thus strategic analysis does not take the culture to be fixed but regards it as changeable albeit with great difficulty.

8 Vision and Strategic Choice

Introduction

There are two components from which a strategic choice needs to be made:

- results of strategic analysis
- vision of the future.

Whilst strategic analysis as its title suggests is analytic and is based on the current state of the organisation and tries to project this forward whilst taking account of environmental influences, it is essentially 'single-loop' thinking. It works from the known into the unknown using basically the same kind of thinking. Whilst it is more sophisticated than long-term planning in that it takes account of changes in the environment, it does not try to think things anew. In this sense there is a missing component, and this is some kind of vision of the future.

The combination of these two components produces strategic options which then have to be evaluated before one is chosen. Strategic issues may provide help in identifying options. (**Activity S15**)

Vision – the added dimension

The missing component is the creative 'double-loop' thinking of trying to envisage how things might be different in the future. It leaps the present and the short term. It looks 10–15 years ahead, sufficient time that things might change radically, and tries to vision the organisation in a new and successful future. This is aspirational but not totally idealistic and tries to provide some correspondence with current circumstances. Thus the vision is not just a projection forward of the present but it does bear some relation to the starting conditions.

Keeping an eye on ideas which have been formulated about the future as part of environmental scanning should assist this process. Undoubtedly those who have never tried to foresee the future find it harder to do so than those who have had some experience of it. There is a need to find cues that assist such thinking.

One contribution to the vision but essentially working forward from the present is to get individuals to write down their hope for the institution (**Activity S16**). By composing a number of sentences which contain statements about future practice of different components of the organisation's work, a picture will emerge of a better future which gives some clues about changes which will need to be made to move towards such a future. In formulating ideas about the future some people may be able to transcend the present and envisage a qualitatively different future. Others will base their ideas on what they would like to see in the present but which they know would require large-scale changes. Bringing the different ideas together should produce a composite. Some components will be incompatible with others and discussion should help to resolve these.

The challenge in strategic choice is to find ways in which individuals can engage in this process in a really free-thinking way and then find ways of communicating their visions. Since this process is visionary unless there are a number of individuals who could engage in this alone and communicate to others, this is probably an activity which lends itself to being carried out in a group. It probably requires some brainstorming to assemble what might be components of work in schools in the future and associated lifestyles. From this array of ideas pictures could be built up. An account could be compiled of how the situation would appear to a visitor. A first-hand account could be written from their perspective. It would need to cover sufficient features to make the account 'come alive' and allow readers and listeners to elaborate the ideas in their own mind (**Activity S17**).

Past experience of foreseeing the future suggests that some developments happen more quickly than expected but many more proceed only slowly. The conservatism which appears to colour most parents' views of schooling should be borne in mind. They constantly compare the school with those of their own school days and are reassured by the constancies whilst expecting that there will be changes and improvements. Thus the difficulty of gaining acceptance for any really major advance should not be underestimated.

❏ Schools of the future?

I have only a few suggestions for possible building blocks of future scenarios. One possibility is that children could undertake more of their learning from computers rather than from teachers. The more systematic instruction, particularly for 'linear' subjects such as mathematics, science and languages could be programmed. Software could be written which tried to replicate through expert systems what an expert teacher would do as children made errors. Whist producing such software would be a great challenge, it would reduce much of the routine teaching done by teachers. This would leave them to concentrate on the more creative aspects of learning and creating the motivation for children to tackle subjects which were more varied in their styles of learning and less easily programmable. In addition to academic learning, schools and teachers would become more important sources of social learning, that is, how to get along with each other and interact.

- If as I argue their social function will increase then there may be a precedent in terms of the way in which many independent schools have adapted from being mainly boarding schools to taking a substantial proportion of day students. In boarding, programmes could count on children 24 hours a day and for seven days a week in order to achieve their objectives. As boarding has declined similar objectives have had to be achieved with a five or five and a half day week and with extended hours but still with time to go home each day.
- Some schools are already thinking of laptop computers for each student. If this is the scenario, then power points and wireless connections for the Internet become important. Teachers could prepare teaching materials on laptops and connect them to large television screens for lessons. Some schools already have the technology.
- Swipe cards for registration are already in existence. Using these for security purposes to gain entry to buildings is only a small step.
- Perhaps a greater international dimension in education will be required. Links with other schools in other countries.

Developing strategies and choosing

Strategies for the future need to combine the results of analysis with the creative vision. One aid to doing this may be to develop strategic issues which, when resolved, help identify courses of action (**Activity S15**). Another possible way of trying to bridge the gap between the two, as has already been mentioned, is the idea of core competences. These are organisational rather than individual but consist of those skills which are likely to be useful in the future in some way. This does not require the specification of the precise ways in which these competences may be valuable but does require that these general capabilities be identified and ways found of developing them. The most promising of these to incorporate are the ones that are already present to some degree. But this is also the opportunity to identify proficiencies that the school does not have at the moment but are predicted to become increasingly important in the future.

❏ Future trends

There are a number that I would suggest will be important:

- developing children's social skills
- use of ICT
- information management
- facilitating change
- managing staff with portfolio careers
- managing para-professionals
- managing other support staff
- managing volunteers.

It is clear that the ability to use ICT in all its forms – for management, communication and for teaching and learning will be increasingly important. This will involve technical capabilities to deal with hardware and software but also the associated teaching technology. How to exploit the opportunities offered by ICT will be the core competence. A requirement related to this concerns the nature of trends in teaching. As technology assists some elements of teaching, others will decline relative to them because technology provides less help. I believe that these latter areas will be seen as increasingly important where a distinctive teaching expertise is required. I think that this is the competence to develop children's social and behavioural skills and abilities reliably and to a high level.

A further three concern the nature of staffing of schools in the future. The first trend which has started and appears set to continue is a greater number of staff who wish to combine two or more jobs or a job and leisure. Whilst there have always been part-time teachers and other staff in schools, this has for many become a permanent situation rather than one which is only temporary. This group has been joined by those who have a specialism which they would prefer to use in a variety of situations including one or more schools rather than have a permanent position in just one school. Both these trends suggest a staffing structure which consists of a core of full-time permanent staff and others who are on the periphery in the sense that they have other commitments beyond the one school and spend only part of their working life in a school. This has implications both for those with portfolio careers and also core staff. Particularly it has implications for leadership and management. Another trend which is already noticeable is the greater number of teaching support staff in schools.

There are two kinds of support staff – those that directly assist in classrooms and those that support teachers more indirectly. The good management of both these groups will be increasingly important. They are likely to be more numerous in the future because they are less costly than teaching staff and are expected to be less difficult to recruit. If there are more of them, that itself is an issue, but it also means that their contribution to the work of a school will increase and need to be managed well. This is a larger issue than it might appear because the management of support staff in classrooms will involve most teachers as will making greater use of other support staff who assist their work less directly.

The other staffing trend concerns a recognition of the increasing number of volunteers of many kinds which help in school and that managing this group is not the same as managing paid staff. A headteacher recently examined the register of visitors to her school for a week and found a large number of parents and others who came into school regularly to provide assistance of many kinds. This group had not been consciously recognised and, consequently, was not managed in any corporate way. This group is likely to expand and involve many more volunteers who are not parents of children at the school. This is a leadership and management issue which needs to be recognised as a core competence.

These and the core competence of being able to learn and change need to be fitted into future school developments.

There will be a number of possibilities which combine selected results from the strategic analysis and also incorporate some aspects of the vision of the future. These need to be developed into a number of options from which a choice can be made. One way of developing these options might be through scenario planning – setting up stories of the way in which the school can develop. These will help those developing the ideas to more fully appreciate their propositions and will also help those who are to make the choice.

The criteria evaluating and choosing one of the alternatives from the options are

- consistency
- suitability
- feasibility
- acceptability.

Consistency requires that the actions that are required to implement the strategy are consistent, that is, that the parts fit together and harmonise rather than appear as discrete and disconnected strands.

Suitability involves assessing the proposed strategy for the extent to which it deals satisfactorily with issues raised by the SWOT analysis. In particular, are any issues raised by clients – parents and children – being addressed (and being seen to be addressed) sufficiently rigorously?

The test of feasibility asks whether the strategy has a good chance of being put into practice. Are the assumptions on which it is based sound, has implementation been subjected to detailed logistical analysis and contingencies considered?

Finally, the test of acceptability asks whether groups who play a part in the decision to accept the strategy and, also, those groups who will be required to implement the strategy will find the strategy acceptable. Much preparation will be required to make more radical strategies acceptable.

Deciding on implementation

The strategic aim will be something which could only be achieved over a period of five to ten years. Thus concerted action over that period needs to be planned and implemented. This will require a route map with some broad intentions for the later years and more detailed plans for the early years. The format of the plan will have been decided at an earlier stage and, once the strategy has been decided, it requires to be operationalised or reduced to a series of manageable steps.

9 Implementation and Monitoring

Introduction

This chapter is concerned with the implementation of a strategic plan and its sub-plans. It deals with systems and structures, staffing, resources and budgeting, and planning and implementing change.

School development and action planning

The first year or more of the development required to progress the strategy can be planned using the school development planning framework. Some realistic targets for one year or more need to be set and then action steps to achieve these targets planned. Using the 'design and build' principles the next year's development can be planned on the assumption of what will be achieved in the first year and so on.

The strategic route map provides direction by sets of broad-brush intentions. These should provide the signposts for shorter term plans to follow. Yearly plans can use the school development planning framework to devise operational plans.

A strategic plan will have a number of sub-plans. The most fundamental is that concerned with the school's organisational structure and decision-making. This identifies any changes to the school's customary ways of working which will be necessary – how are we going to work together to achieve our strategy? The main plan will concern the curricular changes which the strategy incorporates – what is the contribution to children's learning? There are then subordinate plans for:

- staffing (how will staff be recruited and trained to carry out the strategy?)
- finance (how will resources be acquired and deployed?)
- marketing (how will support be built up?).

There should also be plans for constituent units within the school which are consistent with the overall plan for the school. If a strategy is to be effective, it should influence the day-to-day work of teachers and other staff; thus it should influence the plans for development of sections of the school and the development plans of staff.

Systems and structures

One of the requirements of global change is that structures and systems need to be in harmony with the desired direction of the changes. Thus the first requirement is to examine the current organisational structure of roles and responsibilities.

❑ Symbolism
Creating a new responsibility with a new title may be only one element of all the changes required, but it may be symbolic. It will be taken as a sign of an explicit and public declaration of an aim. This also needs to be followed up with more practical steps but its symbolism should not be underestimated. The effect of such symbolic actions will be intensified if there are changes to other positions as well. If some positions are downgraded these will be seen as being incorporated into the ongoing work of the school and this will intensify new priorities for development.

A secondary school which had abandoned a deputy head position to save money found a year later that no progress had been made on staff development which was the missing deputy's brief. Beware painless options!

❑ Pragmatism

In addition to actions which have both symbolic and practical significance there will be other actions which are less obvious but have great importance in practice. Some of these are to ensure that:

- crucial responsibilities are resourced
- policies clearly indicate priorities
- systems reinforce priorities
- policies and systems are consistent.

All these are concerned with trying to ensure that organisation members do not receive 'mixed messages'. If the same actions are encouraged by policies but discouraged by the systems which are in place, it will not be surprising if people are confused and less than wholehearted in their commitment to what are described as priorities. The 'espoused theories' and the 'theories-in-use' need to match.

Staffing

One of the sub-plans of the strategic plan will be a staffing plan. This will contain staffing intentions for the medium term and more precise proposals for the short term. Thus there may be intentions which it would be desirable to incorporate as the opportunities present themselves. These may concern such factors as age balance, gender balance, ethnic balance, etc. and particular core competences which are to be built up. These will be background intentions which influence individual appointments and development activities.

Any strategy should have taken account of the present staff and future needs. These will have implications for the development of current staff and the recruitment of new ones. Such an assessment needs to cover all three types of staff:

- teachers
- teaching support staff (administration, clerical, technical, premises)
- leaders and managers.

Although the plan will start from the current staffing establishment, a shadow staffing structure can be compiled which makes assumptions about future needs. This will deal with particular posts but also groups of staff who can work together and contribute to core competences. This structure should deal with the skills and expertise needed in the future. Many of these will be provided by current staff. But some current staff might leave over the course of the next few years and there may also be opportunities to expand the numbers of staff. If longer-term requirements have been formulated, any replacement staff can be appointed with these in mind.

Schools which find it difficult to recruit high-quality staff and expect this to be an ongoing problem will need to incorporate this as part of their strategy. This may include a series of measures to increase their sources of supply and to increase their chances of being seen as a more desirable school in which to teach. Schools should make best use of taking part in Initial Teacher Training as a contribution to staff development and a source of future recruits.

There are some general trends which should be taken into account such as increasing numbers of

- para-professionals
- job shares
- staff with portfolio careers.

These will need to be managed in ways which are not the same as full-time teachers. Activities of this group will need greater co-ordination as each contributes less than full time or in other ways does not take on full professional responsibilities. The fewer core staff will need to take on increased responsibilities. This will require extra time.

There are already substantial number of volunteers working in schools. There has not always been a recognition that this is a group which needs managing and that this will not be the same as that required for paid staff. The motivation and skills of this group will require particular attention.

Resources

The strategic plan should have a sub-plan which deals with resources – their acquisition and allocation. There will be broad intentions such as raising more income from non-standard sources, increasing efficiency and changing the allocation of resources. These broad intentions will need translation into more operational plans for the short term so that they are likely to be achieved over the longer term.

Long-term resource planning is very difficult in a system that operates annual budgeting. However, trends in student numbers are indicators of rising or falling income if other factors do not change. Thus projections of student numbers will give some advance information about financial trends. The degree of difficulty in reallocating resources is likely to be affected by whether or not a school is static in size or whether the school is growing in size. If the amount of money, in real terms, is likely to remain constant, then spending on a different course of action can only be achieved at the expense of cutting some present expenditure, whereas if there is additional money appearing, then it is possible to look at a standstill budget to keep existing activities functioning and to apportion further money for new developments.

❏ Acquiring resources

There are a number of possibilities which should be explored. Current sources of income should be maximised and additional sources sought. There is a greater expectation of entrepreneurial activity and an increasing the number of sources of funding:

- formula funding
- additional state funding
- additional finance
- resources in kind.

The first and rather obvious suggestion is to ensure that the maximum income accrues through the formula funding of schools. Although this might sound obvious, it is worth reviewing the current LEA formula to ensure that any data provided by a school which brings income has been legitimately maximised. This may require requests to parents to take up free school meals, for example, where this statistic brings in additional income or triggers additional benefits. Investigation may be needed to find ways in which take-up can be increased. A general approach needs to be one of inventiveness, a return to previous issues with new ideas.

The second area includes the many grants which are provided for school improvement, staff development and other earmarked activities. Some come automatically and these need to be scrutinised for their basis of calculation to ensure they are maximised. Others have to be bid for. As a number of schools have discovered, unless this is carefully scrutinised and targeted a lot of time can be spent to achieve only a small amount of extra funding. Writing of bids for this and other income-raising sources is a somewhat specialised activity. Some staff need to acquire expertise and there needs to be back-up administrative help if this is to be done efficiently. There are efficiencies of scale and, so, gearing up to engage in this to a substantial degree is one course of action. Another would be to be very selective about what bids are submitted.

There are a range of potential sources of extra finance

- grants from charities, specific government schemes
- New Opportunities Fund of the National Lottery
- raising income from activities.

There are grants that are available from charities and government schemes. Many of these are targeted at particular groups, particular activities and particular locations such as Education Action Zones and Excellence in Cities projects in England. Knowledge of what is available will need a fair amount of research. Many grants will need a joint application with other organisations or institutions. All sources of contacts with these should be exploited – governors, staff, parents and supporters of the school.

The New Opportunities Fund of the National Lottery has recently come into existence and offers a new source of substantial grants. Their web site gives detail of current schemes, for example out of school hours learning. (http://www.nof.org.uk)

Raising income from school events, parent–teacher associations and other activities have a long history in schools. Letting of buildings and car parks became an additional source when local management of schools was instituted. New activities which can raise funds come along from time to time and need to be exploited. Such activities, however, need to be evaluated for their costs and benefits. Some activities take a great deal of effort and do not raise much income. Unless there are substantial intangible benefits such activities should be culled as the time and effort can probably be deployed better elsewhere.

The final source is resources in kind. These are all the non-financial sources. Local industry and business may provide surplus computers, machinery, etc. They may provide staff time or training facilities. Other professionals and friends of the school may provide some time as a voluntary activity.

Learning and Skills Councils in England may have resources which they can provide for particular schemes. They may provide free consultancy to help gain an Investors in People award. They may have other training resources which they can provide. Education Business Partnerships and Chambers of Commerce may be further sources of help. They have web sites. (http://www.lsc.gov.uk; http://www.nationalebp.org; http://www.chamberonline.co.uk)

As there are more and more sources of potential funding there needs to be ways of obtaining information about them. Some may be available in documentary form and on the Internet, but many more will be available through networks of contacts. Discovering and noting the networks that could be used and are in use will be a valuable research activity.

Allocating resources

It would be prudent to plan for little real expansion in spending over and above that generated by additional student numbers, in which case it is likely to involve the transfer of some expenditure from one current heading to a future one. The interrelationship between resource planning and allocation and the initial resource analysis should be quite clear. Some kind of very simple network analysis might be quite useful to indicate the stages through which the strategy will be achieved. It is then possible to look at the spending implications of each of these to make sure there is not some hiatus towards the end because of some intermediate step which should have been funded.

Development budget

Where the strategic plan requires new activities or extra funding of existing ones, extra finance will be needed. In an expanding school there may be additional finance which can be used for this purpose; for a school with a fixed budget such funding has to come from existing activities. This can be done by creating a 'development budget'. This is a heading within the draft budget which can be allocated to whatever are the development priorities in the particular year. However, since in general terms school budgets are tight, where is the development budget to come from? There are a number of systematic answers to this question:

- arbitrary cut in recurrent spending
- base and development budgets
- programme budgets.

Arbitrary cut in recurrent spending

In order to free up 2 per cent of the budget for development, the planned spending for the coming year can be planned to consume only 98 per cent of previous spending. If this is done too quickly, it will lead to the oft-noted effect that those budgets which are 'easy' to cut are reduced rather than those budgets which ought to be cut. Thus some activities may be only partially funded. This is the least efficient way of operating since resources are being consumed but the activities cannot take place as intended because one element of resourcing is missing – the computers have been purchased but not the software, for example. A programme budget which is referred to later is a way of preventing this happening.

Base and development budgets

The Audit Commission (1991) have suggested that schools should construct a budget called a 'base' budget that represents their minimum spending level. Contrary to what many in schools might think, this is not their current spending level but the level below which they could not offer a satisfactory education or below which teacher unions would not co-operate (for example if class sizes were too great). The Audit Commission recognise that the school might not be able to operate in this mode immediately, even if it wished, because it would involve breaking contracts etc. However, the value of such an activity is to show up the ways a school is currently spending resources in excess of the minimum needed so that these can be subjected to scrutiny and then changed. The difference between the current budget and the base budget represents opportunities foregone, that is, it represents discretion which has been used in a particular way and is no longer available.

The difference between the actual income to the school and the projected base spending level represents, in principle, the sum available for development. A plan could be drawn up to release this sum and to deploy it over a number of years as opportunities allow.

The Audit Commission illustration covers a primary school where most resources are committed by the fixing of class sizes. In secondary schools the situation is more complicated. There are two techniques which provide assistance:

- staff deployment analysis
- activity-led staffing.

Staff deployment analysis

This is more commonly known as COSMOS analysis after the committee which first introduced the techniques devised by T.I. Davies. They have been reproduced in the OFSTED handbook for school inspections. This technique recognises that the main curriculum cost is not in differences between subjects offered but in the sizes of teaching groups. Decisions about how many teaching groups to divide a year group into and how large to have as a maximum for a particular subject are both educational and resourcing decisions. Whilst the educational considerations are discussed, schools rarely understand the 'cost' of these decisions and often are unable to recall when and on what basis in the past these decisions were made. One investigation of two similarly sized secondary schools discovered that in one the smallest teaching groups were in mathematics and in the other they were in CDT. Whilst these may have been rational decisions at some point in time, they tend to get perpetuated year after year and cease to have a clear rationale years later. Staff deployment analysis provides a conceptual framework to investigate the deployment of staffing resources between year groups and can be developed to compare the use of resources between different curriculum subjects in the same year. This technique provides information to inform judgement; it does not replace judgement.

Activity-led staffing (ALS)

Activity-led staffing (Audit Commission, 1986) goes one stage further to include non-teaching activities. It is mainly intended as a planning tool but can be used to analyse an existing situation. In planning mode, decisions are made about the number of teaching periods offered to each year group in each subject of the curriculum and also the maximum size of teaching group for each subject each year. The maximum number of teacher periods required to staff this curriculum can be calculated.

The secondary stage of the calculation is to estimate the amount of time which should be allocated to cover school tasks, teacher-related tasks and student-related tasks. Since the original proposal the concept of 'directed time' of 1,265 hours has appeared and the time allocations would have to be made out of directed time. However, in principle the total time taken for teaching and non-teaching tasks can be aggregated to ensure that school resources are sufficient to cover the total. The value of ALS is that it focuses on the whole-school task.

There is a tendency in allocating resources to provide sufficient teaching periods to staff the curriculum up to a historical proportion of time. Usually in secondary schools this means that the typical teacher teaches for 80 per cent of possible periods in a week. This figure may climb significantly when time to cover for absent colleagues is included. This appears to allocate time for teaching and assume that other tasks can be fitted into the remainder. This should be regarded as an empirical question rather than the answer being assumed. The relative proportions of teaching and non-teaching time need investigation and judgement rather than relying on historical precedent from 20 or more years ago.

Programme budgeting

Programme budgeting is a way of costing areas of activity. Thus the cost of educating a year group can be calculated. This is a way of ensuring that the appropriate resource mix is available rather than discovering that there are plenty of teachers and classroom assistants in a well-equipped and furnished classroom but no paper or pencils. Programme budgeting is a form of zero-based budgeting. This involves devising the cost of carrying out an activity without any prior (historical) assumptions. This is unrealistic in that teachers are already employed and other expenditure is committed, but the programme budget then provides a target budget towards which to aim as circumstances allow.

Marketing

The final sub-plan concerns how to build up support for a school to complete its strategy successfully. Although I have called this a marketing plan it is really more a promotional plan since the marketing component – identifying what clients want in the future – has been subsumed within the process of strategy formation. Thus the major activity is promoting the public image of the school and mobilising support. This will need a plan of activities both externally and internally.

Planning and implementing change

Throughout this book I have referred to the strategic plan as a route map to school improvement. I think that the 'design and build' analogy from engineering in Chapter 2, p. 9 is helpful and indicates an element of the interactive nature of planning. Subsequent actions are influenced by the first ones and the first ones are made in anticipation of subsequent actions. And as development proceeds adjustments are made to the subsequent plans as the first stages are completed and environmental changes occur.

I think that some kind of diagrammatic representation of the route map will be helpful. This will facilitate discussion of progress and deviations, and also engender a sense of progress as early developments are completed. One element of this I think should be a flow chart or network analysis. This can illustrate how detailed plans are part of a longer-term rolling programme. Some estimated timescale for the completion of activities will be needed so that targets and deadlines can be set. These will need to be adjusted in the light of experience but allow work to be co-ordinated.

If staff have played a part in devising the strategy they will have understood its purpose and should better understand their own part in it. Trying to communicate the 'big picture' and the parts which make it up will be a challenge. As schools make greater use of the Internet, devising web pages which help explain the strategic plan and are able to be regularly updated begins to offer new possibilities for communication which have not been available before.

Regular monitoring of progress and periodic checks that the underlying assumptions of the strategic plan are still valid will be essential. Monitoring will provide early warning of problems and also contribute to the sense of progress.

Role of consultant

The roles of subject consultants and process consultants have been referred to previously. Whilst the educational knowledge of subject consultants may be valuable in assessing the performance of current educational activities and suggesting how to improve, it is the process consultant who has most to offer strategic change. The process consultant needs organisational knowledge and experience of practice in many organisations. Such a consultant can then offer advice at the planning stage and follow-up as implementation proceeds.

The consultants need to be individuals who have rapport with the school leader and whom he or she trusts. In this way school leaders can be frank and receive authentic feedback from their consultant.

School leaders often remark on the isolation they feel in their job despite others around with whom they work. The process of major change may mean that there is an even greater need for emotional support to carry through changes that are controversial. A consultant may be one such form of support after the necessary rapport has been established, but other headteachers acting as mentors may offer another.

10 Conclusion

This book has attempted to give an account of how strategic management of school development should be organised. I want to emphasise a number of points from sections of the book as final advice:

- There is a need to understand the concept of strategy to appreciate the difficulties and make a more realistic assessment of what is possible. A clear understanding facilitates adaptation of the process.
- Schools are different from other organisations and how they devise strategy, but that has advantages as well as limitations.
- Leadership is important but so are management and administration. Leadership needs to be contingent and adapt to the internal situation and the external context. For strategy it is the proactive and symbolic elements of leadership which will be important. Strategic thinking and the cognitive processes are vital.
- A long-term approach to school improvement is important. This needs to include the organisational dimension of survival and success. The what and how of school improvement should start from the school's aims and its long-term intentions. An evaluation of these is part of the strategic analysis process. Longer-term aims should be aspirational.
- Three organisational approaches to improvement in the longer term are organisational learning, core competences and benchmarking.
- The strategic planning model for schools has three conceptual stages and three operational stages. Planning the operational stages is vital to ensure a productive planning process. Inevitably the plan of operational stages will need modifying but the plan will give an overview that makes modifications more effective.
- Strategic analysis involves assessing a school's current performance, assessing environmental influences both currently and making predictions about the future, and recognising the values and priorities underlying its current organisational culture. Data collection, analysis, interpretation and judgement are required.
- The added ingredient for an aspirational strategy for the future is to incorporate a vision of the future. This is a vision of what stakeholders would prefer the school to be like in the future. From the results of strategic analysis and the incorporation of a future vision strategic options need to be created. These need to be evaluated before the final choice is compiled.
- Planning the implementation of strategy is vital but expect this to be interactive like 'design and build' rather than rigidly following a precise plan.
- Regard the first attempt at strategic planning as a pilot with lessons to be learned to apply to the next planning process. Hoping for too much from the first exercise is likely to result in disillusionment.
- Take on what is manageable but challenging.
- Develop strategic thinking and become more aware of conceptual frameworks which are being used.
- Encourage others to think strategically and to be on the look-out for ideas and data.

Activities

No	Title	P/S	Area		Activity
		(Primary or secondary schools)			
S1	Success criteria	Both	Strategic analysis (SA)		Prioritising
S2P	School image	P	SA		Rating of items
S2S	School image	S	SA		Rating of items
S3P	Environmental scanning: local	P	SA		Rating of items
S3S	Environmental scanning: local	S	SA		Rating of items
S4P	Environmental scanning: national	P	SA		Rating of items
S4S	Environmental scanning: national	S	SA		Rating of items
S5	Status of children	B	SA (school culture)		Discussion of 3 ideas
S6	Organisational culture	B	SA	"	Identifying 3 positions
S7P	Organisational culture	P	SA	"	Discussion of sentences
S7S	Organisational culture	S	SA	"	Discussion of sentences
S8P	School performance	P	SA	"	Rating of items
S8S	School performance	S	SA	"	Rating of items
S9	Achievement of school aims	B	SA	"	Analysis/completion
S10	Effort on school aims	B	SA	"	Estimation
S11	Contribution to school aims	B	SA	"	Estimation
S12	Staff audit	B	SA	"	Data collection
S13	Accommodation audit	B	SA	"	Data collection
S14	SWOT analysis	B	SA	"	Completion
S15	Strategic issues identification	B	Strategic choice (SC)		Analysis
S16	'Vision of success': statement completion	B	SC		Sentence completion
S17	'Vision of success': scenario building	B	SC		Scenario writing

STRATEGIC MANAGEMENT FOR SCHOOL DEVELOPMENT: (S1)
LEADING YOUR SCHOOL'S IMPROVEMENT STRATEGY

ACTIVITIES

STRATEGIC ANALYSIS (S1)

Title: **Success Criteria**

Objective:
This activity enables the school to identify the success criteria of different school stakeholders.

Background:
Different groups may have different expectations of a school and consequently different criteria by which they will judge its success. These can be POSITIVE achievements or NEGATIVE must-not-do's. Whilst positive success criteria are progressive (the greater their value the better), the must-not-do's are undesirable outcomes which must be avoided by every means.

A school needs to try to find out and decide what these are. It will then need to decide how far it should and could meet these success criteria. Intelligence on changes to these success criteria will need constant up-dating.

Where a school decides that it cannot or does not wish to work towards these success criteria (or they are very low on its list of priorities) it must recognise that it has a potential problem. This may need

    (a)   explanation, or
    (b)   distraction, or
    (c)   education of the disappointed stakeholders.

STRATEGIC MANAGEMENT FOR SCHOOL DEVELOPMENT: (S1)
LEADING YOUR SCHOOL'S IMPROVEMENT STRATEGY

Activity 1

Consider each of the following groups (and any others which are important to the school) and arrange the <u>FIVE</u> most important groups in order from the point of view of the future of the school.

Possible stakeholders:

Government
OFSTED
LEA
Governors
Headteacher
Teachers
Parents
Children
Local Community
Diocesan Board and Church
Local Primary/Secondary Schools
Employers
Further/Higher Education
Other.

Activity 2

For each of these five most important stakeholders identify THREE or more positive criteria of success (in order of importance) and ONE or more negative must-not-do's.

    (a)   Which are the dominant positive success criteria?

    (b)   Which are the dominant negative must-not-do's?

STRATEGIC MANAGEMENT FOR SCHOOL DEVELOPMENT: (S2P)
LEADING YOUR SCHOOL'S IMPROVEMENT STRATEGY

ACTIVITIES

STRATEGIC ANALYSIS (S2P)

Title: **School Image (PRIMARY)**

Objective:

This exercise provides a basis for a school to assess its public image on a number of criteria and compare these with how it would wish to be seen.

Background:

A school needs to assess its public image on a number of criteria and also to decide how it would like to be viewed on these same criteria. The discrepancies between the two assessments provide clues about the strategic marketing plan.

It is important to ensure that the assessments of the public image are well founded. In some way the views of parents and other members of the community will have to be collected by some form of market research.

The criteria here are largely the same as those in exercise S8P to facilitate comparison between the professional assessments of the school provided by S8P and the public perceptions recorded in this exercise. The following comparisons should be of value:

a)   comparison of professional and public assessments of the present performance
   - (i)   if the professional exceeds the public then better promotion of the school's achievement is called for;
   - (ii)   if the public exceeds the professional then professional action to improve the school's performance may be necessary.

b)   comparison of professional and public assessments of future desired performance
   - (i)   if the professional exceeds the public then the public may need convincing of the importance of this aspect of the school's performance;
   - (ii)   if the public exceeds the professional then there may be an internal communication process required to convince teachers of the importance attached by the public to this aspect.

Two vitally important caveats should be borne in mind. First, any judgements recorded here or in S8P will be estimates so the results should not be taken at face value but treated cautiously. Secondly, where a school accepts the results thrown up by this exercise a further degree of prioritisation will be required since any changes desired by the public will not all be of equal value nor, in all probability, will they all be possible to accomplish.

This exercise is intended only to provide pointers and stimulate discussion of important issues.

STRATEGIC MANAGEMENT FOR SCHOOL DEVELOPMENT: **(S2P)**
LEADING YOUR SCHOOL'S IMPROVEMENT STRATEGY

Activity

Rate the present *public image* of the school and the desired school image on the following criteria.

Using the following 7 point scale rate the present public image of the school:

Very Poor		*Average*			*Excellent*	
1	2	3	4	5	6	7

For the 'actual' rating compare each item with other schools in the locality and grade the item as potential parents would on the 7 point scale. The 'other' attribute(s) allow you to write in any other feature which you would like to include.

For the desired public rating you have a further 15 points to distribute. These may be added to any present value of ratings. The points can be concentrated on a small number of items or spread more widely.

The differences between present and desired ratings show up areas for action in the strategic plan.

Where one of the items covers a broad area and it is one particular aspect which is the focus of attention, note this by the side of the desired rating, eg ICT equipment.

The items have been divided into three groups:

- Direct student outcomes
- Processes which impact *directly* or *indirectly* on student outcomes
- Organisational processes.

DIRECT STUDENT OUTCOMES

FEATURE	Present Public Rating	Desired Public Rating
1. Achievements in Literacy		
2. Achievements in Numeracy		
3. Achievements in Science		
4. Achievements in other foundation subjects		
5. Attitudes to learning		
6. Cultural involvement and accomplishments		
7. Sporting achievements and disposition		
8. Spiritual and religious attitudes		
9. ICT education and equipment		
10. Behaviour and appearance of children		
11. Other attribute(s)		

STRATEGIC MANAGEMENT FOR SCHOOL DEVELOPMENT: (S2P)
LEADING YOUR SCHOOL'S IMPROVEMENT STRATEGY

DIRECT AND INDIRECT PROCESSES WHICH IMPACT ON STUDENT OUTCOMES

FEATURE	Present Public Rating	Desired Public Rating
12. Curriculum offered – formal and out-of-school		
13. Quality of teaching		
14. Quality of leadership		
15. Staff development		
16. Attitudes to innovation and improvement		
17. Caring and supportive environment		
18. Calm and orderly environment		
19. Special needs provision and attitudes		
20. Provision of equal opportunities		
21. Multicultural education		
22. Parental involvement		
23. Governor involvement		
24. Community involvement		
25. Other attribute(s)		

ORGANISATIONAL PROCESSES

FEATURE	Present Public Rating	Desired Public Rating
26. Welcoming and friendly reception		
27. Availability of staff		
28. Parental information		
29. School uniform		
30. Place in school league tables		
31. Judgement of the school in the last OFSTED inspection report		
32. Liaison with secondary schools		
33. Other attribute(s)		

STRATEGIC MANAGEMENT FOR SCHOOL DEVELOPMENT: (S2S)
LEADING YOUR SCHOOL'S IMPROVEMENT STRATEGY

ACTIVITIES

STRATEGIC ANALYSIS (S2S)

Title: **School Image (SECONDARY)**

Objective:

This exercise provides a basis for a school to assess its public image on a number of criteria and compare these with how it would wish to be seen.

Background:

A school needs to assess its public image on a number of criteria and also to decide how it would like to be viewed on these same criteria. The discrepancies between the two assessments provide clues about the strategic marketing plan.

It is important to ensure that the assessments of the public image are well founded. In some way the views of parents and other members of the community will have to be collected by some form of market research.

The criteria here are largely the same as those in exercise S8S to facilitate comparison between the professional assessments of the school provided by S8S and the public perceptions recorded in this exercise. The following comparisons should be of value:

a) comparison of professional and public assessments of the present performance
    (i)   if the professional exceeds the public then better promotion of the school's achievement is called for;
    (ii) if the public exceeds the professional then professional action to improve the school's performance may be necessary.
b) comparison of professional and public assessments of future desired performance
    (i)   if the professional exceeds the public then the public may need convincing of the importance of this aspect of the school's performance;
    (ii) if the public exceeds the professional then there may be an internal communication process required to convince teachers of the importance attached by the public to this aspect.

Two vitally important caveats should be borne in mind. Firstly, any judgements recorded here or in S8S will be estimates so the results should not be taken at face value but treated cautiously. Secondly, where a school accepts the results thrown up by this exercise a further degree of prioritisation will be required since any changes desired by the public will not all be of equal value nor, in all probability, will they all be possible to accomplish.

This exercise is intended only to provide pointers and stimulate discussion of important issues.

STRATEGIC MANAGEMENT FOR SCHOOL DEVELOPMENT: (S2S)
LEADING YOUR SCHOOL'S IMPROVEMENT STRATEGY

Activity

Rate the present *public image* of the school and the desired school image on the following criteria.

Using the following 7 point scale rate the present public image of the school:

Very Poor   *Average*   *Excellent*

    1   2   3   4   5   6   7

For the 'actual' rating compare each item with other schools in the locality and grade the item as potential parents would on the 7 point scale. The 'other' attribute(s) allow you to write in any other feature which you would like to include.

For the desired public rating you have a further 15 points to distribute. These may be added to any present value of ratings. The points can be concentrated on a small number of items or spread more widely.

The differences between present and desired ratings show up areas for action in the strategic plan.

Where one of the items covers a broad area and it is one particular aspect which is the focus of attention, note this by the side of the desired rating, eg ICT equipment.

The items have been divided into three groups:

- Direct student outcomes
- Processes which impact *directly* or *indirectly* on student outcomes
- Organisational processes.

DIRECT STUDENT OUTCOMES

FEATURE	Present Public Rating	Desired Public Rating
1. Academic standards and academic ethos		
2. Expertise and achievements in technology		
3. Cultural involvement and accomplishments		
4. Literary and dramatic achievements		
5. Business studies and enterprise awards		
6. Sporting achievements and disposition		
7. Spiritual and religious attitudes		
8. ICT education and equipment		
9. Behaviour and appearance of children		
10. Other attribute(s)		

STRATEGIC MANAGEMENT FOR SCHOOL DEVELOPMENT: **(S2S)**
LEADING YOUR SCHOOL'S IMPROVEMENT STRATEGY

DIRECT AND INDIRECT PROCESSES WHICH IMPACT ON STUDENT OUTCOMES

FEATURE	Present Rating	Desired Rating
11. Curriculum offered – formal and out-of-school		
12. Active and individualised learning styles		
13. Caring and supportive structures		
14. Calm and orderly environment		
15. Vocational courses and outlook		
16. Quality of teaching		
17. Quality of leadership		
18. Special needs provision and attitudes		
19. Provision of equal opportunities		
20. Multicultural education and attitudes		
21. Parental involvement		
22. Governor involvement		
23. Community involvement		
24. Involvement with business		
25. Buildings and physical environment		
26. Staff development		
27. Attitudes to innovation and improvement		
28. Other attribute(s)		

ORGANISATIONAL PROCESSES

FEATURE	Present Rating	Desired Rating
29. Place in the school league tables?		
30. Judgement of the school in the last OFSTED inspection report		
31. Welcoming and friendly reception		
32. Parental information		
33. School uniform		
34. Liaison with feeder schools		
35. Liaison with post 16 provision and FE/HE colleges/universities		
36. Other attribute(s)		

STRATEGIC MANAGEMENT FOR SCHOOL DEVELOPMENT: **(S3P)**
LEADING YOUR SCHOOL'S IMPROVEMENT STRATEGY

ACTIVITIES

STRATEGIC ANALYSIS (S3P)

Title: **Environmental Scanning: Local (PRIMARY)**

Objective:
This exercise contributes to strategic analysis by aiding the identification of forces which will be important in shaping the future of a school by identifying potential local influences.

Background:
The strategic plan of the school should take account of important external influences both now and particularly those likely to be important in the future (5 years' time).

Useful headings for recognising these influences locally are:

> PUPIL NUMBERS
> PARENTAL CHOICE
> OTHER SCHOOLS
> SOCIAL TRENDS.

It is necessary to recognise the strength of the influence, whether it is increasing in importance and its possible effects.

For a school to be proactive and forward looking it is important to recognise trends which are increasing in importance. Thus the most important for current planning are those which are strong and particularly those rising in importance. In addition to being taken into account now their importance needs to be monitored in the future for its impact on the chosen strategy.

STRATEGIC MANAGEMENT FOR SCHOOL DEVELOPMENT: (S3P)
LEADING YOUR SCHOOL'S IMPROVEMENT STRATEGY

Activity

The following is a list of potential influences. It is intended to be a prompt list and a spur to further ideas not a definitive list of the most important influences.

(a) Consider each of the influences below and assess whether over the next FIVE YEARS each will have an influence on the school. Those having no influence designate 'not applicable' (N/A).

(b) Assess the strength of each which is likely to have an influence on a THREE point scale (Weak, Medium, Strong).

(c) Assess whether each is likely to increase in importance over the next FIVE YEARS and indicate those rising in importance with a '+', those declining with a '−' and those not changing with a '0'.

(d) Briefly describe the likely effect on the school.

(e) Are there other potentially important local influences which should be added?

INFLUENCE	STRENGTH	FUTURE IMPORTANCE	EFFECT
Number of children in local area			
House building			
Number of catchment area parental choices			
Number of out-of-catchment area choices			
Number of appeals to get in school			
Parental choice of schools			
Change in catchment area			
Perceived position in results league tables			
Possible position in future value-added league tables			
Perceived quality of school in latest OFSTED inspection report			
Relationship with local media			
Perceived attractiveness to parents of any feeder school(s)			
Perceived attractiveness to parents of school(s) which this school feeds			
Children's role in choice of school			
Schools which might offer a curricular specialism			
Merging schools			
Competitor schools have better facilities			
Competitor schools have better equipment especially computers			
New headteacher at a competitor school			
More nursery provision			
Home–school contract			
Pupils' role in school decision-making			

STRATEGIC MANAGEMENT FOR SCHOOL DEVELOPMENT: **(S3P)**
LEADING YOUR SCHOOL'S IMPROVEMENT STRATEGY

INFLUENCE	STRENGTH	FUTURE IMPORTANCE	EFFECT
Children left at school a long time before school begins in the morning			
Children left at school after school finishes			
Cars collecting and depositing children at school			
Increasing information provided to governors through league tables, inspection reports and benchmarking data			
LEA role in school improvement			
School is a local social centre for parents especially mothers			
Educational action zone nearby			

STRATEGIC MANAGEMENT FOR SCHOOL DEVELOPMENT: (S3S)
LEADING YOUR SCHOOL'S IMPROVEMENT STRATEGY

ACTIVITIES

STRATEGIC ANALYSIS (S3S)

Title: **Environmental Scanning: Local (SECONDARY)**

Objective:
This exercise contributes to strategic analysis by aiding the identification of forces which will be important in shaping the future of a school by identifying potential local influences.

Background:
The strategic plan of the school should take account of important external influences both now and particularly those likely to be important in the future (5 years' time).

Useful headings for recognising these influences locally are:

> PUPIL NUMBERS
> PARENTAL CHOICE
> OTHER SCHOOLS
> SOCIAL TRENDS.

It is necessary to recognise the strength of the influence, whether it is increasing in importance and its possible effects.

For a school to be proactive and forward looking it is important to recognise trends which are increasing in importance. Thus the most important for current planning are those which are strong and particularly those rising in importance. In addition to being taken into account now their importance needs to be monitored in the future for its impact on the chosen strategy.

STRATEGIC MANAGEMENT FOR SCHOOL DEVELOPMENT: (S3S)
LEADING YOUR SCHOOL'S IMPROVEMENT STRATEGY

Activity

The following is a list of potential influences. It is intended to be a prompt list and a spur to further ideas not a definitive list of the most important influences.

(a) Consider each of the influences below and assess whether over the next FIVE YEARS each will have an influence on the school. Those having no influence designate 'not applicable' (N/A).
(b) Assess the strength of each which is likely to have an influence on a THREE point scale (Weak, Medium, Strong).
(c) Assess whether each is likely to increase in importance over the next FIVE YEARS and indicate those rising in importance with a '+', those declining with a '–' and those not changing with a '0'.
(d) Briefly describe the likely effect on the school.
(e) Are there other potentially important local influences which should be added?

INFLUENCE	STRENGTH	FUTURE IMPORTANCE	EFFECT
Number of children in local area			
House building			
Number of catchment area parental choices			
Number of out-of-catchment area parental choices			
Number of appeals for school places			
Change in catchment area			
Change in transport patterns			
Pressure from parental choice of school			
Students' role in choice of school			
Perceived position in results league tables			
Possible position in future value-added league tables			
Perceived quality of school in latest OFSTED inspection report			
Relationship with local media			
Perceived attractiveness to parents of any feeder school(s)			
Perceived attractiveness to parents of school(s) or colleges which this school feeds			
Schools nearby which might become a specialist college			
School nearby changing its curriculum			
Merging schools			
Competitor schools have better facilities			
Competitor schools with better equipment especially computers			
New headteacher at a local school			
Home-school contract			
Students' role in school decision-making			

STRATEGIC MANAGEMENT FOR SCHOOL DEVELOPMENT: (S3S)
LEADING YOUR SCHOOL'S IMPROVEMENT STRATEGY

INFLUENCE	STRENGTH	FUTURE IMPORTANCE	EFFECT
Children left at school a long time before school begins in the morning			
Children left at school after school finishes			
Cars collecting and depositing children at school			
Relations with local employers			
Schools nearby obtaining Investors in People certification			
Increasing information provided to governors through league tables, inspection reports and benchmarking data			
LEA role in school improvement			
Educational action zone nearby			

STRATEGIC MANAGEMENT FOR SCHOOL DEVELOPMENT:　　　**(S4P)**
LEADING YOUR SCHOOL'S IMPROVEMENT STRATEGY

ACTIVITIES

STRATEGIC ANALYSIS (S4P)

Title:　　　**Environmental Scanning: National (PRIMARY)**

Objective:
This exercise contributes to strategic analysis by aiding the identification of forces which will be important in shaping the future of the school by identifying potential national influences.

Background:
The strategic plan of the school should take account of important external influences both now and particularly those likely to be important in the future (5 or more years' time).

Useful headings for recognising these influences are:

> POLITICAL
> ECONOMIC
> SOCIAL TRENDS
> TECHNOLOGICAL
> EDUCATIONAL.

It is necessary to recognise the strength of an influence, whether it is increasing in importance and its possible effects.

For a school to be proactive and forward looking it is important to recognise trends which are increasing in importance. Thus the most important for current planning are those which are strong and particularly those rising in importance. Influences which need particular scrutiny are those which are relatively weak at the moment but predicted to grow in importance. In addition to being taken into account now their importance needs to be monitored in the future for its impact on the chosen strategy.

STRATEGIC MANAGEMENT FOR SCHOOL DEVELOPMENT: (S1)
LEADING YOUR SCHOOL'S IMPROVEMENT STRATEGY

Activity

The following is a list of potential influences. It is intended to be a prompt list and a spur to further ideas not a definitive list of the most important influences.

(a) Consider each of the influences below and assess whether over the next FIVE YEARS each will have an influence on the school. Those having no influence designate strength as 'not applicable' (N/A).

(b) Assess the strength which each currently has on a THREE point scale (Weak, Medium, Strong).

(c) Assess whether each is likely to increase in importance over the next FIVE YEARS and indicate those rising in importance on a THREE POINT SCALE with a '+', those declining with a '-' and those not changing with a '0'.

(d) Briefly describe the likely effect on the school.

(e) Are there other potentially important national influences which should be added?

INFLUENCE	STRENGTH	FUTURE IMPORTANCE	EFFECT
General election			
Local election			
Role of school staff unions			
Role of education in generating economic wealth			
Increasing harmonisation of qualifications and work practices in European Union			
European Union involvement in education			
Highlighting incompetent staff			
Influence of performance management and performance related pay			
Pressure on public expenditure			
Teachers' pay compared to other graduate employment			
Attractiveness of teaching as a career			
Multicultural society			
Number of single parent families			
Families spend less time together			
Greater variety in lifestyles			
Levels of crime			
Behaviour of children			
More TV channels			
Emphasis on equal opportunities			
Use of computers and internet			

STRATEGIC MANAGEMENT FOR SCHOOL DEVELOPMENT: (S4P)
LEADING YOUR SCHOOL'S IMPROVEMENT STRATEGY

INFLUENCE	STRENGTH	FUTURE IMPORTANCE	EFFECT
Potential to use management information systems to inform decision making			
League tables of school results			
Potential tables of value added results			
Systematic school inspections			
Pressure for school improvement			
National curriculum for teacher training and teacher competences			
Expectations of career development for teachers			
TTA qualifications at career stages for teachers			
Influence of a General Teaching Council			
Use of teaching support staff			
More nursery provision			
External pressure on teaching styles			
External pressure on pupil grouping			
Concentration on basic skills			
Specialist subject teaching			
Media attention on pupil grouping, teaching styles and basic skills			
Use of specialist teacher assistants			
Pressure on teaching quality			
School-based IT			
Use of target setting			
Better funding of primary schools			
Increased parental expectation of schools			
Capital funds available from private finance initiative			
Additional sources of school funding			

STRATEGIC MANAGEMENT FOR SCHOOL DEVELOPMENT: **(S4S)**
LEADING YOUR SCHOOL'S IMPROVEMENT STRATEGY

ACTIVITIES

STRATEGIC ANALYSIS (S4S)

Title: **Environmental Scanning: National (SECONDARY)**

Objective:
This exercise contributes to strategic analysis by aiding the identification of forces which will be important in shaping the future of the school by identifying potential national influences.

Background:
The strategic plan of the school should take account of important external influences both now and particularly those likely to be important in the future (5 or more years' time).

Useful headings for recognising these influences are:

> POLITICAL
> ECONOMIC
> SOCIAL TRENDS
> TECHNOLOGICAL
> EDUCATIONAL.

It is necessary to recognise the strength of an influence, whether it is increasing in importance and its possible effects.

For a school to be proactive and forward looking it is important to recognise trends which are increasing in importance. Thus the most important for current planning are those which are strong and particularly those rising in importance. Influences which need particular scrutiny are those which are relatively weak at the moment but predicted to grow in importance. In addition to being taken into account now their importance needs to be monitored in the future for its impact on the chosen strategy.

STRATEGIC MANAGEMENT FOR SCHOOL DEVELOPMENT: (S4S)
LEADING YOUR SCHOOL'S IMPROVEMENT STRATEGY

Activity

The following is a list of potential influences. It is intended to be a prompt list and a spur to further ideas not a definitive list of the most important influences.

(a)   Consider each of the influences below and assess whether over the next FIVE YEARS each will have an influence on the school. Those having no influence designate strength as 'not applicable' (N/A).

(b)   Assess the strength which each currently has on a THREE point scale (Weak, Medium, Strong).

(c)   Assess whether each is likely to increase in importance over the next FIVE YEARS and indicate those rising in importance on a THREE POINT SCALE with a '+', those declining with a '-' and those not changing with a '0'.

(d)   Briefly describe the likely effect on the school particularly the curriculum and teaching.

(e)   Are there other potentially important national influences which should be added?

INFLUENCE	STRENGTH	FUTURE IMPORTANCE	EFFECT
General election			
Local election			
Role of school staff unions			
Role of education in generating economic wealth			
Harmonisation of qualifications and work practices in European Union			
European Union involvement in education			
Highlighting incompetent staff			
Influence of performance management and performance related pay			
Pressure on public expenditure			
Teachers' pay compared to other graduate employment			
Attractiveness of teaching as a career			
Multicultural society			
Number of single parent families			
Families spend less time together			
Variety in lifestyles			
Levels of crime			
Behaviour of children			
More TV channels			
Equal opportunities			
Inclusion			

STRATEGIC MANAGEMENT FOR SCHOOL DEVELOPMENT: (S4S)
LEADING YOUR SCHOOL'S IMPROVEMENT STRATEGY

INFLUENCE	STRENGTH	FUTURE IMPORTANCE	EFFECT
Use of computers and internet			
Potential to use management information systems to inform decision making			
League tables of school results			
Potential tables of value added results			
Systematic school inspections			
Pressure for school improvement			
National curriculum for teacher training and teacher competences			
Expectations of career development for teachers			
TTA qualifications at career stages for teachers			
Influence of a General Teaching Council			
Use of teaching support staff			
Use of specialist teacher assistants			
Vocational 14–18 curricula			
Vocational sixth form curricula			
Relations between employers and schools			
Pressure on teaching quality			
School-based ITT			
Use of target setting			
Parental expectations of schools			
Capital funds available from private finance initiative			
Additional funding from European Union			
Additional sources of funding for schools			

STRATEGIC MANAGEMENT FOR SCHOOL DEVELOPMENT: (S5)
LEADING YOUR SCHOOL'S IMPROVEMENT STRATEGY

ACTIVITIES

STRATEGIC ANALYSIS: SCHOOL CULTURE (S5)

Title: **Status of Children**

Objective:

This activity throws further light on the school culture by examining the various aspects of the treatment of children by the school.

Background:

Charles Handy has suggested that the status of children in a school could be interpreted as (Handy & Aitken, 1986, p. 43)

Co-Workers   A worker is a member of the organisation who cooperates in a joint endeavour.

Clients   A client is a benificiary of the organisation who is served by the endeavour.

Products   A product is the output of the organisation which is shaped and developed by the organisation.

Activity 1

Take each of these views in turn and list the features of the ways in which children would be treated if that view represented a school's approach to children.

Activity 2

(a) List any features of your school's operation which are consistent with each of these interpretations of the status of children.

(b) Look at the overall picture of your school's treatment of children. Does this reflect the treatment of children which your school wishes to give?

(c) What features would need to change? Who would be involved? How might the change be accomplished?

STRATEGIC MANAGEMENT FOR SCHOOL DEVELOPMENT: (S6)
LEADING YOUR SCHOOL'S IMPROVEMENT STRATEGY

ACTIVITIES

STRATEGIC ANALYSIS: SCHOOL CULTURE (S6)

Title: **ORGANISATIONAL CULTURE**

Objective:

This exercise contributes to strategic analysis by helping to identify the culture and values presently exhibited by a school

Background:

In order to obtain a full picture of a school, its culture and values need to be made more explicit. This both identifies the current positon of the school and helps identify the perspective from which both external opportunities and threats are viewed and internal strengths and weaknesses.

STRATEGIC MANAGEMENT FOR SCHOOL DEVELOPMENT: (S6)
LEADING YOUR SCHOOL'S IMPROVEMENT STRATEGY

Activity

The grid below identifies nine features of a school culture. Six of them are concerned with how a school relates to or is seen by the world outside and three are concerned with how work is conducted inside the school. For each feature three contrasting positions are presented.

Consider each feature and mark which position most closely resembles that of your school. You may find that it is between two adjacent positons.

What is the predominant pattern?

What changes would be desirable?

Internal orientation	Position 1	Position 2	Position 3
Leadership style	*Participative* (major decisions are jointly made)	*Consultative* (head asks for views and opinions)	*Autocratic* (head makes most decisions)
Working together	*Collaborative* (staff agree on common procedures)	*Co-operative* (staff plan together but operate autonomously)	*Independent* (staff mostly work alone)
Relationship with children	*Friendly* (staff treat children as co-workers)	*Business-like* (staff treat children as clients)	*Repressive* (staff control children)
Attitude to innovation	*Prospector* (actively searches for all new ideas to bring into school)	*Defender* (selectively accepts new ideas)	*Reactor* (resists innovation)
School aims (Social-academic)	*Social* (acquiring skills for life)	*Balanced* (all activities have their place)	*Academic* (exclusive focus on exam results)
School aims (Cultural-academic)	*Cultural* (art, music, drama are renowned)	*Balanced* (all activities have their place)	*Academic* (exclusive focus on exam results)
Multicultural orientation	*Celebrated* (differences prized)	*Tolerated* (differences accepted but as second best)	*Hidden* (treated as an all white school)
Equal opportunities	*Compensatory* (equality of outcome)	*Open* (opportunities open to all)	*Elitist* (able and talented are prized)
Parents treated as	*Customers* ('customer is always right')	*Partners* (parents participate in their child's education)	*Apprentices* ('teachers know best')

STRATEGIC MANAGEMENT FOR SCHOOL DEVELOPMENT: (S7P)
LEADING YOUR SCHOOL'S IMPROVEMENT STRATEGY

ACTIVITIES

STRATEGIC ANALYSIS: SCHOOL CULTURE (S7P)

Title: **Organisational Culture (PRIMARY)**

Objective:

This activity provides a means of recognising the all-pervasive school culture. It should alert the reader to the individual school's 'recipe'.

Background:

The organisational culture describes the norms and values of an individual school or 'the way we do things around here'. It is these features which differentiate one school from another and which have to be taken into account in formulating a strategic plan. These features represent the 'recipe' or automatic assumptions about how things should be done and what is important.

In trying to recognise the organisational culture it may be helpful to try to identify what adjustments would have to be made by a new teacher coming in from another school if he or she were to act in the same way as an established teacher in the school.

Some of the school's ways of working will be written down in the staff handbook but many of the norms and practices which are the subtle indicators of prevailing attitudes and values are not formally written down anywhere.

STRATEGIC MANAGEMENT FOR SCHOOL DEVELOPMENT: (S7P)
LEADING YOUR SCHOOL'S IMPROVEMENT STRATEGY

Activity

Suppose that you have to tell a teacher new to the school how the school really operates so that they could behave as if they have been in the school for years. You can assume that they have taught in other schools and that they are competent. These things which they would have to be told illustrate ideas which other teachers take for granted and are facets of the school's culture.

1. What kind of actions and behaviour from teachers are highly valued by the school?

2. What kind of actions and behaviour from pupils are highly valued by the school?

3. What are the criteria for the promotion of teachers?

4. What are the actions by teachers which will get them disliked in the school (a) by other teachers, (b) by children, (c) by support staff, (d) by parents?

5. How decentralised is decision-making in the school? Are powers clearly delegated?

6. Who controls access to resources? How are materials obtained from the stock cupboard?

7. Who are the important employees in the school? Why? How do they exercise power?

8. Are there heroes and heroines from the past or present? What do they represent?

9. Describe the relationships between teachers of different classes in the school.

10. What part do parents and other adult helpers play in the school? Who is allowed in the staff room?

11. What counts as success for the school? What is regarded as a disaster?

12. Does the school have rituals and traditions? What do they indicate?

13. What part do governors play?

14. What are staff attitudes to staff development?

15. What are staff attitudes to personal professional development?

16. What are staff attitudes to performance related pay?

17. What part do teacher unions play in school affairs?

18. How are OFSTED inspections viewed?

19. How are league tables of test results viewed?

20. What are relationships like between staff and the head and senior management team?

21. What are staff attitudes to parents?

22. What are staff attitudes to change and school improvement?

23. What are staff attitudes to neighbouring schools?

24. What are staff attitudes to the local education authority?

25. Are there other features which make this school different from other comparable schools?

ACTIVITIES

STRATEGIC ANALYSIS: SCHOOL CULTURE (S7S)

Title: **Organisational Culture (SECONDARY)**

Objective:

This exercise provides a means of recognising the all-pervasive school culture. It should alert the reader to the individual school's 'recipe'.

Background:

The organisational culture describes the norms and values of the individual school or 'the way we do things around here'. It is these features which differentiate one school from another and which have to be taken into account in formulating a strategic plan. These features represent the 'recipe' or automatic assumptions about how things should be done and what is important.

In trying to recognise the organisational culture it may be helpful to try to identify what adjustments would have to be made by a new teacher coming in from another school if he or she were to act in the same way as an established teacher in the school.

Some of the school's ways of working will be written down in the staff handbook but many of the norms and practices which are the subtle indicators of prevailing attitudes and values are not formally written down anywhere.

STRATEGIC MANAGEMENT FOR SCHOOL DEVELOPMENT: (S7S)
LEADING YOUR SCHOOL'S IMPROVEMENT STRATEGY

Activity

Suppose that you have to tell a teacher new to the school how the school really operates so that they could behave as if they have been in the school for years. You can assume that they have taught in other schools and that they are competent. These things which they would have to be told illustrate ideas which other teachers take for granted and are facets of the school's culture.

1. What kind of actions and behaviour from teachers are highly valued by the school?

2. What kind of actions and behaviour from pupils are highly valued by the school?

3. What are the criteria for the promotion of teachers?

4. What are the actions by teachers which will get them disliked in the school (a) by other teachers, (b) by children, (c) by support staff, (d) by parents?

5. What are expectations about taking part in out-of-school activities?

6. What are acceptable starting and finishing times of work at school?

7. What is the marking policy? What is the practice?

8. How important are sports in the curriculum?

9. How decentralised is decision-making in the school? Are powers clearly delegated?

10. How much of the school's structure, distribution of management responsibilities, financial allocations and timetables are made public?

11. Who are the important employees in the school? Why? How do they exercise power?

12. Describe the relationships between (a) departments (b) academic and pastoral leaders.

13. Are there heroes and heroines from the past or present? What do they represent?

14. What counts as success for the school?

15. What counts as a disaster for the school?

16. Does the school have rituals and traditions? What do they indicate?

17. What part do governors play?

18. What are staff attitudes to staff development?

19. What are staff attitudes to personal professional development?

20. What are staff attitudes to performance related pay?

21. What part do teacher unions play in school affairs?

22. How are OFSTED inspections viewed?

23. How are the league tables viewed?

24. What are relationships like between staff and the head and senior management team?

25. What are staff attitudes to parents?

26. What are staff attitudes to change and school improvement?

27. What are staff attitudes to neighbouring schools?

28. What are staff attitudes to the local education authority?

29. Are there other features which make this school different from other comparable schools?

STRATEGIC MANAGEMENT FOR SCHOOL DEVELOPMENT: **(S8P)**
LEADING YOUR SCHOOL'S IMPROVEMENT STRATEGY

ACTIVITIES

STRATEGIC ANALYSIS (S8P)

Title: **School Performance (PRIMARY)**

Objective:
This activity provides a basis for a school to assess its own achievements and compare these with its future hopes.

Background:
A school needs to assess its own performance on a number of criteria and also to decide how it would like to perform on these same criteria. The discrepancies between the two assessments provide clues about the strategic plan.

The criteria on which the school rates itself particularly highly also suggest areas in which the school should be promoting its image. Although these will also need to be criteria which stakeholders value.

The criteria here are largely the same as those in exercise S2P to facilitate comparison between the public assessments of the school provided by S2P and the professional perceptions recorded in this exercise. The following comparisons should be of value:

- (a)   comparison of professional and public assessments of the present performance
    - (i)   if the professional exceeds the public then better promotion of the school's achievement is called for;
    - (ii)   if the public exceeds the professional then professional action to improve the school's performance may be necessary.
- b)   comparison of professional and public assessments of future desired performance
    - (i)   if the professional exceeds the public then the public may need convincing of the importance of this aspect of the school's performance;
    - (ii)   if the public exceeds the professional then there may be an internal communication process required to convince teachers of the importance attached by the public to this aspect.

Two vitally important caveats should be borne in mind. First, any judgements recorded here or in S2P will be estimates so the results should not be taken at face value but treated cautiously. Secondly, where a school accepts the results thrown up by this exercise a further degree of prioritisation will be required since any changes desired by the public will not all be of equal value nor, in all probability, will they all be possible to accomplish.

This exercise is intended only to provide pointers and stimulate discussion of important issues.

STRATEGIC MANAGEMENT FOR SCHOOL DEVELOPMENT:　　　**(S8P)**
LEADING YOUR SCHOOL'S IMPROVEMENT STRATEGY

Activity

Rate the present performance of the school and the desired school performance on the following criteria.

Using the following 7 point scale rate the present performance of the school:

Very Poor			*Average*			*Excellent*	
1	2	3	4	5	6	7	

For the 'actual' rating compare each item with other schools in the locality and grade the item as professional educators would on the 7 point scale. The 'other' attribute(s) allow you to write in any other feature which you would like to include.

For the desired professional rating you have a further 19 points to distribute. These may be added to any present value of ratings. The points can be concentrated on a small number of items or spread more widely.

The differences between present and desired ratings show up areas for action in the strategic plan.

Where one of the items covers a broad area and it is one particular aspect which is the focus of attention, note this by the side of the desired rating, eg ICT equipment.

The items have been divided into three groups:

- Direct student outcomes
- Processes which impact *directly* or *indirectly* on student outcomes
- Organisational processes.

DIRECT STUDENT OUTCOMES

FEATURE	Present Professional Rating	Desired Professional Rating
1. Achievements in Literacy		
2. Achievements in Numeracy		
3. Achievements in Science		
4. Achievements in other foundation subjects		
5. Attitudes to learning		
6. Cultural involvement and accomplishments		
7. Sporting achievements and disposition		
8. Spiritual and religious attitudes		
9. ICT education and equipment		
10. Behaviour and appearance of children		
11. Other attribute(s)		

STRATEGIC MANAGEMENT FOR SCHOOL DEVELOPMENT: **(S8P)**
LEADING YOUR SCHOOL'S IMPROVEMENT STRATEGY

DIRECT AND INDIRECT PROCESSES WHICH IMPACT ON STUDENT OUTCOMES

FEATURE	Present Professional Rating	Desired Professional Rating
12. Curriculum offered – formal and out-of-school		
13. Active and individualised learning styles		
14. Student involvement		
15. Quality of teaching		
16. Quality of leadership		
17. Staff involvement		
18. Staff development		
19. Attitudes to innovation and improvement		
20. Caring and supportive environment		
21. Calm and orderly environment		
22. Special needs provision and attitudes		
23. Provision of equal opportunities		
24. Multicultural education		
25. Extent and quality of support to teachers and children by non-teaching staff		
26. Parental involvement		
27. Governor involvement		
28. Community involvement		
29. Other attribute(s)		

STRATEGIC MANAGEMENT FOR SCHOOL DEVELOPMENT: **(S8P)**
LEADING YOUR SCHOOL'S IMPROVEMENT STRATEGY

ORGANISATIONAL PROCESSES

FEATURE	Present Professional Rating	Desired Professional Rating
30. Welcoming and friendly reception		
31. Availability of staff		
32. Parental information		
33. School uniform		
34. Place in school league tables		
35. Possible place in future value-added-league tables		
36. Judgement of the school in the last OFSTED inspection report		
37. Liaison with secondary schools		
38. Co-operation with other primary schools		
39. Co-operation with nursery schools and play groups		
40. Promotion of the school		
41. Fund raising		
42. Other attribute(s)		

STRATEGIC MANAGEMENT FOR SCHOOL DEVELOPMENT: **(S8S)**
LEADING YOUR SCHOOL'S IMPROVEMENT STRATEGY

ACTIVITIES

STRATEGIC ANALYSIS (S8S)

Title: **School Performance (SECONDARY)**

Objective:
This activity provides a basis for a school to assess its own achievements and compare these with its future hopes.

Background:
A school needs to assess its own performance on a number of criteria and also to decide how it would like to be viewed on these same criteria. The discrepancies between the two assessments provide clues about the strategic plan.

The criteria on which the school rates itself particularly highly also suggest areas in which the school should be promoting its image. Although these will also need to be criteria which stakeholders value.

The criteria here are largely the same as those in exercise S2S to facilitate comparison between the public assessments of the school provided by S2S and the professional perceptions recorded in this exercise. The following comparisons should be of value:

    (a)   comparison of professional and public assessments of the present performance
        (i)   if the professional exceeds the public then better promotion of the school's achievement is called for;
        (ii)   if the public exceeds the professional then professional action to improve the school's performance may be necessary.
    (b)   comparison of professional and public assessments of future desired performance
        (i)   if the professional exceeds the public then the public may need convincing of the importance of this aspect of the school's performance;
        (ii)   if the public exceeds the professional then there may be an internal communication process required to convince teachers of the importance attached by the public to this aspect.

Two vitally important caveats should be borne in mind. First, any judgements recorded here or in S2S will be an estimate so the results should not be taken at face value but treated cautiously. Secondly, where a school accepts the results thrown up by this exercise a further degree of prioritisation will be required since any changes desired by the public will not all be of equal value nor, in all probability, will they all be possible to accomplish.

This exercise is intended only to provide pointers and stimulate discussion of important issues.

STRATEGIC MANAGEMENT FOR SCHOOL DEVELOPMENT: (S8S)
LEADING YOUR SCHOOL'S IMPROVEMENT STRATEGY

Activity

Rate the present performance of the school and the desired school performance on the following criteria.

Using the following 7 point scale rate the present performance of the school:

Very Poor		*Average*			*Excellent*	
1	2	3	4	5	6	7

For the 'actual' rating compare each item with other schools in the locality and grade the item as professional educators would on the 7 point scale. The 'other' attribute(s) allow you to write in any other feature which you would like to include.

For the desired professional rating you have a further 20 points to distribute. These may be added to any present value of ratings. The points can be concentrated on a small number of items or spread more widely.

The differences between present and desired ratings show up areas for action in the strategic plan.

Where one of the items covers a broad area ad it is one particular aspect which is the focus of attention, note this by the side of the desired rating, eg ICT equipment.

The items have been divided into three groups:

- Direct student outcomes
- Processes which impact *directly* or *indirectly* on pupil outcomes
- Organisational processes.

DIRECT STUDENT OUTCOMES

FEATURE	Present Professional Rating	Desired Professional Rating
1. Academic standards and academic ethos		
2. Expertise and achievements in technology		
3. Cultural involvement and accomplishments		
4. Literary and dramatic achievements		
5. Business studies and enterprise awards		
6. Sporting achievements and disposition		
7. Spiritual and religious attitudes		
8. ICT education and equipment		
9. Behaviour and appearance of children		
10. Attitudes to learning		
11. Other attribute(s)		

STRATEGIC MANAGEMENT FOR SCHOOL DEVELOPMENT: **(S8S)**
LEADING YOUR SCHOOL'S IMPROVEMENT STRATEGY

DIRECT AND INDIRECT PROCESSES WHICH IMPACT ON STUDENT OUTCOMES

FEATURE	Present Rating	Desired Rating
12. Curriculum offered – formal and out-of-school		
13. Active and individualised learning styles		
14. Caring and supportive structures		
15. Calm and orderly environment		
16. Vocational courses and outlook		
17. Quality of teaching		
18. Quality of leadership		
19. Special needs provision and attitudes		
20. Provision of equal opportunities		
21. Multicultural education and attitudes		
22. Parental involvement		
23. Governor involvement		
24. Community involvement		
25. Involvement with business		
26. Buildings and physical environment		
27. Staff development		
28. Attitudes to innovation and improvement		
29. Extent and quality of support to teachers and students by non-teaching staff		
30. Other attribute(s)		

STRATEGIC MANAGEMENT FOR SCHOOL DEVELOPMENT: **(S8S)**
LEADING YOUR SCHOOL'S IMPROVEMENT STRATEGY

ORGANISATIONAL PROCESSES

FEATURE	Present Rating	Desired Rating
31. Place in the school league tables?		
32. Possible place in future value-added league tables		
33. Judgement of the school in the last OFSTED inspection report		
34. Welcoming and friendly reception		
35. Availability of staff		
36. Parental information		
37. School uniform		
38. Liaison with feeder schools		
39. Liaison with other secondary schools		
40. Liaison with post 16 provision and FE/HE colleges/universities		
41. Promotion of the school		
42. Fund raising		
43. Other attribute(s)		

STRATEGIC MANAGEMENT FOR SCHOOL DEVELOPMENT: **(S9)**
LEADING YOUR SCHOOL'S IMPROVEMENT STRATEGY

ACTIVITIES

STRATEGIC ANALYSIS (S9)

Title: **Achievement of School Aims**

Objective:

This activity investigates the way in which school aims are achieved. What are the processes and actions by which current aims are intended to be achieved. This involves an examination of whether current school aims are being achieved. This requires a reappraisal of school aims and an evaluation of how any revised aims are to be achieved.

Background:

The current school aims represent formally what a school is trying to achieve. There should be mechanisms by which they are put into effect and activities which contribute to their achievement.

An examination of current school aims and their more precise objectives may reveal that some are only being weakly pursued. This may be clearer when the activities which are intended to achieve the aims are examined in some detail.

This provides an opportunity to reappraise the school aims to see whether they are still appropriate and whether they give an appropriate impression to those outside the school about its intentions. Some additional aims or a rewording of existing aims may be required. There will also need to be a consideration of how they are to be achieved.

The means include:

- Assemblies
- Classroom teaching
- Teaching outside the classroom
- Out-of-school activities
- Pastoral activities
- Social activities of students.

More detail about each of these will be needed in relation to each aim and objective.

STRATEGIC MANAGEMENT FOR SCHOOL DEVELOPMENT: **(S9)**
LEADING YOUR SCHOOL'S IMPROVEMENT STRATEGY

Activity

Carry out the analysis suggested below on the existing aims of the school, the more detailed objectives, the means by which these are to be achieved and any obstacles to their achievement.

Are the aims appropriate?

Are the objectives appropriate?

What priorities are indicated?

Aims	Objectives	Means of achievement	Obstacles

STRATEGIC MANAGEMENT FOR SCHOOL DEVELOPMENT: **(S10)**
LEADING YOUR SCHOOL'S IMPROVEMENT STRATEGY

ACTIVITIES

STRATEGIC ANALYSIS (S10)

Title: **Effort on School Aims**

Objective:

This activity investigates the way in which school aims are achieved. What are the processes and actions by which current aims are intended to be achieved and what is the proportion of the school's effort which is expended on each aim?

Background:

The current school aims represent formally what a school is trying to achieve. There should be mechanisms by which they are put into effect and activities which contribute to their achievement.

An examination of current school aims and their more precise objectives may reveal that some are only being weakly pursued. This may be clearer when the activities which are intended to achieve the aims are examined in some detail and the extent of the school's effort which is devoted to each is examined.

This provides an opportunity to reappraise the school aims to see whether some are only being pursued rather weakly. Any that are receiving little effort may be less important aims or it may be that they should be pursued more vigorously.

School aims may be interconnected and it may be a little artificial to examine each one independently. However, the purpose of this exercise is not to be able to calculate the precise effort devoted to each but to develop an appreciation of the approximate amount of effort devoted to each to see if this corresponds with the importance of the aim.

STRATEGIC MANAGEMENT FOR SCHOOL DEVELOPMENT:
LEADING YOUR SCHOOL'S IMPROVEMENT STRATEGY

(S10)

Activity

Carry out the analysis suggested below on the existing aims of the school, if necessary by examining the more detailed objectives. Calculate the importance of the school's aims as a proportion of 100%. Calculate the school's effort devoted to each aim as a proportion of 100%. What is the correspondence between the two figures for each aim? Is any mismatch indicated?

Aims	Importance of each %	Effort devoted to each %
1		
2		
3		
4		
5		
more		
Total	**100%**	**100%**

STRATEGIC MANAGEMENT FOR SCHOOL DEVELOPMENT: **(S11)**
LEADING YOUR SCHOOL'S IMPROVEMENT STRATEGY

ACTIVITIES

STRATEGIC ANALYSIS (S11)

Title: **Contribution to School Aims**

Objective:

This activity investigates the way in which school aims are achieved. It examines the relative contributions of the school and parents to the achievement of each aim.

Background:

The current school aims represent formally what a school is trying to achieve. There should be mechanisms by which they are put into effect and activities which contribute to their achievement. A school is unlikely to assume that it can achieve its aims without a contribution of each parent to each aim.

An examination of current school aims and their more precise objectives may reveal some are more dependent on the help of parents than others. Such an examination may reveal that more parental help needs to be mobilised.

This provides an opportunity to reappraise the school aims to see whether some are only being pursued rather weakly. Any that are receiving little effort may be less important aims or it may be that they should be pursued more vigorously.

School aims may be interconnected and it may be a little artificial to examine each one independently. However, the purpose of this exercise is not to be able to calculate the precise effort devoted to each but to develop an appreciation of the approximate amount of effort devoted to each by parents and the school.

STRATEGIC MANAGEMENT FOR SCHOOL DEVELOPMENT: (S11)
LEADING YOUR SCHOOL'S IMPROVEMENT STRATEGY

Activity

Carry out the analysis suggested below on the existing aims of the school, if necessary by examining the more detailed objectives, Calculate the relative contribution to each aim by parents and by the school. Compare the current distribution with that which would be required to be successful. Is any mismatch indicated?

Aims	Contribution of parents to each aim %	Contribution of the school to each aim %	Total %
1			100
2			100
3			100
4			100
5			100
more			

**STRATEGIC MANAGEMENT FOR SCHOOL DEVELOPMENT:
LEADING YOUR SCHOOL'S IMPROVEMENT STRATEGY**

ACTIVITIES

STRATEGIC ANALYSIS (S12)

Title: **Staff Audit**

Objective:
This exercise entails the collection of details on teaching staff and teaching support staff to identify existing and potential strengths.

Background:
The strategic plan of the school should take account of resource capabilities, both present and future ones. The most important resources in a school are the human resources. In most schools there is much untapped potential in both teaching and teaching support staff.

The exercise will both highlight existing strengths and also provide a database from which future proposed strategies can be tested. If a proposed strategy requires new skills or experience, the database will reveal whether among the staff there are such skills and experience or the likelihood of their development.

The two pro-formas associated with this exercise provide a basis for collecting data about the human resources in the school. The pro-formas may need modification for any particular school.

Although some of this data may already exist unless it has been recently collected it should be checked. The collection of this information may lead to a dialogue from which other valuable information about human resource potential also emerges.

(S12)

STRATEGIC MANAGEMENT FOR SCHOOL DEVELOPMENT: LEADING YOUR SCHOOL'S IMPROVEMENT STRATEGY

Activity

Carry out a staff audit for both teaching and teaching support staff.

Teaching Staff

Name	Post	Temp FT/ perm PT	Incremental point	Resp point	Age	Length of teaching	Years in school	Age range of students	Main Subject Spec	Subsid Subject Spec	IT expertise	Qualifications	Recent INSET (3 yrs)	Interests relevant to teaching	Previous non-teaching jobs

Addresses and phone & fax numbers, e-mail addresses of all staff

(S12)

STRATEGIC MANAGEMENT FOR SCHOOL DEVELOPMENT:
LEADING YOUR SCHOOL'S IMPROVEMENT STRATEGY

Teaching Support Staff

Name	Job Title	Pay Scale	Hours per week	Weeks per year	Age	Years in school	Qualifications	IT expertise	Recent INSET	Safety course	Other work experience	Interests relevant to school

Addresses and phone & fax numbers, e-mail addresses of all staff

STRATEGIC MANAGEMENT FOR SCHOOL DEVELOPMENT: **(S13)**
LEADING YOUR SCHOOL'S IMPROVEMENT STRATEGY

ACTIVITIES

STRATEGIC ANALYSIS (S13)

Title: **Accommodation Audit**

Objective:
This exercise enables the creation of an accommodation database for teaching and non-teaching space.

Background:
The school buildings are an important resource for the school. An accommodation audit provides information on the school facilities including their size, equipment and state of decoration and repair.

This may signal areas in need of repair, redecoration or refurbishment. The potential for energy saving measures should also be investigated.

The number of pupils which a school may accommodate is determined by the amount of teaching space and its intended use. Data from the pro-forma allows a check on the published capacity of the school. Open plan areas need to be assessed for their respective teaching and circulation spaces.

If the strategic plan calls for a change to teaching or non-teaching accommodation, the data on the pro-forma permits an overview of the effects of making changes to the present accommodation.

The general state of the structure and fabric of buildings should also be assessed periodically.

(S13)

STRATEGIC MANAGEMENT FOR SCHOOL DEVELOPMENT: LEADING YOUR SCHOOL'S IMPROVEMENT STRATEGY

Activity
Carry out an accommodation audit of teaching and non-teaching space.

Teaching Space (Page 1)

Basic Features of

Room No	Uses/ spec areas	Level (from ground)	L(m)	W(m)	Area(m²)	H(m)	Open plan area	Perm/ Temp	Chairs (number)	Tables (number)	Lights (type and number)	Floor (type)	Window area	Storage space	Sink or other facility	Security locks	Fire escape	Fire extinguisher	Disabled access

**STRATEGIC MANAGEMENT FOR SCHOOL DEVELOPMENT:
LEADING YOUR SCHOOL'S IMPROVEMENT STRATEGY**

Teaching Space (Page 2)

Condition of Structure and Decoration of

Room No	Doors	Floor	Windows (inc blinds curtains)	Walls	Ceiling	Furniture (and equipment)	Fittings (inc. Blackboard)	Power points	Internet access pts	Computers (specify)	Printers or other peripherals	OHP	Data Projector	Comments

(S13)

STRATEGIC MANAGEMENT FOR SCHOOL DEVELOPMENT: LEADING YOUR SCHOOL'S IMPROVEMENT STRATEGY

Carry out a similar survey of non-teaching space

Non-Teaching Space

Offices	Staff rooms	Toilets	Cloakrooms	Halls	Reception

STRATEGIC MANAGEMENT FOR SCHOOL DEVELOPMENT: (S14)
LEADING YOUR SCHOOL'S IMPROVEMENT STRATEGY

ACTIVITIES

STRATEGIC ANALYSIS (S14)

Title: **SWOT Analysis**

Objective:

This exercise will enable an assessment of the internal strengths and weaknesses of a school and the external opportunities and threats.

Background:

For a school to identify a successful strategy SWOT analysis is helpful. The strengths and weaknesses of a school are related to its total internal resources. Strengths are those features where its skills, facilities, reputation etc are superior to other comparable schools, whereas weaknesses are those features where the school is less good. These must either be judged to be comparatively unimportant or improved. All of these are related to its present operations.

Opportunities and threats come from the external environment. Some of the environmental influences can be regarded as opportunities because they can be used to enable the school to achieve its objectives. Threats are those environmental influences which tend to prevent the school achieving what it would like to do.

A weakness of a SWOT analysis is that it uses the perceptions of insiders to compile it. These are conditioned by the current expectations of the school. Unless steps are taken to challenge these a SWOT may perpetuate the status quo. Steps to minimise this possibility include – seeking external perspectives on the school's performance, trying to make the school's cultural assumption more explicit and to seek to justify any identification of the elements of the SWOT by evidence.

A successful strategy is one which maximises strengths by using opportunities and minimises weaknesses and avoids threats. This strategy has to take account of the culture and values of the school.

STRATEGIC MANAGEMENT FOR SCHOOL DEVELOPMENT: (S14)
LEADING YOUR SCHOOL'S IMPROVEMENT STRATEGY

Activity
Carry out a SWOT analysis on the school.

INTERNAL	STRENGTHS	
	WEAKNESSES	

STRATEGIC MANAGEMENT FOR SCHOOL DEVELOPMENT: **(S14)**
LEADING YOUR SCHOOL'S IMPROVEMENT STRATEGY

	OPPORTUNITIES	
EXTERNAL		
	THREATS	

STRATEGIC MANAGEMENT FOR SCHOOL DEVELOPMENT: **(S15)**
LEADING YOUR SCHOOL'S IMPROVEMENT STRATEGY

ACTIVITIES

STRATEGIC CHOICE (S15)

Title: **Strategic Issues Identification**

Objective:

This exercise is intended to help identify the strategic questions which a school needs to resolve in order to point the direction of its strategic plan.

Background:

Strategic issues are those fundamental policy questions which affect the school's mission and values. The questions can be about ends or means.

The questions should be sufficiently fundamental such that when they are resolved other more minor questions begin to be answered.

STRATEGIC MANAGEMENT FOR SCHOOL DEVELOPMENT: (S15)
LEADING YOUR SCHOOL'S IMPROVEMENT STRATEGY

Activity

Identify SIX strategic issues for your school. The resolution of these issues should broadly point the way forward.

The issues will be individual to the school but they may involve such questions as:

What is the school's attitude to parents?

What is the school's attitude to other schools?

Are feeder schools popular? Are schools which this school feeds popular?

What is the school's attitude to the community?

What should children have acquired by the time they leave the school?

How do children learn? Do they come willingly to school?

What are the pupils' attitudes to each other?

What is the role of the teacher?

What are the staff's attitudes to each other?

Has the school an appropriate public image?

Does the school's future look secure?

What is the school's attitude to change?

What is the physical condition of the school buildings and its surroundings?

Are pupils' achievements appropriately high compared to other schools?

Should this school acquire a specialism?

Can the school recruit sufficient children? Do these reflect an appropriate spread of ability?

Does the school have a well-defined catchment area?

Is the parental group relatively homogenous? Are there shared aspirations?

STRATEGIC MANAGEMENT FOR SCHOOL DEVELOPMENT: (S16)
LEADING YOUR SCHOOL'S IMPROVEMENT STRATEGY

ACTIVITIES

STRATEGIC CHOICE (S16)

Title: **'Vision of Success': Statement completion**

Objective:

This exercise provides a way to visualise how the school will look and operate in five years' time or more if the school is successful.

Background:

In order to plan for the future it is important to form a picture of what the school will be like and how it will operate in FIVE OR MORE YEARS' TIME if it develops as you hope. Sharing this vision with others will provide feedback on its feasibility. It will also be possible to identify the changes required and vulnerable features.

The 'vision' might include:

> Buildings
> Facilities
> Equipment
> Academic Achievement
> Pastoral Care
> Curriculum Content
> Curriculum Process
> Activities
> Achievements
> Relationships
> Attitudes and Values.

STRATEGIC MANAGEMENT FOR SCHOOL DEVELOPMENT: LEADING YOUR SCHOOL'S IMPROVEMENT STRATEGY

Exercise

Compose 5 statements: for each of the following:

'The school will..........'

'The pupils will..........'

'The teachers will..........'

'The headteacher will..........'

'The parents will..........'

'The governors will..........'

STRATEGIC MANAGEMENT FOR SCHOOL DEVELOPMENT: **(S17)**
LEADING YOUR SCHOOL'S IMPROVEMENT STRATEGY

ACTIVITIES

STRATEGIC CHOICE (S17)

Title: **'Vision of Success': Scenario Building**

Objective:

This exercise provides a way to visualise how the school will look and operate in five years' time if the school is successful.

Background:

In order to plan for the future it is important to form a picture of what the school will be like and how it will operate in FIVE OR MORE YEARS' TIME if it develops as you hope. Sharing this vision with others will provide feedback on its feasibility. It will also be possible to identify the changes required and vulnerable features.

The 'vision' might include:

> Buildings
> Facilities
> Equipment
> Academic Achievement
> Pastoral Care
> Curriculum Content
> Curriculum Process
> Activities
> Achievements
> Relationships
> Attitudes and Values.

STRATEGIC MANAGEMENT FOR SCHOOL DEVELOPMENT:　　(S17)
LEADING YOUR SCHOOL'S IMPROVEMENT STRATEGY

Activity

Imagine that a newspaper reporter visits your school in seven years' time and writes a description of what he or she observes. This might take the form of a description of the features which the reporter observes from the time they enter the school and might cover:

　　how they are received

　　the behaviour and attitudes of pupils and staff

　　what happens in classrooms

　　the equipment children and teachers are using

　　interviews with children, teachers and parents about the work of the school.

References

Argyris, C. and Schon, D.A. (1974) *Theories in Practice*. San Francisco, CA: Jossey-Bass.

Audit Commission (1991) *Management within Primary Schools*. London: HMSO.

Audit Commission (1986) *Towards Better Management of Secondary Education*. London: HMSO.

Ball, R. (1984) *Management Techniques and Quantitative Methods*. London: Heinemann.

Belbin, R.M. (1981) *Team Roles at Work*. Oxford: Heinemann.

Bell, J. (1999) *Doing Your Research Project* (3rd edn). Buckingham: Open University Press.

Bennett, N., Glatter, R. and Levačić, R. (eds) (1994) *Improving Educational Management through Research and Consultancy*. London: Paul Chapman Publishing.

Bolman, L.G. and Deal, T.E. (1997) *Reframing Organizations: Artistry, Choice and Leadership* (2nd edn). San Francisco, CA: Jossey-Bass.

Bridges, E.M. (1967) 'A model of shared decision making in school principalship', *Educational Administration Quarterly*, 3:49–61.

Bryson, J.M. (1988) *Strategic Planning for Public and Nonprofit Organizations: A Guide to Strengthening and Sustaining Organizational Achievement*. San Francisco, CA: Jossey-Bass.

Casey, D. (1985) 'When is a team not a team?', *Personnel Management*, January: 26–9.

Chell, E. (1993) *The Psychology of Behaviour in Organizations* (2nd edn). Basingstoke: Macmillan.

Cherrington, D.J. (1989) *Organizational Behavior*. Boston, MA: Allyn & Bacon.

Chin, R. and Benne, K.D. (1976), 'General Strategies for Effecting Change in Human Systems', in W.G. Bennis, K.D. Benne, R. Chin and K.E. Corey (eds), *The Planning of Change*. New York: Holt, Rinehart & Winston.

Dalkey, N. and Helmer, O. (1963) 'An experimental application of the Delphi method to the use of experts', *Management Science*, 9: 458–67.

Everard, B. and Morris, G. (1996) *Effective School Management* (3rd edn). London: Paul Chapman Publishing.

Fidler, B. and Bowles, G. (eds) (1989) *Effective Local Management of Schools*. Harlow: Longman.

Fidler, B. and Bowles, G., with Hart, J. (1991) *Effective Local Management of Schools Workbook: Planning Your School's Strategy*. Harlow: Longman.

Francis, D. (1990) *Effective Problem Solving*. London: Routledge.

Gear, T. (1975) 'Applications of decision trees to educational planning' and 'Network planning', in L. Dobson, T. Gear and A. Westoby (eds), *Management in Education (Reader 2): Some Techniques and Systems*. London: Ward Locke Educational.

Hamel, G. and Prahalad, C.K. (1994) *Competing for the Future*. Boston, MA: Harvard Business School Press.

Handy, C. (1984) Taken for Granted: *Understanding Schools as Organisations*. York: Longman Resource Unit.

Handy, C. and Aitken, R. (1986) *Understanding Schools as Organizations*, Harmondsworth: Penguin.

Harris, A. and Hopkins, D. (2000) 'Introduction to special feature: alternative perspectives on school improvement', *School Leadership and Management*, 20:1, 9–14.

Harvey-Jones, J. (1988) *Making It Happen: Reflections on Leadership*. Glasgow: Fontana/Collins.

Honey, P. and Mumford, A. (1986) *The Manual of Learning Styles* (2nd edn). Maidenhead: Honey.

Hoy, W.K. and Miskel, C.G. (1991) *Educational Administration: Theory, Research and Practice* (4th edn). New York: McGraw-Hill.

Jackson, K.F. (1975) *The Art of Solving Problems*. London: Heinemann.

Jaques, D. (1984) *Learning in Groups*. London: Croom Helm.

Johnson, G. and Scholes, K. (1999) *Exploring Corporate Strategy: Text and cases* (5th edn). Harlow: Pearson Education.

Kast, F.E. and Rosenzweig, J.E. (1985) *Organization and Management: A systems and contingency approach* (4th edn). New York: McGraw-Hill.

Lewin, K. (1951) *Field Theory in Social Science*. New York: Harper & Row.

Majoro, S. (1992) *Managing Ideas for Profit: The Creative Gap*. Maidenhead: McGraw-Hill.

McMahon, A., Bolam, R., Abbott, R. and Holly, P. (1984) *Guidelines for Review and Internal Development in Schools (GRIDS): Primary and Secondary Handbooks*. York: Longman for Schools Council.

Miles, M.B. and Ekholm, M. (1985) 'What is school improvement?', in W.G. Van Velzen, M.B. Miles, M. Ekholm, U. Hameyer and D. Robin (eds), *Making School Improvement Work: A Conceptual Guide to Practice*. Leuven: ACCO.

Morrisey, G.L. (1976) *Management by Objectives and Results in the Public Sector*. Reading, MA: Addison-Wesley.

Mortimore, P., Sammons, P., Stoll, L. Lewis, D. and Ecob, R. (1988) *School Matters: The Junior Years*. Wells: Open Books.

Murgatroyd, S. and Morgan, C. (1992) *Total Quality Management and the School*. Buckingham: Open University Press.

Murnighan, J.K. (1981) 'Group decision making: what strategies should you use?', *Management Review*, February: 55–62.

Murnighan, J.K. (1982) 'Game theory and the structure of decision-making groups', in R.A. Guzzo (ed.), *Improving Group Decision Making in Organizations: Approaches from Theory and Research*. London: Academic Press.

Peters, T.J. and Waterman, R.M. (1982) *In Search of Excellence: Lessons from America's Best-Run Companies*. New York: Harper and Row.

Quinn, J.B. (1980) *Strategies for Change: Logical Incrementalism*. Homewood, IL: Irwin.

Rae, L. (1983) *The Skills of Training*. Aldershot: Gower.

Sammons, P., Hillman, J. and Mortimore, P. (1995) *Key Characteristics of Effective Schools: A Review of School Effectiveness Research*. London: OFSTED.

Sammons, P., Thomas, S. and Mortimore, P. (1997) *Forging Links: Effective Schools and Effective Departments*. London: Paul Chapman Publishing.

Schmuck, R.A. and Runkel, P.J. (1994) The Handbook of Organization Development in Schools and Colleges (4th edn). Prospect Heights, IL: Waveland Press.

Simon, H.A. (1957) *Administrative Behavior* (2nd edn). New York: Macmillan.

Stein, M.I. (1982) 'Creativity, groups and management', in R.A. Guzzo (ed.), *Improving Group Decision Making in Organizations: Approaches from Theory and Research*. London: Academic Press.

Van de Ven, A.H. and Delbecq, A.L. (1974) 'The effectiveness of nominal, delphi, and interacting group decision making processes', *Academy of Management Journal*, 17:4, 605–21.

Vaughan, B.W. (1978) *Planning in Education*. Cambridge: Cambridge University Press.

Wilkins, A.L. and Patterson, K.J. (1985) 'You can't get there from here: What will make culture-change projects fail?', in R.H. Kilman, M.J. Saxton, R. Serpa and Associates (eds), *Gaining Control of the Corporate Culture*. San Francisco, CA: Jossey-Bass.

Further Reading

In addition to sources that have been referred to in the text there are some further sources which may be worth following up:

Bate, P. (1994) *Strategies for Cultural Change*. Oxford: Butterworth-Heinemann.

Bolman, L.G. and Deal, T.E. (1997) *Reframing Organizations: Artistry, Choice and Leadership* (2nd edn). San Francisco, CA: Jossey-Bass.

Earley, P., Fidler, B. and Ouston, J. (eds) (1996) *Improvement through Inspection? Complementary Approaches to School Development*. London: David Fulton.

Fidler, B., with Edwards, M., Evans, B., Mann, P. and Thomas, P. (1996) *Strategic Planning for School Improvement*. London: Pitman.

Fidler, B., Russell, S. and Simkins, T. (eds) (1997) *Choices for Self-managing Schools: Autonomy and Accountability*. London: Paul Chapman Publishing.

Gray, H.L. (ed.) (1988) *Management Consultancy in Schools*. London: Cassell.

Hamel, G. and Prahalad, C.K. (1994) *Competing for the Future*. Boston, MA: Harvard Business School Press.

Hoyle, E. (1986) *The Politics of School Management*. London: Hodder & Stoughton.

Owens, R.G. (1991) *Organizational Behavior in Education* (4th edn). Boston, MA: Allyn & Bacon.

Rodger, A. and Rawling, K. (1985) *The Seven Point Plan and New Perspectives Fifty Years On*. Windsor: NFER-Nelson.

Schein, E.H. (1992) *Organizational Culture and Leadership* (2nd edn). San Francisco, CA: Jossey-Bass.

Schmuck, R.A. and Runkel, P.J. (1994) *The Handbook of Organization Development in School* (4th edn). Prospect Heights, IL: Waveland Press.

Willms, J.D. (1992) *Monitoring School Performance: A Guide for Educators*. Lewes: Falmer.

Index